# 7th Workshop on Language Technology for Cultural Heritage, Social Sciences, and Humanities

# (LaTeCH 2013)



**Sofia, Bulgaria**
**8 August 2013**

ISBN: 978-1-62748-998-0

**Printed from e-media with permission by:**

Curran Associates, Inc.
57 Morehouse Lane
Red Hook, NY 12571

**Some format issues inherent in the e-media version may also appear in this print version.**



Printed by Curran Associates, Inc. (2013)

For permission requests, please contact the Association for Computational Linguistics at the address below.

Association for Computational Linguistics
209 N. Eighth Street
Stroudsburg, Pennsylvania 18360

Phone: 1-570-476-8006
Fax: 1-570-476-0860

acl@aclweb.org

**Additional copies of this publication are available from:**

Curran Associates, Inc.
57 Morehouse Lane
Red Hook, NY 12571 USA
Phone: 845-758-0400
Fax: 845-758-2634
Email: curran@proceedings.com
Web: www.proceedings.com

LaTeCH 2013

# Proceedings of the 7th Workshop on Language Technology for Cultural Heritage, Social Sciences, and Humanities (LaTeCH 2013)

August 8, 2013
Sofia, Bulgaria

# Preface

We are delighted to present you with this volume containing the papers accepted for presentation at the 7th Workshop on Language Technology for Cultural Heritage, Social Sciences, and Humanities, endorsed by the ACL SIGHUM interest group.

Language technology has by now pervaded core processing procedures targeting the cleaning, searching, linking, enriching, and mining of digitized data from these fields. After six previous LaTeCH workshops, we are happy to carry on with aggregating and disseminating the most interesting studies – selected by a thorough peer-review process – concerning current hot topics in the area of natural language processing. Acceptance rate for LaTeCH-2013 was 62%. We would especially like to thank the members of the programme committee for willing to share their expertise by providing detailed reviews and insightful input to all the submitting authors.

On top of the regular paper presentations, the organisers are proud to integrate the SIGHUM annual business meeting into the programme.

We wish you a well-spent workshop day!

Piroska Lendvai and Kalliopi Zervanou
Chairs of LaTeCH-2013

# Organizers

**Workshop Chairs:**

Piroska Lendvai, Research Institute for Linguistics (Hungary)
Kalliopi Zervanou, Radboud University Nijmegen (The Netherlands)

**Organizing Committe:**

Piroska Lendvai, Research Institute for Linguistics (Hungary)
Caroline Sporleder, Saarland University / Trier University, Germany
Antal van den Bosch, Radboud University Nijmegen (The Netherlands)
Kalliopi Zervanou, Radboud University Nijmegen (The Netherlands)

**Program Committee Members:**

Ion Androutsopoulos, Athens University of Economics and Business, Greece
David Bamman, Carnegie Mellon University, USA
Rens Bod, Universiteit van Amsterdam, The Netherlands
Toine Bogers, Royal School of Library and Information Science, Copenhagen, Denmark
Paul Buitelaar, DERI Galway, Ireland
Mick O'Donnell, Universidad Autonoma de Madrid, Spain
Julio Gonzalo, Universidad Nacional de Educacion a Distancia, Spain
Ben Hachey, Macquarie University, Australia
Iris Hendrickx, Radboud University Nijmegen, The Netherlands
Elias Iosif, Technical University of Crete, Greece
Jaap Kamps, Universiteit van Amsterdam, The Netherlands
Vangelis Karkaletsis, NCSR Demokritos, Greece
Mike Kestermont, University of Antwerp / Research Foundation Flanders, Belgium
Dimitrios Kokkinakis, University of Gothenburg, Sweden
Stasinos Konstantopoulos, NCSR Demokritos, Greece
Barbara McGillivray, Oxford University Press, UK
Joakim Nivre, Uppsala University, Sweden
Csaba Oravecz, Research Institute for Linguistics, Hungary
Petya Osenova, Bulgarian Academy of Sciences, Bulgaria
Katerina Pastra, Cognitive Systems Research Institute, Greece
Michael Piotrowski, University of Zurich, Switzerland
Georg Rehm, DFKI Berlin, Germany
Martin Reynaert, Tilburg University, The Netherlands
Eszter Simon, Research Institute for Linguistics, Hungary
Herman Stehouwer, Max Planck Institute for Psycholinguistics, The Netherlands
Mark Stevenson, University of Sheffield, UK
Mariët Theune, University of Twente, The Netherlands
Suzan Verberne, Radboud University Nijmegen, The Netherlands
Cristina Vertan, University of Hamburg, Germany
Menno van Zaanen, Tilburg University, The Netherlands
Svitlana Zinger, TU Eindhoven, The Netherlands

# Table of Contents

# Conference Program

**Thursday August 8, 2013**

9:00-9:15 Opening

9:15–9.35 *Generating Paths through Cultural Heritage Collections*
Samuel Fernando, Paula Goodale, Paul Clough, Mark Stevenson, Mark Hall and Eneko Agirre

9:35–9.55 *Using character overlap to improve language transformation*
Sander Wubben, Emiel Krahmer and Antal van den Bosch

9:55–10:15 *Comparison between historical population archives and decentralized databases*
Marijn Schraagen and Dionysius Huijsmans

10:15–10:30 *Semi-automatic Construction of Cross-period Thesaurus*
Chaya Liebeskind, Ido Dagan and Jonathan Schler

10:30-11:00 Coffee Break

11:00–11:15 *Language Technology for Agile Social Media Science*
Simon Wibberley, David Weir and Jeremy Reffin

11:15–11:30 *Morphological annotation of Old and Middle Hungarian corpora*
Attila Novák, György Orosz and Nóra Wenszky

11:30–11:45 *Argument extraction for supporting public policy formulation*
Eirini Florou, Stasinos Konstantopoulos, Antonis Koukourikos and Pythagoras Karampiperis

11:45-12:30 SIGHUM annual business meeting

12:30-14:00 Lunch Break

14:00–14:20 *Towards a Tool for Interactive Concept Building for Large Scale Analysis in the Humanities*
Andre Blessing, Jonathan Sonntag, Fritz Kliche, Ulrich Heid, Jonas Kuhn and Manfred Stede

14:20–14:40 *Learning to Extract Folktale Keywords*
Dolf Trieschnigg, Dong Nguyen and Mariët Theune

**Thursday August 8, 2013 (continued)**

14:40–15:00 *Towards Creating Precision Grammars from Interlinear Glossed Text: Inferring Large-Scale Typological Properties*
Emily M. Bender, Michael Wayne Goodman, Joshua Crowgey and Fei Xia

15:00–15:15 *Using Comparable Collections of Historical Texts for Building a Diachronic Dictionary for Spelling Normalization*
Marilisa Amoia and José Manuel Martínez

15:15–15:30 *Integration of the Thesaurus for the Social Sciences (TheSoz) in an Information Extraction System*
Thierry Declerck

15:30-16:00 Coffee Break

16:00–16:15 *The (Un)faithful Machine Translator*
Ruth Jones and Ann Irvine

16:15–16:30 *Temporal classification for historical Romanian texts*
Alina Maria Ciobanu, Anca Dinu, Liviu Dinu, Vlad Niculae and Octavia-Maria Şulea

16:30–16:50 *Multilingual access to cultural heritage content on the Semantic Web*
Dana Dannells, Aarne Ranta, Ramona Enache, Mariana Damova and Maria Mateva

16:50-17:00 Closing

# Generating Paths through Cultural Heritage Collections

**Samuel Fernando[1], Paula Goodale[2], Paul Clough[2],**
**Mark Stevenson[1], Mark Hall[2], Eneko Agirre[3]**
[1]Department of Computer Science, University of Sheffield
[2]Information School, University of Sheffield
[3]Computer Science Department, University of the Basque Country
{s.fernando, p.goodale, p.d.clough,
r.m.stevenson, m.mhall}@sheffield.ac.uk
e.agirre@ehu.es

## Abstract

Cultural heritage collections usually organise sets of items into exhibitions or guided tours. These items are often accompanied by text that describes the theme and topic of the exhibition and provides background context and details of connections with other items. The PATHS project brings the idea of guided tours to digital library collections where a tool to create virtual paths are used to assist with navigation and provide guides on particular subjects and topics. In this paper we characterise and analyse paths of items created by users of our online system. The analysis highlights that most users spend time selecting items relevant to their chosen topic, but few users took time to add background information to the paths. In order to address this, we conducted preliminary investigations to test whether Wikipedia can be used to automatically add background text for sequences of items. In the future we would like to explore the automatic creation of full paths.

## 1 Introduction

Paths (or trails) have been studied as a means of assisting users with the navigation of digital collections as an alternative to standard keyword-based search (Furuta et al., 1997; Reich et al., 1999; Shipman et al., 2000; White and Huang, 2010). Paths can be particularly useful to users who are unfamilar with the content of digital collections (e.g. historical documents) and may find it difficult to formulate appropriate queries (Wilson et al., 2010). Paths can be used to assist users with the navigation of collections through the provision of narratives and subject guides. From an educational perspective paths can provide tangible learning objects, created by teachers and followed by students. Alternatively from a cultural heritage perspective paths can be used to create activity trails and guided tours support exploration by visitors through collections of cultural artefacts. This echoes the organised galleries and guided tours found in physical museums. The existance of tools, such as Walden's paths[1], Trailmeme[2] and Storify[3], provide functionalities for users to record and share paths through web resources and digital libraries. From this perspective everyone can take on role of curator and provide access to their own personal collections.

We have developed an online system called PATHS that allows curators and end-users to create and view paths to navigate through the Europeana[4] cultural heriage collection. As part of evaluations of the prototype PATHS system participants have created paths on various topics. In this paper we describe a number of these paths and their characteristics. Analysing paths that are created manually and characterising them can be seen as a first step towards developing methods to support the creation of paths automatically and semi-automatically. Within the context of the PATHS project this is being considered to deal with the following limitations of manual creation of paths. Firstly, the effort required in generating them often means that a sufficient number of paths on a variety of topics are not available. Secondly, the manual creation of paths is a very time-consuming process that would benefit from computational support in whatever form this might take. This paper presents initial work in automatically creating paths and provides the following novel con-

[1]`http://www.csdl.tamu.edu/walden/`
[2]`http://open.xerox.com/Services/xerox-trails`
[3]`http://storify.com/`
[4]`http://www.europeana.eu/`

tributions: (1) we present results of user studies describing what people want from paths and how they use them to navigate digital collections; (2) we analyse a set of manually-created paths to identify their properties and be able to characterise them; and (3) we present work on automatically generating background text for sequences of items, thus providing an efficient way to enrich paths with additional information with little manual input required.

The paper is structured as follows: Section 2 describes related work on the use of narratives in cultural heritage and previous approaches to automatically generate paths; Section 3 defines the problem of generating paths and describes the datasets used in the experiments; Section 4 presents analysis of manually-created paths; Section 5 shows results of using automatic methods to generate background text; and finally Section 6 concludes the paper and provides avenues for further work.

## 2 Related Work

### 2.1 Narratives and Cultural Heritage

The potential of narrative in digital CH to support learning, creativity and exploration is clear, providing opportunities for supporting a more active user interaction, including deeper engagement with context, representation of the collecting process, and facilitation of a more entertaining experience of learning (Mulholland and Collins, 2002). Walker et al. (2013) also propose narrative as a major element of interaction and informal learning, suggesting that meaning is made when the links between people and artefacts, and interpretation and ideas are surfaced, especially within social groups. Their experiments involve the use of mobile and handheld technologies in a physical museum environment, capturing audio annotations, but have much in common with experimental systems designed for path creation online. In a similar vein the StoryBank project utilises collections of photographs and audio narratives to create and share stories as information in the developing world (Frohlich and Rachovides, 2008).

Whilst technologies have aided the creation and sharing of narratives in physical cultural encounters, Manovich (1999) critiques the lack of narrative in digital cultural environments, offering that online collections and many CH web sites are databases with constantly changing content that inevitably lack a cohesive and persistent story. However, since "narrative is constructed by linking elements of this database in a particular order" (Manovich, 1999), it is possible to offer users any number of explicit 'trajectories' (narratives) through a digital information space, and by merging database and narrative in this way, creating a more dynamic, discovery-led experience. This view might be interpreted at its simplest level as a virtual representation of the guided tours routinely offered in physical CH spaces, and indeed there is a small strand of research into the creation of systems for generating and exploring online exhibitions and tours from items held within digital collections. A scenario of users creating and editing trails in a CH context is described by Walker (2006), including functionality for collecting, ordering and annotating museum objects.

### 2.2 Automatically Creating Paths

Generation of implicit trails through physical and virtual museum spaces has been related to the learning process (Peterson and Levene, 2003). In this example, trails are automatically created by users as they navigate their way through an information space, and may be used for individual or collaborative purposes. Research on the application of curated pathways in web environments has often focused on providing trails pre-prepared by experts (e.g. curators, educationalists) as a means of assisting novice users to navigate information online (Shipman et al., 2000). Indeed, it has been found that domain knowledge or expertise can considerably enhance the quality of trails created (Yuan and White, 2012). Automatic extraction and generation of trails in information spaces has been explored as a means of harnessing the wisdom of crowds, using the mass actions of earlier user behaviour to establish relevance, and recommend content or navigation routes to later users. Such trails can be readily mined from search engine transaction logs and have been shown to provide added value (White and Huang, 2010; Hassan and White, 2012; Liao et al., 2012). West and Leskovec (2012) take this notion a stage further and attempt to identify wayfinding strategies employed by browsers in Wikipedia, with the goal of assisting future users in their navigation by surfacing potentially useful hyperlinks.

Guided tours or pathways are essentially more structured, purposeful forms of trails, taking the user through a specific sequence of information nodes and may also be automatically generated, rather than manually curated as in the examples above. Wheeldon and Levene (2003) offer an algorithm for generating trails from site-search, enabling elements of structure and context to be incorporated into the trails created in this way, but noting potential scalability issues for web scale search tasks. In the CH domain, a small number of projects have attempted to automatically generate digital content in the form of exhibitions, tours and trails. Mäkelä et al. (2007) describe a system which utilises semantically annotated content to generate personalised 'exhibitions' from a structured narrative-based search query. Similarly, Zdrahal et al. (2008) demonstrate how pathways can be generated through a collection of semantically related documents to provide a means of exploration, using non-NLP clustering and path creation techniques. Sophisticated approaches such as linear programming and evolutionary algorithms have also been proposed for generating summaries and stories (McIntyre and Lapata, 2010; Woodsend and Lapata, 2010). In contrast, Wang et al. (2007) use a recommender system approach to generate museum tours on the basis of ratings stored within a dynamic user model, and Pechenizkiy and Calders (2007) propose the additional use of data mining techniques on log data to improve this type of tour personalisation.

In summary, online tours and trails are made possible either through manually curated content generated through the efforts of experts or other end users, or have been automatically generated from the mining of large scale search logs, or from collections benefitting from semantically-linked content and/or detailed user models.

## 3 Methodology

This study brings together work from several areas of the PATHS project. An analysis of what paths might be used for and what form they are expected to take, has had implications for the system design and functionality and evaluation measures. A user study focused upon evaluation of the first prototype has provided manually-created paths as a basis for analysing path content and attributes, which in turn informs the desired characteristics of automated paths and the algorithm designed for generating paths automatically.

### 3.1 Utilisation of Paths

Initial user requirements interviews with 22 expert users in the heritage, education and professional domains found a strong affinity with the path metaphor, revealing a range of different interpretations of what it means in the CH context and how they could be employed in an online environment to engage with key audiences. Eight interpretations of the path metaphor emerged:

1. Path as search history
2. Path as information seeking journey
3. Path as linked metadata
4. Path as a starting point or way in
5. Path as a route through
6. Path as augmented reality
7. Path as information literacy journey / learning process
8. Path as transaction process

The first three of these are closest to the idea of hypertext trails, with trails defined by user interaction in 1 and 2, and trails defined automatically, by the system in 3. Variations 4-6 are more creative interpretations, all suggesting opportunities for guiding the user into and through collections, encouraging exploration and/or offering an immersive experience, conducive with our initial vision for the PATHS system.

In addition to expert-defined routes, 5 also incorporates the idea of users being able to see and follow "well-trodden path" defined by the cumulative interactions of other users, thus extending the opportunities for utilizing search histories. Conversely, 7 and 8 are both process oriented, although 7 is experiential, user-defined, learning-oriented, typified by trial and error and unique to the individual, whilst 8 is a rigid process designed to escort all users consistently through a standard process of pre-defined steps.

A strong emphasis was placed on path content being carefully selected or 'curated' by the path-creator, with the addition of context and interpretation so that the objects within the path convey a narrative or meaning. Content may be derived from one collection, but there were seen to be significant benefits from including objects from diverse collections, along with other materials from external web sites.

Paths facilitate topic-based information retrieval typified by the berry-picking mode of interaction (Bates, 1989), rather than known item searching. Furthermore, paths may be a useful tool for personal information management in both formal and informal research scenarios, enabling the user to record, reuse and share their research activity, or helping them to organize their ideas. Creativity is also encouraged, as user-generated paths provide the means to repurpose CH objects into users' own narratives for private or public consumption.

A summary of specific user scenarios highlighted by participants is given below:

- Teachers/lecturers presentations and classroom activities
- Museum personnel curating collections, giving an overview, or covering a topic in depth
- Leisure users browsing, collecting interesting and/or visually appealing content
- Researchers to aid image-based research, sharing and discussing findings with fellow researchers and supervisors
- Non-academic specialists (e.g. local historians) collecting and sharing items of interest with other enthusiasts

### 3.2 Defining the Problem

To create a path or narrative that guides a user through a set of items from a collection, whether as a manual process or automatically, there are three main activities: (1) the selection of items to include in the path; (2) the arrangement of items to form a path or narrative and (3) the annotation of the path to with descriptive text and background information. We envision techniques to automate the entire process; however, a first step is to analyse existing manually-created paths to identify their characteristics and inform the automatic creation of similar structures.

### 3.3 User Study

The manually generated paths used for this study were created as part of a more detailed user study to evaluate the first prototype, conducted using a protocol informed by the Interactive IR evaluation framework (Borlund, 2003). Twenty-two users, including subject experts, students and general users (subject novices), each completed a 2-hour session, during which they participated in the following activities:

- Profile questionnaire and cognitive style test
- Familiarisation with the system
- 4x short information seeking tasks (5 minutes each)
- 1x long simulated work task - path creation (30 minutes)
- Task feedback questionnaire
- Session/system feedback questionnaire
- Think-after interview based upon the complex task

Of most interest here is the simulated work task, with associated observations, feedback and reflections. This task focused on the creation of a path, using a scenario adapted to the type of user. Freedom was given in choosing a subject for the path, and limited instructions were provided in what might be needed to complete the task, for example:

"Imagine you are a student who has been asked to create a path as part of a university assignment. You have been asked to use primary source materials to create a mini online exhibition suitable for a target group within the general public and/or school visitor categories. Your goal is to introduce a historical or art-focussed topic in a popular, accessible way, and to encourage further use and exploration of cultural heritage resources."

Data on the tasks was captured via log files, as well as screen recording and observations using the Morae usability software. Detailed analysis was undertaken of user behaviour in the process of completing the task, and of the paths created, from both quantitative and qualitative perspectives.

## 4 Analysing Manually-created Paths

In this section we describe the results of analysing the 22 paths created manually in the PATHS prototype system.

### 4.1 User behaviour

On average users spend 25.3 mins on creating a path (min=11.7; max=33.6) with an average of 201 mouse clicks (min=53; max=380). From the observations, it was noted that some participants spent quite a lot of time thinking about the task and pondering their next move, whilst others engaged in more rapid fire activity in the face of uncertainty. Analysis of the screen recordings showed a variety of primary interaction styles for this task, with a fairly even split between serial searching (33%) and serial browsing (39%), as the two most popular strategies. Serial searching involves repetitive search and reformulation, with only a page or two of search results viewed before searching again, and serial browsing involves very few searches, with large numbers of search results pages viewed (over 50 pages in some cases). These are then in effect, polar opposites of interaction. Only 6% engaged primarily in exploring behaviour (using the explore and similar items content), and 22% of participants occupied the middle ground, utilising a mix of search, browse and explore, with no strong preference for any one style.

### 4.2 Properties of paths

The mean number of items in a path was 10.7 (std dev=6.7 items) with a minimum of 5 items and maximum of 29 items. Most popular bin is 6-10 items in a path (59%). We found 85% of the items included in the paths included an image with the metadata. The paths created were manually categorised by theme to ascertain whether there are any distinct preferences for the subject matter of content included. The most popular categories were paths about places (23%), art subjects (23%) and history subjects (32%). These themes are likely to have been influenced at least partly by what content is currently available in our collection, although the amount of art-related content is much less than for history, and also appear to have been influenced by the topics covered in existing paths in the system (e.g. places, topics related to the world wars). There were, however a significant number of expert users who attempted to build paths related to their own research interests, with varying degrees of success.

### 4.3 Descriptions and ordering

Once items have been selected and they have been transferred in the path creation workspace, users have the opportunity to modify and enhance their path with a number of tools for adding content and metadata, and for re-ordering the content. On creating the path, most users immediately went to the metadata fields and added information for the path description and duration fields, as well as a number of tags (or keywords). A short 1-2 line description of the path appears to be the norm and was added in 91% of cases. Tags were added by 82% of users and a duration by only 46% of users. It is clear from further investigation that the tags were added incorrectly (without commas between them) by a significant number of users and a tip for successful use is required.

The items within a path can be annotated with the user's own contextual information, and can be re-ordered into a more meaningful sequence, such as a chronological or narrative sequence. These more advanced features were used by significantly fewer users, which could indicate a learning issue, a lack of need, or a time constraint. On reviewing the paths created by our evaluation participants it is found that in 41% of cases, contextual information was not added to any items in the path. There are however 32% in which annotations were added to all items (generally these were shorter paths with fewer items), and a further 27% where annotations were added to some or most of the items.

In 72% of cases the items in the paths created were re-ordered to some degree, with 17% spending a considerable amount of time on this activity. This finding is encouraging, as the default is for items to be included in the path in the order they were saved to the workspace, and re-ordering indicates that users are thinking about their path as a whole and trying to make sense of the information it is intended to convey. Typical types of ordering included chronology (32%), narrative (23%), geography (for example, a walking tour - 9%), theme (9%) and 'interestingness' (5%).

## 5 Enriching paths with background information

This section describes preliminary work on the task of semi-automated path creation. In particular we describe efforts to enrich paths with background contextual information using relevant Wikipedia articles. The related work described in Section 2.2 shows that there have been previous efforts to automatically select cultural heritage items to form paths, trails and exhibitions. However to our knowledge no significant effort has been made to automatically annotate such paths with descriptive or contextual information. The interviews described in Section 3.1 highlighted the importance CH experts placed on having additional information to give context for the items in the path. It was also noted during the manual path-creation exercise (Section 4.3) that a significant number of the users did not add any such information to the path. The reasons for this are unclear, but nevertheless there seems to be sufficient motivation to devise automatic methods for this task. Although the methods have previously been well established in other tasks[5] , we believe

[5]INEX Tweet Contextualization Track (https://inex.mmci.uni-saarland.de/tracks/qa/) and Link-the-wiki Track (http://www.inex.otago.ac.nz/tracks/wiki-link/wiki-link.asp)

this is the first time they have been applied for the task of annotating sequences of items in this way.

### 5.1 Method

Manually generated paths contain sequences of items selected from Europeana on some topic or theme. Creators provide their own title, subject keywords and description for the path. To aid creation of paths we explore whether background information could be generated automatically for such paths. An approach is presented here which shows promise as a potential way to achieve this task. The input for this approach is a sequence of items and a key Wikipedia article which describes the overall topic of the path. The output comprises sentences taken from a relevant Wikipedia article. The aim is for this output to provide useful and interesting additional background information related to the items and theme of the path. In this paper experiments are focussed on how to select good quality text to present as additional information for the path. For this reason the key Wikipedia article is manually chosen, and the task is to find a good approach for selecting the most relevant sentences from this key article for the text.

Two methods are tested in this paper. The first method simply takes the first $n$ sentences of the article and outputs this. Since Wikipedia articles are always structured to have a summary of the article in the first paragraph we can expect this text to perform well as a summary of the path topic.

The second method is more advanced and attempts to find text in the article that is relevant to the actual items that have been chosen for the path. This approach uses the Wikipedia Miner software (Milne and Witten, 2008) to add inline links to the text in the items for this approach. This software disambiguates terms in the text and then detects links using various features such as the commonness of the term, the overall relatedness of the terms in the text and so on. The result is text enriched with inline links to relevant Wikipedia articles. Each link also has an associated confidence value which indicates how sure the software is that the link is correctly disambiguated and relevant to the text.

The approach works as follows for a sequence of items $S$ and a key article $K$. First Wikipedia Miner is run over the items in $S$. The text input to Wikipedia Miner comprises the title, subject and description fields of each item. The output is a set of article titles $W$ comprising the titles of all the linked articles which were found in the text fields of $S$. For each title in $W$ we also have the associated confidence value for the link as calculated by Wikipedia Miner. The next step is to select from $K$ the most relevant sentences to output as the generated text. For each sentence in $K$ a score is assigned if any of the words in the sentence match one of the titles in $W$. The score is then simply the sum of the confidence values associated with these titles. The top scoring sentences are then output as the background text. This method can be considered to be a kind of query based summarisation (Jurafsky and Martin, 2008).

### 5.2 Results

The automatic approaches for generating background text were run over the items in the 22 manually created paths described in the previous section. To ensure a fair test the user-added text was was discarded and only the original Europeana metadata for the items was used as source for the methods.

For each path a single key Wikipedia article was manually found which best captured the overall theme or topic of the path. For all paths at least one reasonably good article was found, although for some paths the articles were better matches for the path topic than for others. Some examples are shown in Table 1.

With the input ready, the approaches described were run over the items and key articles to generate the additional text. This was limited to 3 sentences to provide a short but useful piece of text for viewers of the paths. For example one path was entitled "Bronze Age metallurgy". The user provided description was as follows:

*Bronze Age metalsmiths produce a variety of objects, however, we learn as much from the tools, leftover debris and the way in which objects were deposited as we do from the finished objects themselves.*

The key article chosen for the path was "Bronze Age". The items in the path included various artifacts and working debris from the Bronze Age. For the first approach the output is the first 3 sentences from this article:

*The Bronze Age is a period characterized by the use of copper and its alloy bronze as the chief hard materials in the manufacture of some implements and weapons. Chronologically, it stands be-*

| Path title | Key Wikipedia article |
|---|---|
| Canals in England | Canals of the United Kingdom |
| A brief history of Sheffield | History of Sheffield |
| Art and Criticism of John Ruskin | John Ruskin |
| Early medieval features in English Parish Churches | Architecture of the medieval cathedrals of England |
| Brooches through the ages | Brooch |

Table 1: Key articles for paths

*tween the Stone Age and Iron Age. The term Stone Age implies the inability to smelt any ore, the term Bronze Age implies the inability to smelt iron ore and the term Iron Age implies the ability to manufacture artifacts in any of the three types of hard material.*

For the second approach the top 3 highest scoring sentences were output:

*A region could be in the Bronze Age either by smelting its own copper and alloying with tin or by trading for bronze from production areas elsewhere. The Bronze Age in Ireland commenced around 2000 BC, when copper was alloyed with tin and used to manufacture Ballybeg type flat axes and associated metalwork. The Bronze Age is a period characterized by the use of copper and its alloy bronze as the chief hard materials in the manufacture of some implements and weapons.*

These sentences scored most highly since they contained the most high-confidence terms from the items, for example terms such as 'copper', 'alloy' and 'Bronze Age'.

### 5.3 Evaluation

To evaluate the two approaches, 5 annotators were presented with the paths and the text and asked to rate each path on 3 dimensions:

- The *relevance* of the text to the theme and items of the path. Text which relates strongly to the path is scored highly while off-topic or irrelevant text is given a low score.
- The *coherence* or quality of the text itself. Text which appears well-written and well-structured is scored highly, while poorly written or incoherent text is given a low score.
- The *contextualisation* of the text in relation to the path. To achieve a high score the text should offer useful or interesting additional information which is not found elsewhere within the content, i.e. the text helps to provide a context for items in the path.

Annotators were asked to grade from A (very good) to E (very poor) on each dimension. The results are shown in Figure 1. The results for the first 3 sentences are shown as **First3** and for the weighted approach as **Weighted**. For each dimension, the distribution of judgements across the paths is shown. The **First3** approach was found to be superior in every dimension. For relevance scores 90% of the scores were either A or B compared to 63% for the **Weighted** approach. Similarly for the coherence judgements 97% were A or B compared to 62% for the weighted approach. The reason for this superior performance seems to be that the first few sentences of Wikipedia articles are deliberately created to give a short summary introduction of the topic of the article. This explains the high scores for relevance and coherence.

Both approaches scored lower on the contextualisation dimension, with **First3** getting 67% A or B grades and the **Weighted** approach getting 43%. There may be several reasons for this. Firstly one problem is that the auto-generated text sometimes repeats information that is already in the path and item descriptions; thus the text fails to meet the requirement of 'useful additional information'. Secondly the text is sometimes quite general and vague, rather than focussing on specific details which might be most relevant to the items chosen for the path.

To measure the agreement among the annotators the following approach was used. First the scores were converted to numeric values; A to 1, B to 2 and so on. Then the scores for each annotator were compared to the average of the scores of all the other annotators. The correlation was computing using Spearman's correlation coefficient. These scores were then averaged amongst all annotators to give a final agreement value. The results are shown in Table 2.

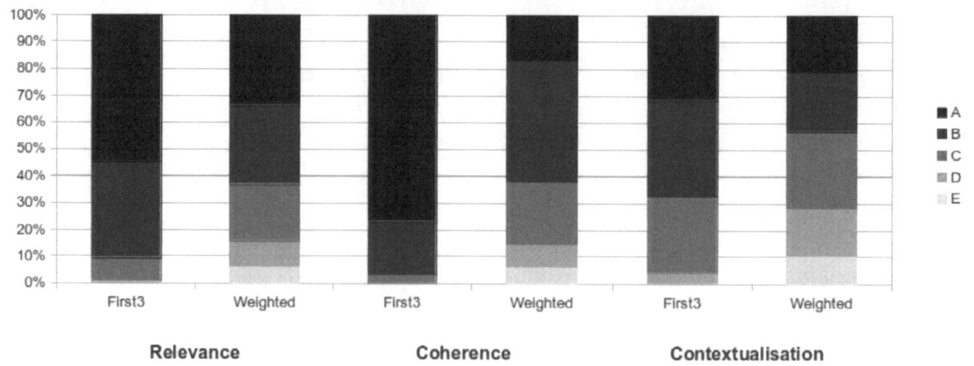


Figure 1: Comparing the results of the two methods.

| | **First3** | **Weighted** |
|---|---|---|
| Relevance | 0.57 | 0.57 |
| Coherence | 0.28 | 0.56 |
| Contextualisation | 0.56 | 0.78 |

Table 2: Agreement amongst annotators.

For both approaches there was good agreement on the Relevance dimension. For the Coherence dimension the **First3** approach got quite a low score. This may be because one annotator gave lower scores for all paths, while the others all gave consistently high scores, which seems to have skewed the correlation co-efficient. For the contextualisation dimension the correlation scores for high for both approaches, and the **Weighted** approach in particular achieved a very high agreement value.

## 6 Conclusions

This paper presented results of interviews about creating paths through cultural heritage collections. These results inform us on how people want to navigate through cultural heritage collections using the path metaphor, how they wish to make use of paths for their work and education, and what information and qualities they consider it important for a path to contain. The paper also presents results from studies using the PATHS prototype software where users were able to search and explore a large digital library collection and create their own paths of items from the collection on topics of their interest.

From the interviews it was clear that the experts considered it important that the paths contain additional information to convey contextual information to understand the meaning of the items in the path. The results from the user studies showed that this need was not being met in a significant number of cases; users were putting items together on a topic but adding little or no descriptive text about the topic and the items in the path. Therefore we identified this as a key task which might benefit from automatic methods. The simpler approach which output the first $n$ sentences from the key Wikipedia article was found to generate the best results. The resulting generated text was found to be relevant and coherent. In most cases the text was also found to add useful context about the topic.

Future work will further refine the text generation approach. The approach depends on successfully identifying a good key article for each path. In these experiments the key article was manually chosen, however we are devising methods to select this article automatically. To correct the problem with repeated information a filtering approach could eliminate information that is already contained within the paths.

## Acknowledgments

The research leading to these results was carried out as part of the PATHS project (`http://paths-project.eu`) funded by the European Community's Seventh Framework Programme (FP7/2007-2013) under grant agreement no. 270082.

## References

Marcia J Bates. 1989. The design of browsing and berrypicking techniques for the online search interface. *Online Information Review*.

Pia Borlund. 2003. The IIR evaluation model: a framework for evaluation of interactive information retrieval systems. *Information research*, 8(3).

David M Frohlich and Dorothy Rachovides. 2008. Using digital stories for local and global information sharing. In *Community and International Development, CHI 2008 Workshop*.

R. Furuta, F.. Shipman, C. Marshall, D. Brenner, and H. Hsieh. 1997. Hypertext paths and the World-Wide Web: experiences with Walden's Paths. In *Proceedings of the eighth ACM conference on Hypertext*, pages 167–176, New York, NY.

Ahmed Hassan and Ryen W White. 2012. Task tours: helping users tackle complex search tasks. In *Proceedings of the 21st ACM international conference on Information and knowledge management*, pages 1885–1889. ACM.

Daniel Jurafsky and James H. Martin. 2008. *Speech and Language Processing (2nd Edition) (Prentice Hall Series in Artificial Intelligence)*. Prentice Hall.

Zhen Liao, Yang Song, Li-wei He, and Yalou Huang. 2012. Evaluating the effectiveness of search task trails. In *Proceedings of the 21st international conference on World Wide Web*, pages 489–498. ACM.

Eetu Mäkelä, Osma Suominen, and Eero Hyvönen. 2007. Automatic exhibition generation based on semantic cultural content. In *Proc. of the Cultural Heritage on the Semantic Web Workshop at ISWC+ ASWC*, volume 2007.

Lev Manovich. 1999. Database as symbolic form. *Convergence: The International Journal of Research into New Media Technologies*, 5(2):80–99.

Neil McIntyre and Mirella Lapata. 2010. Plot induction and evolutionary search for story generation. In *Proceedings of the 48th Annual Meeting of the Association for Computational Linguistics*, pages 1562–1572. Association for Computational Linguistics.

D. Milne and I.H. Witten. 2008. Learning to link with wikipedia. In *Proceeding of the 17th ACM conference on Information and knowledge management*, pages 509–518. ACM.

Paul Mulholland and Trevor Collins. 2002. Using digital narratives to support the collaborative learning and exploration of cultural heritage. In *Database and Expert Systems Applications, 2002. Proceedings. 13th International Workshop on*, pages 527–531. IEEE.

Mykola Pechenizkiy and Toon Calders. 2007. A framework for guiding the museum tours personalization. In *Proceedings of the Workshop on Personalised Access to Cultural Heritage (PATCH07)*, pages 11–28.

Don Peterson and Mark Levene. 2003. Trail records and navigational learning. *London review of Education*, 1(3):207–216.

S. Reich, L. Carr, D. De Roure, and W. Hall. 1999. Where have you been from here? Trails in hypertext systems. *ACM Computing Surveys*, 31.

Frank M Shipman, Richard Furuta, Donald Brenner, Chung-Chi Chung, and Hao-wei Hsieh. 2000. Guided paths through web-based collections: Design, experiences, and adaptations. *Journal of the American Society for Information Science*, 51(3):260–272.

K. Walker, A. Main, and Fass. J. 2013. User-Generated Trails in Third Places. In *HCI-3P Workshop on Human Computer Interaction for Third Places at Computer Human Interaction 2013*.

Kevin Walker. 2006. Story structures. building narrative trails in museums. In *Technology-Mediated Narrative Environments for Learning*, pages 103–114. Sense Publishers.

Yiwen Wang, Lora M Aroyo, Natalia Stash, and Lloyd Rutledge. 2007. Interactive user modeling for personalized access to museum collections: The rijksmuseum case study. In *User Modeling 2007*, pages 385–389. Springer.

Robert West and Jure Leskovec. 2012. Human wayfinding in information networks. In *Proceedings of the 21st international conference on World Wide Web*, pages 619–628. ACM.

Richard Wheeldon and Mark Levene. 2003. The best trail algorithm for assisted navigation of web sites. In *Web Congress, 2003. Proceedings. First Latin American*, pages 166–178. IEEE.

Ryen W White and Jeff Huang. 2010. Assessing the scenic route: measuring the value of search trails in web logs. In *Proceedings of the 33rd international ACM SIGIR conference on Research and development in information retrieval*, pages 587–594. ACM.

M. Wilson, Kulesm B., M. Schraefel, and B. Schneiderman. 2010. From keyword search to exploration: Designing future search interfaces for the web. *Foundations and Trends in Web Science*, 2(1):1–97.

Kristian Woodsend and Mirella Lapata. 2010. Automatic generation of story highlights. In *Proceedings of the 48th Annual Meeting of the Association for Computational Linguistics*, pages 565–574. Association for Computational Linguistics.

Xiaojun Yuan and Ryen White. 2012. Building the trail best traveled: effects of domain knowledge on web search trailblazing. In *Proceedings of the 2012 ACM annual conference on Human Factors in Computing Systems*, pages 1795–1804. ACM.

Zdenek Zdrahal, Paul Mulholland, and Trevor Collins. 2008. Exploring pathways across stories. In *Proc. of International Conference on Distributed Human-Machine Systems.*

# Using character overlap to improve language transformation

**Sander Wubben**
Tilburg University
P.O. Box 90135
5000 LE Tilburg
The Netherlands
s.wubben@uvt.nl

**Emiel Krahmer**
Tilburg University
P.O. Box 90135
5000 LE Tilburg
The Netherlands
e.j.krahmer@uvt.nl

**Antal van den Bosch**
Radboud University Nijmegen
P.O. Box 9103
6500 HD Nijmegen
The Netherlands
a.vandenbosch@let.ru.nl

## Abstract

Language transformation can be defined as translating between diachronically distinct language variants. We investigate the transformation of Middle Dutch into Modern Dutch by means of machine translation. We demonstrate that by using character overlap the performance of the machine translation process can be improved for this task.

## 1 Introduction

In this paper we aim to develop a system to paraphrase between diachronically distinct language variants. For research into history, historical linguistics and diachronic language change, historical texts are of great value. Specifically from earlier periods, texts are often the only forms of information that have been preserved. One problem that arises when studying these texts is the difference between the language the text is written in and the modern variant that the researchers who want to study the texts know and speak themselves. It takes a great deal of deciphering and interpretation to be able to grasp these texts. Our aim is to facilitate scholars such as historians who do not possess extensive knowledge of Middle Dutch who are studying medieval texts. We do this by attempting to generate literal translations of the sentences in the text into modern language. In particular we focus on the task of translating Middle Dutch to modern Dutch. The transformation between language variants, either synchronically or diachronically, can be seen as a paraphrase and a translation task, as it is often impossible to categorize two languages as either variants or different languages.

We define Middle Dutch as a collection of closely related West Germanic dialects that were spoken and written between 1150 and 1500 in the area that is now defined as the Netherlands and parts of Belgium. One of the factors that make Middle Dutch difficult to read is the fact that at the time no overarching standard language existed. Modern Dutch is defined as Dutch as spoken from 1500. The variant we investigate is contemporary Dutch. An important difference with regular paraphrasing is the amount of parallel data available. The amount of parallel data for the variant pair Middle Dutch - Modern Dutch is several orders of magnitude smaller than bilingual parallel corpora typically used in machine translation (Koehn, 2005) or monolingual parallel corpora used for paraphrase generation by machine translation (Wubben et al., 2010).

We do expect many etymologically related words to show a certain amount of character overlap between the Middle and Modern variants. An example of the data is given below, from the work 'Van den vos Reynaerde' ('About Reynard the Fox'), part of the Comburg manuscript that was written between 1380-1425. Here, the first text is the original text, the second text is a modern translation in Dutch by Walter Verniers and a translation in English is added below that for clarity.

"Doe al dat hof versamet was,
Was daer niemen, sonder die das,
Hine hadde te claghene over Reynaerde,
Den fellen metten grijsen baerde."

"Toen iedereen verzameld was,
was er niemand -behalve de das-
die niet kwam klagen over Reynaert,
die deugniet met zijn grijze baard."

"When everyone was gathered,
there was noone -except the badger-
who did not complain about Reynaert,
that rascal with his grey beard."

We can observe that although the two Dutch texts are quite different, there is a large amount of character overlap in the words that are used. Our aim is to use this character overlap to compensate for the lower amount of data that is available. We compare three different approaches to translate Middle Dutch into Modern Dutch: a standard Phrase-Based machine translation (PBMT) approach, a PBMT approach with additional preprocessing based on Needleman-Wunsch sequence alignment, and a character bigram based PBMT approach. The PBMT approach with preprocessing identifies likely translations based on character overlap and adds them as a dictionary to improve the statistical alignment process. The PBMT approach based on character bigrams rather than translating words, transliterates character bigrams and in this way improves the transformation process. We demonstrate that these two approaches outperform standard PBMT in this task, and that the PBMT transliteration approach based on character bigrams performs best.

## 2 Related work

Language transformation by machine translation within a language is a task that has not been studied extensively before. Related work is the study by Xu et al. (2012). They evaluate paraphrase systems that attempt to paraphrase a specific style of writing into another style. The plays of William Shakespeare and the modern translations of these works are used in this study. They show that their models outperform baselines based on dictionaries and out-of-domain parallel text. Their work differs from our work in that they target writing in a specific literary style and we are interested in translating between diachronic variants of a language.

Work that is slightly comparable is the work by Zeldes (2007), who extrapolates correspondences in a small parallel corpus taken from the Modern and Middle Polish Bible. The correspondences are extracted using machine translation with the aim of deriving historical grammar and lexical items. A larger amount of work has been published about spelling normalization of historical texts. Baron and Rayson (2008) developed tools for research in Early Modern English. Their tool, VARD 2, finds candidate modern form replacements for spelling variants in historical texts. It makes use of a dictionary and a list of spelling rules. By plugging in other dictionaries and spelling rules, the tool can be adapted for other tasks. Kestemont et al. (2010) describe a machine learning approach to normalize the spelling in Middle Dutch Text from the 12th century. They do this by converting the historical spelling variants to single canonical (present-day) lemmas. Memory-based learning is used to learn intra-lemma spelling variation. Although these approaches normalize the text, they do not provide a translation.

More work has been done in the area of translating between closely related languages and dealing with data sparsity that occurs within these language pairs (Hajič et al., 2000; Van Huyssteen and Pilon, 2009). Koehn et al. (2003) have shown that there is a direct negative correlation between the size of the vocabulary of a language and the accuracy of the translation. Alignment models are directly affected by data sparsity. Uncommon words are more likely to be aligned incorrectly to other words or, even worse, to large segments of words (Och and Ney, 2003). Out of vocabulary (OOV) words also pose a problem in the translation process, as systems are unable to provide translations for these words. A standard heuristic is to project them into the translated sentence untranslated.

Various solutions to data sparsity have been studied, among them the use of part-of-speech tags, suffixes and word stems to normalize words (Popovic and Ney, 2004; De Gispert and Marino, 2006), the treatment of compound words in translation (Koehn and Knight, 2003), transliteration of names and named entities, and advanced models that combine transliteration and translation (Kondrak et al., 2003; Finch et al., 2012) or learn unknown words by analogical reasoning (Langlais and Patry, 2007).

Vilar et al. (2007) investigate a way to handle data sparsity in machine translation between closely related languages by translating between characters as opposed to words. The words in the parallel sentences are segmented into characters. Spaces between words are marked with a special character. The sequences of characters are then used to train a standard machine translation model and a language model with n-grams up to $n = 16$. They apply their system to the translation between the related languages Spanish and Catalan, and find that a word based system outperforms their letter-based system. However, a combined system performs marginally better in terms of BLEU scores.

Tiedemann (2009) shows that combining character-based translation with phrase-based translation improves machine translation quality in terms of BLEU and NIST scores when translating between Swedish and Norwegian if the OOV-words are translated beforehand with the character-based model.

Nakov and Tiedemann (2012) investigate the use of character-level models in the translation between Macedonian and Bulgarian movie subtitles. Their aim is to translate between the resource poor language Macedonian to the related language Bulgarian, in order to use Bulgarian as a pivot in order to translate to other languages such as English. Their research shows that using character bigrams shows improvement over a word-based baseline.

It seems clear that character overlap can be used to improve translation quality in related languages. We therefore use character overlap in language transformation between two diachronic variants of a language.

## 3 This study

In this study we investigate the task of translating from Middle Dutch to Modern Dutch. Similarly to resource poor languages, one of the problems that are apparent is the small amount of parallel Middle Dutch - Modern Dutch data that is available. To combat the data sparseness we aim to use the character overlap that exists between the Middle Dutch words and their Modern Dutch counterparts. Examples of overlap in some of the words given in the example can be viewed in Table1. We are interested in the question how we can use this overlap to improve the performance of the translation model. We consider three approaches: (A) Perform normal PBMT without any preprocessing, (B) Apply a preprocessing step in which we pinpoint words and phrases that can be aligned based on character overlap and (C) perform machine translation not to words but to character bigrams in order to make use of the character overlap.

We will first discuss the PBMT baseline, followed by the PBMT + overlap system and the character bigram PBMT transliteration system in Section 4. We then describe the experiment with human judges in Section 6, and its results in Section 7. We close with a discussion of our results in Section 8.

| Middle Dutch | Modern Dutch |
|---|---|
| versamet | verzameld |
| was | was |
| niemen | niemand |
| die | de |
| das | das |
| claghene | klagen |
| over | over |
| Reynaerde | Reynaert |
| metten | met zijn |
| grijsen | grijze |
| baerde | baard |

Table 1: Examples of character overlap in words from a fragment of 'Van den vos Reynaerde'

## 4 Language transformation Models

### 4.1 PBMT baseline

For our baseline we use the Moses software to train a phrase based machine translation (PBMT) model (Koehn et al., 2007). In general, a statistical machine translation model normally finds a best translation $\tilde{E}$ of a text in language $F$ for a text in language $E$ by combining a translation model $P(F|E)$ with a language model $P(E)$:

$$\tilde{E} = arg \max_{E \in E^*} P(F|E)P(E)$$

In phrase-based machine translation the sentence $F$ is segmented into a sequence of $I$ phrases during decoding. Each source phrase is then translated into a target phrase to form sentence $E$. Phrases may be reordered.

The GIZA++ statistical alignment package (Och and Ney, 2003) is used to perform the word alignments, which are later combined into phrase alignments in the Moses pipeline to build the language transformation model. GIZA++ implements IBM Models 1 to 5 and an HMM word alignment model to find statistically motivated alignments between words. We first tokenize our data. We then lowercase all data and use all sentences from the Modern Dutch part of the corpus to train an $n$-gram language model with the SRILM toolkit (Stolcke, 2002). Then we run the GIZA++ aligner using the training pairs of sentences in Middle Dutch and Modern Dutch. We execute GIZA++ with standard settings and we optimize using minimum error rate training with BLEU scores. The Moses decoder is used to generate the translations.

### 4.2 PBMT with overlap-based alignment

Before using the Moses pipeline we perform a preprocessing alignment step based on character overlap. Word and phrase pairs that exhibit a large amount of character overlap are added to the parallel corpus that GIZA++ is trained on. Every time we find a phrase or word pair with large overlap it is added to the corpus. This helps bias the alignment procedure towards aligning similar words and reduces alignment errors. To perform the preprocessing step we use the Needleman-Wunsch algorithm (Needleman and Wunsch, 1970). The Needleman-Wunsch algorithm is a dynamic programming algorithm that performs a global alignment on two sequences. Sequence alignment is a method to find commonalities in two (or more) sequences of some items or characters. One often used example is the comparison of sequences of DNA to find evolutionary differences and similarities. Sequence alignment is also used in linguistics, where it is applied to finding the longest common substring or the differences or similarities between strings.

The Needleman-Wunsch algorithm is a sequence alignment algorithm that optimizes a score function to find an optimal alignment of a pair of sequences. Each possible alignment is scored according to the score function, where the alignment giving the highest similarity score is the optimal alignment of a pair of sequences. If more than one alignment yields the highest score, there are multiple optimal solutions. The algorithm uses an iterative matrix to calculate the optimal solution. All possible pairs of characters containing one character from each sequence are plotted in a 2-dimensional matrix. Then, all possible alignments between those characters can be represented by pathways through the matrix. Insertions and deletions are allowed, but can be penalized by means of a gap penalty in the alignment.

The first step is to initialize the matrix and fill in the gap scores in the top row and leftmost column. In our case we heuristically set the values of the scores to +1 for matches, -2 for mismatches and -1 for gaps after evaluating on our development set. After initialization, we can label the cells in the matrix $C(i,j)$ where $i = 1,2,...,N$ and $j = 1,2,...,M$, the score of any cell $C(i,j)$ is then the maximum of:

$$\begin{aligned} q_{diag} &= C(i-1,j-1) + s(i,j) \\ q_{down} &= C(i-1,j) + g \\ q_{right} &= C(i,j-1) + g \end{aligned}$$

Here, $s(i,j)$ is the substitution score for letters $i$ and $j$, and $g$ is the gap penalty score. If $i$ and $j$ match, the substitution score is in fact the matching score. The table is filled this way recursively, filling each cell with the maximum score of the three possible options (diagonally, down and right). After this is done, an optimal path can be found by performing a traceback, starting in the lower right corner of the table and ending in the upper left corner, by visiting cells horizontally, vertically or diagonally, but only those cells with the highest score. After this process we end up with an alignment.

We use the Needleman-Wunsch algorithm to find an optimal alignment of the Middle Dutch - Modern Dutch sentence pairs. We regard each line as a sentence. In case of rhyming text, a frequent phenomenon in Middle Dutch text, lines are usually parts of sentences. We then consider each line a string, and we try to align as many characters and whitespaces to their equivalents in the parallel line. We split the aligned sentences in each position where two whitespaces align and we consider the resulting aligned words or phrases as alignments. For each aligned word or phrase pair we calculate the Jaccard coefficient and if that is equal or higher than a threshold we add the aligned words or phrases to the training material. We heuristically set this threshold to 0.5. By using this method we already can find many-to-one and one-to-many alignments. In this way we help the GIZA++ alignment process by biasing it towards aligning words and phrases that show overlap. Table 2 illustrates this process for two lines.

### 4.3 Character bigram transliteration

Another somewhat novel approach we propose for Language Transformation is Character-based transliteration. To circumvent the problem of

| Middle Dutch: | hine | hadde+ | ++te | claghene | over | Reynaerde | , |
|---|---|---|---|---|---|---|---|
| Modern Dutch: | di+e | ++niet | kwam | klag+en+ | over | Reynaer+t | , |
| Jaccard | 0.4 | 0.14 | 0 | 0.63 | 1 | 0.70 | 1 |

| Middle Dutch: | +den | fe++llen | met++ten | grijsen | baerde | . |
|---|---|---|---|---|---|---|
| Modern Dutch: | die+ | deugniet | met zijn | grijze+ | baard+ | . |
| Jaccard | 0.50 | 0.09 | 0.50 | 0.71 | 0.8 | 1 |

Table 2: Alignment of lines with Jaccard scores for the aligned phrases. A + indicates a gap introduced by the Needleman Wunsch alignment.

OOV-words and use the benefits of character overlap more directly in the MT system, we build a translation model based on character bigrams, similar to (Nakov and Tiedemann, 2012). Where they use this approach to translate between closely related languages, we use it to translate between diachronic variants of a language. The sentences in the parallel corpus are broken into character bigrams, with a special character representing whitespaces. These bigrams are used to train the translation model and the language model. An example of the segmentation process is displayed in Table 3. We train an SRILM language model on the character bigrams and model sequences of up to 10 bigrams. We then run the standard Moses pipeline, using GIZA++ with standard settings to generate the phrase-table and we use the Moses decoder to decode the bigram sequences. A number of sample entries are shown in Table 4. As a final step, we recombine the bigrams into words. The different sizes of the Phrase-table for the different approaches can be observed in Table 5.

| original | segmented |
|---|---|
| Hine | #H Hi in ne e# |
| hadde | #h ha ad dd de e# |
| te | #t te e# |
| claghene | #c cl la ag gh he en ne e# |
| over | #o ov ve er r# |
| Reynaerde | #R Re ey yn na ae er rd de e# |
| , | #, ,# |

Table 3: Input and output of the character bigram segmenter

## 5 Data Set

Our training data consists of various Middle Dutch literary works with their modern Dutch translation. A breakdown of the different works is in

| | |
|---|---|
| #d da at t# | en n# #d da aa ar |
| #d da at t# | et t# #s st |
| #d da at t# | et t# #s |
| #d da at t# | ie et t# #s st |
| #d da at t# | ie et t# #s |
| #d da at t# | la an n# |
| #d da at t# | le et t# |
| #d da at t# | n# #d da aa ar ro |
| #d da at t# | n# #d da aa ar |
| #d da at t# | n# |
| #d da at t# | rd da at t# |
| #d da at ts s# | #d da at t# |
| #d da at ts si i# | #h he eb bb be en |
| #d da at ts | #d da at t# |
| #d da at ts | #w wa at t# |
| #d da at tt tu | #w wa at t# #j |

Table 4: Example entries from the character bigram Phrase-table, without scores.

| system | lines |
|---|---|
| PBMT | 20,092 |
| PBMT + overlap | 27,885 |
| character bigram transliteration | 93,594 |

Table 5: Phrase-table sizes of the different models

Table 6. All works are from the Digital Library of Dutch Literature[1]. "Middle Dutch" is a very broad definition. It encompasses all Dutch language spoken and written between 1150 and 1500 in the Netherlands and parts of Belgium. Works stemming from different centuries, regions and writers can differ greatly in their orthography and spelling conventions. No variant of Dutch was considered standard or the norm; Middle Dutch can be considered a collection of related lects (regiolects, dialects). This only adds to the problem of data

[1] http://www.dbnl.org

sparsity. Our test set consists of a selection of sentences from the Middle Dutch work Beatrijs, a Maria legend written around 1374 by an anonymous author.

| source text | lines | date of origin |
|---|---|---|
| Van den vos Reynaerde | 3428 | around 1260 |
| Sint Brandaan | 2312 | 12th century |
| Gruuthuuse gedichten | 224 | around 1400 |
| 't Prieel van Trojen | 104 | 13th century |
| Various poems | 42 | 12th-14th cent. |

Table 6: Middle Dutch works in the training set

| | |
|---|---|
| Middle Dutch | Si seide: 'Ic vergheeft u dan.<br>Ghi sijt mijn troest voer alle man |
| Modern Dutch | Ze zei: 'ik vergeef het je dan.<br>Je bent voor mij de enige man |
| PBMT | Ze zei : ' Ik vergheeft u dan .<br>Gij ze alles in mijn enige voor al man |
| PBMT + Overlap | Ze zei : ' Ik vergheeft u dan .<br>dat ze mijn troest voor al man |
| Char. Bigram PBMT | Ze zeide : ' Ik vergeeft u dan .<br>Gij zijt mijn troost voor alle man |
| Middle Dutch | Dat si daer snachts mochte bliven.<br>'Ic mocht u qualijc verdriven,' |
| Modern Dutch | omdat ze nu niet verder kon reizen.<br>'Ik kan u echt de deur niet wijzen,' |
| PBMT<br>' | dat ze daar snachts kon bliven .<br>Ik kon u qualijc verdriven , ' |
| PBMT + Overlap | dat ze daar s nachts kon blijven .<br>' Ik kon u qualijc verdriven , ' |
| Char. Bigram PBMT | dat zij daar snachts mocht blijven .<br>' Ik mocht u kwalijk verdrijven , |

Table 7: Example output

## 6 Experiment

In order to evaluate the systems, we ran an experiment to collect human rankings of the output of the systems. We also performed automatic evaluation.

### 6.1 Materials

Because of the nature of our data, in which sentences often span multiple lines, it is hard to evaluate the output on the level of separate lines. We therefore choose to evaluate pairs of lines. We randomly choose a line, and check if it is part of a sensible sentence that can be understood without more context. If that is the case, we select it to include in our test set. In this way we select 25 pairs of lines. We evaluate the translations produced by the three different systems for these sentences. Examples of the selected sentences and the generated corresponding output are displayed in Table 7.

### 6.2 Participants

The participants in this evaluation study were 22 volunteers. All participants were native speakers of Dutch, and participated through an online interface. All participants were adults, and 12 were male and 10 female. In addition to the 22 participants, one expert in the field of Middle Dutch also performed the experiment, in order to be able to compare the judgements of the laymen and the expert.

### 6.3 Procedure

The participants were asked to rank three different automatic literal translations of Middle Dutch text. For reference, they were also shown a modern (often not literal) translation of the text by Dutch author Willem Wilmink. The order of items to judge was randomized for each participant, as well as the order of the output of the systems for each sentence. The criterium for ranking was the extent to which the sentences could be deciphered and understood. The participants were asked to always provide a ranking and were not allowed to assign the same rank to multiple sentences. In this way, each participant provided 25 rankings where each pair of sentences received a distinct rank. The pair with rank 1 is considered best and the pair with 3 is considered worst.

| system | mean rank | 95 % c. i. |
|---|---|---|
| PBMT | 2.44 (0.03) | 2.38 - 2.51 |
| PBMT + Overlap | 2.00 (0.03) | 1.94 - 2.06 |
| char. bigram PBMT | 1.56 (0.03) | 1.50 - 1.62 |

Table 8: Mean scores assigned by human subjects, with the standard error between brackets and the lower and upper bound of the 95 % confidence interval

## 7 Results

### 7.1 Human judgements

In this section we report on results of the experiment with judges ranking the output of the systems. To test for significance of the difference in the ranking of the different systems we ran repeated measures analyses of variance with system (PBMT, PBMT + Overlap, character bigram MT) as the independent variable, and the ranking of the output as the dependent variable. Mauchly's test for sphericity was used to test for homogeneity of

| PBMT | PBMT + overlap | char. bigram PBMT | $X^2$ |
|---|---|---|---|
| 2.05 | 2.59 | 1.36 | 16.636** |
| 2.77 | 1.82 | 1.41 | 21.545** |
| 2.50 | 1.27 | 2.23 | 18.273** |
| 1.95 | 1.45 | 2.59 | 14.273** |
| 2.18 | 2.36 | 1.45 | 10.182** |
| 2.45 | 2.00 | 1.55 | 9.091* |
| 2.91 | 1.77 | 1.32 | 29.545** |
| 2.18 | 2.27 | 1.55 | 6.903* |
| 2.14 | 2.00 | 1.86 | 0.818 |
| 2.27 | 1.73 | 2.00 | 3.273 |
| 2.68 | 1.68 | 1.64 | 15.364** |
| 2.82 | 1.95 | 1.23 | 27.909** |
| 2.68 | 2.09 | 1.23 | 23.545** |
| 1.95 | 2.55 | 1.50 | 12.091** |
| 2.77 | 1.86 | 1.36 | 22.455** |
| 2.32 | 2.23 | 1.45 | 9.909** |
| 2.86 | 1.91 | 1.23 | 29.727** |
| 2.18 | 1.09 | 2.73 | 30.545** |
| 2.05 | 2.09 | 1.86 | 0.636 |
| 2.73 | 2.18 | 1.09 | 30.545** |
| 2.41 | 2.27 | 1.32 | 15.545** |
| 2.68 | 2.18 | 1.14 | 27.364** |
| 1.82 | 2.95 | 1.23 | 33.909** |
| 2.73 | 1.95 | 1.32 | 21.909** |
| 2.91 | 1.77 | 1.32 | 29.545** |

Table 9: Results of the Friedman test on each of the 25 sentences. Results marked * are significant at $p < 0.05$ and results marked ** are significant at $p < 0.01$

variance, but was not significant, so no corrections had to be applied. Planned pairwise comparisons were made with the Bonferroni method. The mean ranking can be found in Table 8 together with the standard deviation and 95 % confidence interval. We find that participants ranked the three systems differently, $F(2,42) = 135,604, p < .001, \eta_p^2 = .866$. All pairwise comparisons are significant at $p < .001$. The character bigram model receives the best mean rank (1.56), then the PBMT + Overlap system (2.00) and the standard PBMT system is ranked lowest (2.44). We used a Friedman test to detect differences across multiple rankings. We ran the test on each of the 25 K-related samples, and found that for 13 sentences the ranking provided by the test subjects was equal to the mean ranking: the PBMT system ranked lowest, then the PBMT + Overlap system and the character bigram system scored highest for each of these cases at $p < .005$. These results are detailed in Table 9. When comparing the judgements of the participants with the judgements of an expert, we find a significant medium Pearson correlation of .65 ($p < .001$) between the judgements of the expert and the mean of the judgements of the participants. This indicates that the judgements of the laymen are indeed useful.

### 7.2 Automatic judgements

In order to attempt to measure the quality of the transformations made by the different systems automatically, we measured NIST scores by comparing the output of the systems to the reference translation. We do realize that the reference translation is in fact a literary interpretation and not a literal translation, making automatic assessment harder. Having said that, we still hope to find some effect by using these automatic measures. We only report NIST scores here, because BLEU turned out to be very uninformative. In many cases sentences would receive a BLEU score of 0. Mauchly‘s test for sphericity was used to test for homogeneity of variance for the NIST scores, and was not significant. We ran a repeated measures test with planned pairwise comparisons made with the Bonferroni method. We found that the NIST scores for the different systems differed significantly ($F(2,48) = 6.404, p < .005, \eta_p^2 = .211$). The average NIST scores with standard error and the lower and upper bound of the 95 % confidence interval can be seen in Table 10. The character bigram transliteration model scores highest with 2.43, followed by the PBMT + Overlap model with a score of 2.30 and finally the MT model scores lowest with a NIST score of 1.95. We find that the scores for the PBMT model differ significantly from the PBMT + Overlap model ($p < .01$) and the character bigram PBMT model ($p < .05$), but the scores for the PBMT + Overlap and the character bigram PBMT model do not differ significantly. When we compare the automatic scores to the human assigned ranks we find no significant Pearson correlation.

## 8 Conclusion

In this paper we have described two modifications of the standard PBMT framework to improve the transformation of Middle Dutch to Modern Dutch

| system | mean NIST | 95 % c. i. |
|---|---|---|
| PBMT | 1.96 (0.18) | 1.58 - 2.33 |
| PBMT + overlap | 2.30 (0.21) | 1.87 - 2.72 |
| char. bigram PBMT | 2.43 (0.20) | 2.01 - 2.84 |

Table 10: Mean NIST scores, with the standard error between brackets and the lower and upper bound of the 95 % confidence interval

by using character overlap in the two variants. We described one approach that helps the alignment process by adding words that exhibit a certain amount of character overlap to the parallel data. We also described another approach that translates sequences of character bigrams instead of words. Reviewing the results we conclude that the use of character overlap between diachronic variants of a language is beneficial in the translation process. More specifically, the model that uses character bigrams in translation instead of words is ranked best. Also ranked significantly better than a standard Phrase Based machine translation approach is the approach using the Needleman-Wunsch algorithm to align sentences and identify words or phrases that exhibit a significant amount of character overlap to help the GIZA++ statistical alignment process towards aligning the correct words and phrases. We have seen that one issue that is encountered when considering the task of language transformation from Middle Dutch to Modern Dutch is data sparseness. The number of lines used to train on amounts to a few thousand, and not millions as is more common in SMT. It is therefore crucial to use the inherent character overlap in this task to compensate for the lack of data and to make more informed decisions. The character bigram approach is able to generate a translation for out of vocabulary words, which is also a solution to the data sparseness problem. One area where the character bigram model often fails, is translating Middle Dutch words into Modern Dutch words that are significantly different. One example can be seen in Table 7, where 'mocht' is translated by the PBMT and PBMT + Overlap systems to 'kon' and left the same by the character bigram transliteration model. This is probably due to the fact that 'mocht' still exists in Dutch, but is not as common as 'kon' (meaning 'could'). another issue to consider is the fact that the character bigram model learns character mappings that are occurring trough out the language. One example is the disappearing silent 'h' after a 'g'. This often leads to transliterated words of which the spelling is only partially correct. Apparently the human judges rate these 'half words' higher than completely wrong words, but automatic measures such as NIST are insensitive to this.

We have also reported the NIST scores for the output of the standard PBMT approach and the two proposed variants. We see that the NIST scores show a similar patterns as the human judgements: the PBMT + Overlap and character bigram PBMT systems both achieve significantly higher NIST scores than the normal PBMT system. However, the PBMT + Overlap and character bigram PBMT models do not differ significantly in scores. It is interesting that we find no significant correlation between human and automatic judgements, leading us to believe that automatic judgements are not viable in this particular scenario. This is perhaps due to the fact that the reference translations the automatic measures rely on are in this case not literal translations but rather more loosely translated literary interpretations of the source text in modern Dutch. The fact that both versions are written on rhyme only worsens this problem, as the author of the Modern Dutch version is often very creative.

We think techniques such as the ones described here can be of great benefit to laymen wishing to investigate works that are not written in contemporary language, resulting in improved access to these older works. Our character bigram transliteration model may also play some role as a computational model in the study of the evolution of orthography in language variants, as it often will generate words that are strictly speaking not correct, but do resemble Modern Dutch in some way. Automatic evaluation is another topic for future work. It would be interesting to see if an automatic measure operating on the character level correlates better with human judgements.

## References

Alistair Baron and Paul Rayson. 2008. VARD 2: A tool for dealing with spelling variation in historical corpora. In *Proceedings of the Postgraduate Conference in Corpus Linguistics*, Birmingham, UK. Aston University.

A. De Gispert and J. B. Marino. 2006. Linguistic knowledge in statistical phrase-based word alignment. *Natural Language Engineering*, 12(1):91–108.

Andrew Finch, Paul Dixon, and Eiichiro Sumita. 2012. Rescoring a phrase-based machine transliteration system with recurrent neural network language models. In *Proceedings of the 4th Named Entity Workshop (NEWS) 2012*, pages 47–51, Jeju, Korea, July. Association for Computational Linguistics.

Jan Hajič, Jan Hric, and Vladislav Kuboň. 2000. Machine translation of very close languages. In *Proceedings of the sixth conference on Applied natural language processing*, pages 7–12. Association for Computational Linguistics.

Mike Kestemont, Walter Daelemans, and Guy De Pauw. 2010. Weigh your words—memory-based lemmatization for Middle Dutch. *Literary and Linguistic Computing*, 25(3):287–301, September.

Philipp Koehn and Kevin Knight. 2003. Feature-rich statistical translation of noun phrases. In *ACL '03: Proceedings of the 41st Annual Meeting on Association for Computational Linguistics*, pages 311–318, Morristown, NJ, USA. Association for Computational Linguistics.

Philip Koehn, Franz Josef Och, and Daniel Marcu. 2003. Statistical phrase-based translation. In *Proceedings of the 2003 Conference of the North American Chapter of the Association for Computational Linguistics on Human Language Technology-Volume 1*, pages 48–54. Association for Computational Linguistics.

Philipp Koehn, Hieu Hoang, Alexandra Birch, Chris C. Burch, Marcello Federico, Nicola Bertoldi, Brooke Cowan, Wade Shen, Christine Moran, Richard Zens, Chris Dyer, Ondrej Bojar, Alexandra Constantin, and Evan Herbst. 2007. Moses: Open source toolkit for statistical machine translation. In *ACL*. The Association for Computer Linguistics.

P. Koehn. 2005. Europarl: A parallel corpus for statistical machine translation. In *MT summit*, volume 5.

Grzegorz Kondrak, Daniel Marcu, and Kevin Knight. 2003. Cognates can improve statistical translation models. In *HLT-NAACL*.

Philippe Langlais and Alexandre Patry. 2007. Translating unknown words by analogical learning. In *EMNLP-CoNLL*, pages 877–886. ACL.

Preslav Nakov and Jörg Tiedemann. 2012. Combining word-level and character-level models for machine translation between closely-related languages. In *Proceedings of the 50th Annual Meeting of the Association for Computational Linguistics (Volume 2: Short Papers)*, pages 301–305, Jeju Island, Korea, July. Association for Computational Linguistics.

S. B. Needleman and C. D. Wunsch. 1970. A general method applicable to the search for similarities in the amino acid sequence of two proteins. *Journal of molecular biology*, 48(3):443–453, March.

Franz Josef Och and Hermann Ney. 2003. A systematic comparison of various statistical alignment models. *Computational Linguistics*, 29(1):19–51.

Maja Popovic and Hermann Ney. 2004. Towards the use of word stems and suffixes for statistical machine translation. In *LREC*. European Language Resources Association.

Andreas Stolcke. 2002. SRILM - an extensible language modeling toolkit. In *In Proc. Int. Conf. on Spoken Language Processing*, pages 901–904, Denver, Colorado.

Jörg Tiedemann. 2009. Character-based PSMT for closely related languages. In Lluís Marqués and Harold Somers, editors, *Proceedings of 13th Annual Conference of the European Association for Machine Translation (EAMT'09)*, pages 12 – 19, Barcelona, Spain, May.

Gerhard B Van Huyssteen and Suléne Pilon. 2009. Rule-based conversion of closely-related languages: a dutch-to-afrikaans convertor. *20th Annual Symposium of the Pattern Recognition Association of South Africa*, December.

David Vilar, Jan-Thorsten Peter, and Hermann Ney. 2007. Can we translate letters? In *Second Workshop on Statistical Machine Translation*, pages 33–39, Prague, Czech Republic, jun. Association for Computational Linguistics.

Sander Wubben, Antal van den Bosch, and Emiel Krahmer. 2010. Paraphrase generation as monolingual translation: Data and evaluation. In B. Mac Namee J. Kelleher and I. van der Sluis, editors, *Proceedings of the 10th International Workshop on Natural Language Generation (INLG 2010)*, pages 203–207, Dublin.

Wei Xu, Alan Ritter, Bill Dolan, Ralph Grishman, and Colin Cherry. 2012. Paraphrasing for style. In *COLING*, pages 2899–2914.

Amir Zeldes. 2007. Machine translation between language stages: Extracting historical grammar from a parallel diachronic corpus of Polish. In Matthew Davies, Paul Rayson, Susan Hunston, and Pernilla Danielsson, editors, *Proceedings of the Corpus Linguistics Conference CL2007*. University of Birmingham.

# Comparison between historical population archives and decentralized databases

**Marijn Schraagen and Dionysius Huijsmans**
Leiden Institute of Advanced Computer Science (LIACS)
Leiden University, The Netherlands
{schraage,huijsman}@liacs.nl

### Abstract

Differences between large-scale historical population archives and small decentralized databases can be used to improve data quality and record connectedness in both types of databases. A parser is developed to account for differences in syntax and data representation models. A matching procedure is described to discover records from different databases referring to the same historical event. The problem of verification without reliable benchmark data is addressed by matching on a subset of record attributes and measuring support for the match using a different subset of attributes. An application of the matching procedure for comparison of family trees is discussed. A visualization tool is described to present an interactive overview of comparison results.

## 1 Introduction

In the historical demographics and genealogy domain, research data can be collected from centralized databases such as a historical census or civil registry. Alternatively, decentralized data can be collected from, e.g., personal archives or local organizations. Complementary and conflicting information between these sources can be valuable for research if the overlap, i.e., matching records, is correctly identified. This paper describes a method to discover matching records in centralized and decentralized data for the problem of family reconstruction. An overview of related work is presented in Section 2. Section 3 describes the two different data formats. Section 4 provides a mapping procedure between the different data formats. In Section 5 the matching procedure is explained at the conceptual and technical level. Section 6 provides a verification procedure and results for a test database. An application of the matching in a family tree visualization tool is provided in Section 7. A conclusion and directions for future research are provided in Section 8.

The most important concepts used throughout this paper are defined as follows:

**Record**. Unit of matching and linkage. A record refers to a Genlias certificate (Section 3) or a Gedcom certificate reconstruction (Sections 3 and 4), unless stated otherwise.

**Record match**. A pair of records that refer to the same event (birth, marriage, or death).

**Record link**. A pair of records that refer to related events (e.g., birth and death of the same person).

**Field similarity measure**. Similarity between field values, e.g., number of days between dates.

**Record similarity measure**. Similarity requirements for selected fields and relations between the requirements.

**Edit distance**. Minimum number of character insertions, deletions and/or substitutions needed to transform one string into another (Levenshtein distance).

**Name sequence**. Concatenation of person names from a record.

**Person name**. Single name, i.e., given name or family name.

## 2 Related work

Automatic matching and linkage of historical records has been researched for several decades. An early example can be found in (Winchester, 1970), using Soundex as field similarity measure to compare census data. An approach from the French-speaking Canadian province of Quebec, using a custom phonetic code, is described in (Bouchard and Pouyez, 1980). In this approach different types of data are merged together. The researchers state that "the most fundamental rule is that we never try to link individuals, but rather pairs of individuals; that is: couples [...] It can be demonstrated easily that individual linkage is liable to result in uncertain, false, or missed links, whereas the result of the linkage of couples is very reliable". The approach is implemented as follows: "we accept as candidates for linkage those pairs which have at least two exactly identical elements". Experience with the dataset used in the current research has resulted in a similar approach (see Section 5). Linkage on the Quebec dataset has been developed by the same authors (Bouchard, 1992). The 1992 paper discusses the use of field values: "the various fields can serve as identifiers (linkage), controls (validation), or variables (analysis)." The notion of internal validation is discussed further in Section 6. Later approaches to record linkage have focussed on scalability of linkage methods for large amounts of data, see, e.g., (Christen and Gayler, 2008).

A detailed overview of elements from genealogical records and the application of each element for linkage is provided in (Wilson, 2011). Besides historical and/or genealogical data, various other types of data have been used for development and testing of algorithms, such as hospital records, phone book records, customer records, etc. However, algorithms generally assume a certain level of uniformity in data representation, both at a technical and at a conceptual level. This means that generally pedigrees are linked to other pedigrees but not to civil certificates, and vice versa. Events and individuals (actors) have been modelled together using NLP techniques (Segers et al., 2011), however these approaches are mostly not applicable for genealogical data both because of the lack of natural language resources to identify and link instances of actors and events, as well as the difference in scope of the model (participants of historically significant events vs. every person that existed during a certain time period). Some attempts have been made to facilitate data exchange and accessability in the genealogical domain, either by presenting a standardized format (the Gedcom standard (GEDCOM Team, 1996) being the most succesful example), by conversion into a standardized format (Kay, 2006; Kay, 2004), by enforcing a Semantic Web ontology (Zandhuis, 2005), or by defining a framework that accepts custom data models as metadata to be provided upon exchange of the genealogical data itself (Woodfield, 2012). Algorithmic solutions for merging of pedigrees have been proposed (Wilson, 2001) that take into account matches between individuals and matching links between individuals. More elaborate linkage of pedigree data is described in (Quass and Starkey, 2003), using feature weights and thresholds to increase linkage performance.

Using various definitions of *record*, such as a single individual, multiple individuals, families (i.e., multiple individuals in a family relation), or events (i.e., multiple individuals in a certain relation at a specific point in time), most research in record linkage is either directed towards matching of records, i.e., asserting equal reference, or linkage of related (but not equal) records using matching of record elements (e.g., a birth record linked to a marriage record based on a match between the child and the bridegroom). In social networks research a different type of linkage is common, where records are linked but not matched (e.g., two people sharing common interests). Occasionally this type of link is used in historical record linkage as well (Smith and Giraud-Carrier, 2006).

Test corpora have been developed (Schone et al., 2012), (Bouchard, 1992), however these are intrinsically domain- and language-specific. Moreover, these corpora are generally not readily available for research.

## 3 Data formats

The centralized data used in the experiments is extracted from the Dutch Genlias[1] database. Genlias contains civil certificates (around 15 million in total) from the Netherlands, for the events of birth, marriage and death. Most documents originate from the 19th and early 20th century. A record (see Figure 1 for an example) consists of the type of event, a serial number, date and place, and participant details. The parents are also listed for the main subject(s) of the document, i.e., the newborn child, bride and groom, and deceased person for birth, marriage and death certificates, respectively. The documents do not contain identifiers for individuals. No links are provided between documents or individuals.

The decentralized data is extracted from a family tree database in the Gedcom (Genealogical Data Communication) format. In this format genealogical data is stored based on individuals and nuclear (immediate) families, instead of events as

[1] The Genlias data is currently maintained by WieWasWie, see `http://www.wiewaswie.nl` (in Dutch)

```
Type: birth certificate
Serial number: 176
Date: 16 - 05 - 1883
Place: Wonseradeel
Child: Sierk Rolsma
Father: Sjoerd Rolsma
Mother: Agnes Weldring
```

Figure 1: Genlias birth certificate.

```
0 @F294@ FAM
1 HUSB @I840@
1 WIFE @I787@
1 MARR
2 DATE 30 MAY 1874
2 PLAC Wonseradeel
1 CHIL @I847@
1 CHIL @I848@
1 CHIL @I849@
0 @I840@ INDI
1 NAME Sjoerd/Rolsma/
1 BIRT
2 DATE 13 FEB 1849
1 DEAT
2 DATE 17 JAN 1936
1 FAMS @F294@
0 @I787@ INDI
1 NAME Agnes/Welderink/
1 SEX F
1 BIRT
2 DATE ca 1850
1 FAMS @F294@
0 @I849@ INDI
1 NAME Sierk/Rolsma/
1 BIRT
2 DATE 16 MAY 1883
2 PLAC Wonseradeel
2 SOUR
3 REFN 176
1 FAMC @F294@
```

Figure 2: Gedcom database fragment, showing a selection of fields from a FAM record (family) and three INDI records (individual).

in Genlias. Every individual or family in Gedcom is assigned a unique identifier. Records for individuals usually contain personal information like names, birth and death date, etc. The families in which the individual participates, either as child or as parent, are also indicated. A family record lists the individuals and their roles. Marriage information (date, place) can also be present in a family record. Using the record identifiers, a link network between individuals and families can be constructed.

Gedcom is a text-based free entry format. The standard (GEDCOM Team, 1996) states that "A record is represented as a sequence of tagged, variable-length lines, arranged in a hierarchy. A line always contains a hierarchical level number, a tag, and an optional value. A line may also contain a cross-reference identifier or a pointer." (see Figure 2 for an example). The Gedcom standard is used by a wide variety of genealogical applications, ranging from full-featured commercially available software to small scripts. The implementation of the standard can differ between applications, as well as the content format entered by users. The next section describes a parsing procedure designed to process this kind of data.

## 4 Parsing

Prior to the actual record matching, a mapping between the data formats must be performed. This requires either a reconstruction of events from the Gedcom file, or vice versa a reconstruction of individuals and nuclear families from Genlias. The first option requires links between Gedcom records, for example to construct a birth record from the three individual records of the child and parents using the intermediate family record. The second option requires links between Genlias certificates, for example to construct a family record from the birth certificates of several children. Record links are available in Gedcom only, and therefore reconstruction of events from Gedcom is the preferred option.

There are various tools available to perform the required data transformation. Many genealogy programs can export Gedcom data to, e.g., XML or SQL databases which can be queried to construct events. Alternatively, dedicated Gedcom parsers exist for a number of programming languages (such as Perl (Johnson, 2013), C (Verthez, 2004), Python (Ball, 2012), XSLT (Kay, 2004)) that provide data structures to manipulate the Gedcom data from within code. However, the data structures are still centered around individuals and families and the performance of the tools is to a greater or lesser degree sensitive to violations of (some version of) the Gedcom standard. The rest of this section describes a more general parsing algorithm that can be applied to any kind of level-numbered textual data.

The parser (see Figure 3) uses a Prolog DCG-style grammar to specify the elements of target records (see Figure 4 for an example). Tags found in lines from the database file are pushed on a stack one by one. Before a tag is pushed, all cur-

```
S ← ∅
while L ← readline(database) do
    if(L.level = 0) then
        id ← L.value
    while(S.top.level ≥ L.level) do
        S.pop()
    S.push(L.tag)
    foreach terminalList ∈ grammar do
        if(S = terminalList) then
            index(id,terminalList) ← L.value
foreach id ∈ index do
    foreach target ∈ grammar do
        if(pointerList ∈ target) then
            duplicate(target,id,pointerList)
        foreach protoRecord ∈ ({target} ∪ duplicates) do
            foreach terminalList ∈ protoRecord do
                output ← index(id,terminalList)
            output ← record separator
```

Figure 3: Parser algorithm.

```
birthcertificate --> [@],[fam,chil(+)]:birthbasic,
    [fam,husb]:personname, [fam,wife]:personname.
birthbasic --> birthdate, birthplace, birthref, personname.
birthdate --> [indi,birt,date].
birthplace --> [indi,birt,plac].
birthref --> [indi,birt,sour,refn].
personname --> [@],[indi,name].
target --> birthcertificate.
```

Figure 4: Grammar fragment. Special characters: '@' level 0-value (record id), '+' pointer list, ':' pointer dereference.

rent elements with an equal or higher level number are popped, which makes the stack correspond to the current branch in the database hierarchy. If the stack corresponds to a list of terminal symbols in the grammar, then the current line is indexed for later use by the value at level 0. All grammar rules are expanded to terminal symbols and subsequently dereferenced for each of the index values in the previous step. If an expanded rule contains a pointer list (indicated by a + symbol) then the rule is duplicated for each element of the pointer list associated to the current index value before dereferencing. As an example the algorithm in Figure 3 applied to the database in Figure 2 using the grammar in Figure 4 on the index value @F294@ will produce three duplicate protorecords which can be dereferenced to certificates. Figure 5 provides an example that matches the Genlias certificate in Figure 1. Note that the family name of the mother differs between the databases.

The use of a domain-independent grammar provides a flexible parser for Gedcom or structurally

*Protorecord*

[@], [fam,chil(2)]:[indi,birt,date], [fam,chil(2)]:[indi,birt,plac], [fam,chil(2)]:[indi,birt,sour,refn], [fam,chil(2)]:[@], [fam,chil(2)]:[indi,name], [fam,husb]:[@], [fam,husb]:[indi,name], [fam,wife]:[@], [fam,wife]:[indi,name]

*Certificate*

@F294@, 16 MAY 1883, Wonseradeel, 176, @I849@, Sierk/Rolsma/, @I840@, Sjoerd/Rolsma/, @I787@, Agnes/Welderink/

Figure 5: Parsing example for index value @F294@ using the pointer [@F294@,CHIL(2)], which is @I849@.

similar data formats. Additionally, only information that corresponds to an element of a target record is indexed, resulting in a light-weight procedure. The output of the parser can be directly used for record matching, which is described in the next section.

## 5 Matching

After parsing, both databases are represented in the same data format. This enables a definition of similarity between records based on the values of corresponding fields. In the current experiments a partial similarity measure is used, meaning that any sufficiently large subset of the corresponding fields must be similar whereas the complement set remains unchecked. This approach assumes sparseness of high-dimensional data, which implies that the set of field values of each record is unique and moreover any large subset of field values is also unique. This property can easily be verified on a given database and if it holds, the similarity measure can be simplified accordingly. For the current experiments this allows for name variation in civil certificates which is hard to detect automatically by similarity measures. A certificate, as discussed in Section 3, generally contains at least three individuals, which amounts to six names in total (given names and family names). If one of the names is subject to large variation in two matching records (for example *Elizabeth* vs. *Lisa*), this match might be undetected when using all names in the record comparison. However, by ignoring this field in a partial comparison the match will be discovered.

A partial record similarity measure can be defined by stating similarity requirements for each of the fields used in the measure and relations between the requirements. As an example, consider the matching between marriage certificates based on the year of marriage and the names of the bride and bridegroom (four names in total) which is used in the current experiments, as stated in Figure 6. Note that the first clause in this definition requires an exact match on person names. This has the conceptual advantage that exact matching is more reliable than similarity matching based on, e.g., edit distance. Additionally, exact matching allows for straightforward string indexing and efficient look-up. Memory consumption is less efficient, the example index of two names out of four requires $\binom{4}{2} = 6$ entries per record. Therefore it might be necessary to adjust the similarity measure to meet computational resources.

> At least two out of four names are exactly equal, *and*
>
> > the year of marriage is equal or different by a small margin, *or*
> >
> > the year of marriage is different by a larger margin and the edit distance between name sequences is below a small threshold, *or*
> >
> > the year of marriage in a record is specified as a range and the year of marriage in another record is within this range, and the edit distance between name sequences is below a small threshold.

Figure 6: Record similarity measure for marriage certificates.

## 6 Results and verification

The record similarity measure in Figure 6 is applied to the Genlias database and a sample Gedcom database containing 1327 individuals and 423 families. As preprocessing, given names are reduced to the first token (for example: *Quentin Jerome Tarantino* → *Quentin Tarantino*). Separate family name prefixes, which are common in Dutch, are stripped using a stop list (for example: *Vincent van Gogh* → *Vincent Gogh*). The edit distance threshold and year margins required by the similarity measure are set according to empirical knowledge of the domain. A subset of the Gedcom records is used to match the timeframe of the Genlias database (1796–1920). Settings and matching results are displayed in Table 1. The matching is performed for the three main types of civil certificates: birth, marriage and death. For birth and death certificates the marriage record similarity measure (Figure 6) is used replacing the roles of bride and bridegroom by mother and father of the child or deceased person for birth and death certificates respectively (i.e., the name of the child or deceased person itself is not used). To avoid confusion with other siblings, the small year margin for birth and death certificates is set to zero. If multiple matching candidates are found using the record similarity measure, the match with the smallest edit distance between name sequences is used. The large amount of missed matches for birth and death certificates is expected, because the Genlias database is still under active development and a significant number of birth and death certificates are not yet digitized. Moreover, Gedcom databases generally contain many peripheral individuals for which no parents are listed (usually inlaws of the family of interest), prohibiting the reconstruction of birth and death certificates.

| | | |
|---|---|---|
| Edit distance threshold | | 5 |
| Large year margin | | 10 |
| Small year margin | | |
| *marriage* | | 2 |
| *birth, death* | | 0 |
| Marriage | match | 153 |
| | no match | 23 |
| Birth | match | 335 |
| | no match | 276 |
| Death | match | 100 |
| | no match | 239 |

Table 1: Matching parameters and results.

Verification of record matches should ideally be performed using a test set of known matches (a *gold standard*). However, for this particular combination of databases such a test set is not available. The lack of test sets extends to the majority of decentralized historical data, as well as Genlias itself (which does not have any kind of internal links or verification sets). This is a quite undesirable situation given the large variation in data quality and coverage between databases in the historical domain. Because the characteristics of any two databases regarding the contents can differ to a large degree, the performance of a matching algorithm obtained on one database is not indicative for other databases. Put differently: every application of a matching algorithm has to perform its own verification, which is difficult in the absence of test sets.

### 6.1 Internal verification

A possible solution for the verification problem is to re-use the sparseness assumption to obtain a measure of support for a match. The matches returned by the similarity measure are based on a subset of fields. If other field values are equal or similar as well, they provide additional support for the match independent of the similarity measure. Note that this solution is only applicable if there are fields available which are not used in the record similarity measure. Moreover these fields should have a certain discriminative power, which rules out categorical variables like gender or religion. For many linkage tasks extra fields are not available, for example linking a marriage certificate of a person to the marriage certificate of this person's parents, in which case the only available information about the parents are the person names. However, in the current experiments a certificate from one database is being matched to the same certificate in another database, therefore the amount of available information is much larger.

A candidate field for verification is the serial number, which has been recorded since the start of the civil registry in the Netherlands. The numbers are assigned per year by the municipality issuing the certificate, meaning that the combination of municipality, year and serial number uniquely references a certificate (also known as a *persistent identifier* or PID). A shared PID between two records in a match therefore provides strong support for this match. However, in a Gedcom database serial numbers are not necessarily included. The source of the data can be something different than the civil registry, such as church records, or the database author might just have omitted the serial number. Moreover, if the source of the Gedcom record is the civil registry, then the match is not very indicative of the performance of the similarity measure in combining different data sources. Therefore, the serial number is of limited use only for verification purposes. Other candidate fields are dates and toponyms (location names). The year is used in the similarity measure, but the day and month can be used for support. For the current experiments three levels of support are defined: exact date match, a difference of 1 to 7 days, or a difference of more than 7 days.

In case of limited support from the verification fields, edit distance (or any other string similarity measure) can be used as an indication of the correctness of a match.

### 6.2 Toponym mapping

Toponyms cannot always be compared directly, because of the difference in use between Genlias and most Gedcom databases. In Genlias the toponym that denotes the location of the event is always the municipality that has issued the certificate. In a Gedcom database often the actual location of the event is used, which can be a town that is part of a larger municipality. A comparison between toponyms is therefore more informative after mapping each toponym to the corresponding municipality. In the current experiments a reference database of Dutch toponyms is used to perform the mapping. Because the municipal organization in the Netherlands changes over time, the year of the event is required for a correct mapping. Ambiguity for toponyms (i.e., multiple locations with the same name) can generally be resolved using the province of the event. In case that the province is not recorded the toponym can be disambiguated by choosing the location with the most inhabitants by default.

### 6.3 Interpretation of support figures

Table 2 shows the results of verification using serial numbers, dates and mapped toponyms as support fields. The support figures should be interpreted with the distribution of data values in mind. The first two rows of Table 2 represent matches with equal serial numbers. Most of these matches have equal PIDs (toponym and year equal as well). Given that each PID is unique these matches are correct. Differences in toponym are usually small for matches with equal serial numbers, therefore a PID match can be assumed (although support is higher for true PID matches). The third row represents matches with the same toponym and date, and also two names equal (by definition of the similarity measure). Note again that the match was selected using the names and the year only, and verified using the toponym and the full date. These matches could be incorrect, because it is possible that different couples with (partially) the same name got married on the same day in the same place, for example. In the Genlias database this is the case for around 0.3% of all marriage certificates. Therefore, the sparseness assumption largely holds for this set of fields and these matches can also be considered correct. Similarly, other verification field values can be interpreted in terms of confidence in a match (based on the validity of the sparseness assumption) or counterevidence against a match (in case of large differences in field values). For the current experiments, the last row of matches should be considered incorrect. The relatively large number of incorrect matches for birth and death certificates can be attributed to the lack of coverage in Genlias. The best match is returned, however this assumes true matches to be present in the data set. The record similarity match can be adjusted using the verification fields, however it is preferred to keep similarity computation and verification separated.

| field | | | | marriage | birth | death |
|---|---|---|---|---|---|---|
| *s* | *t* | *d* | *e* | | | |
| + | + | + | | 69 | 170 | 9 |
| + | - | + | | 2 | 30 | 0 |
| – | + | + | | 41 | 20 | 1 |
| – | + | $\sim$ | | 0 | 33 | 6 |
| – | + | – | | 2 | 1 | 0 |
| – | – | + | | 10 | 2 | 7 |
| – | – | $\sim$ | | 2 | 5 | 10 |
| – | – | – | $\leq 3$ | 11 | 2 | 3 |
| – | – | – | $> 3$ | 16 | 72 | 64 |
| total | | | | 153 | 335 | 100 |

Table 2: Verification results. Columns: (s)erial number, (t)oponym, (d)ate, (e)dit distance. Support level: + equal, $\sim$ 1–7 days difference,– not equal (*s,t*) or $>$ 7 days difference (*d*). Edit distance is only used for the matches without support from the verification fields (final two rows).

## 7 Application

The previous sections have discussed matching records from different databases that refer to the same event. However, most research in historical record linkage is focussed on links between events, such as a birth and the marriage of the parents listed in the birth certificate. These links can be added to a database by manual annotation or using automatic linkage methods. Different databases in the same population domain are likely to contain complementary and conflicting links, which can be used to increase the quality and quantity of links in both databases. To compare links between databases the records need to be matched first, which can be achieved using the record matching method from the current research.

To demonstrate the application of the method, a comparison is performed on links between marriage certificates in Genlias and corresponding links in the sample Gedcom database used in the matching experiments. A marriage certificate contains the marriage couple and the parents of both bride and bridegroom. A link can be defined between a marriage and the marriage of one of the parent couples (see Figure 7). For the Genlias database links have been constructed by selecting all record pairs with a maximum Levenshtein edit distance of 3 between name sequences. Additional record links are computed by converting each name to a base form and selecting record pairs with matching base name sequences. The details of the link computation are beyond the scope of this paper, for the current experiments

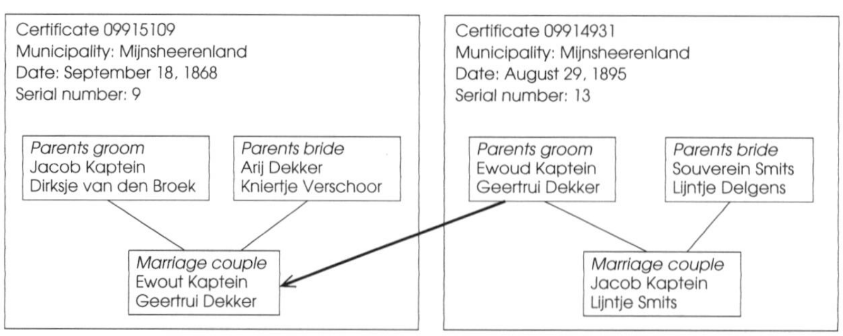


Figure 7: Example of a link between two Genlias marriage certificates, containing a small spelling variation: *Ewout* vs. *Ewoud*.

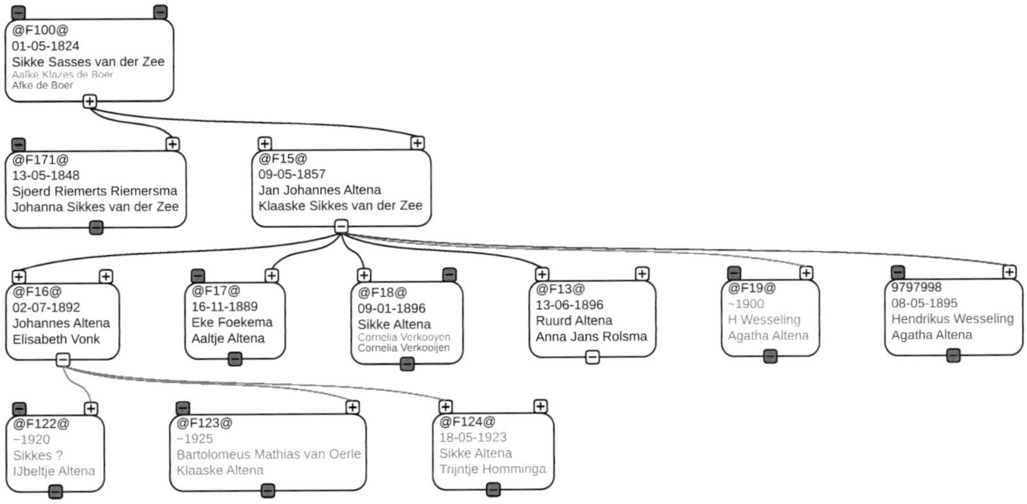


Figure 8: Visualization of link comparison.

only the resulting set of links between Genlias marriage certificates is of interest. In the Gedcom database links between marriages are already present. The link comparison procedure is as follows: first, marriage certificates are matched using the method described in Section 5. For every matched certificate the marriages of the children are identified using the links from Genlias and the Gedcom database (cf. Figure 7). These two sets of marriages are aligned using a slightly more strict version of the record similarity measure in Figure 6, to accomodate for the inherent similarity in names and timeframe of sibling marriages. Using the alignment, the links can be divided into three categories: present in both databases, present in the Gedcom database only, or present in Genlias only. A visualization tool is developed that shows the results of the comparison in a link tree (see Figure 8), which can be browsed by expanding or collapsing record links. Colours indicate differences between databases (red and blue for the Gedcom database and Genlias, respectively). Records @F19@ and 9797998 are an example of a false negative. The lower row is found in the Gedcom database only because these records are outside of the Genlias timeframe. The tool enables users to provide their own Gedcom database and identify differences with the nation-wide Genlias database. Due to data licensing issues the tool has not yet been released, however it could be integrated in the Genlias website in the future.

## 8 Conclusion and future work

In this paper a method is described to compare a dataset based on events (Genlias) to a dataset based on individuals (the Gedcom model). This method is complementary to most current approaches in record linkage, in which only datasets with the same conceptual structure are compared. The parser (Section 4) facilitates the transformation of data formats. A combination of multiple string indexing and field similarity measures provides a computationally efficient and flexible record matching method, as described in Section 5. The problem of verification without gold standard test data is addressed in Section 6. An application of the method in a visualization tool is presented in Section 7.

In future research, other Gedcom databases can be presented to the matching procedure. A crowdsourcing set-up can be envisioned to perform large-scale data collection and evaluation of the approach. The matching procedure itself can be refined by improving the record similarity measure or by incorporating a network approach in which record links can contribute to matching. Finally, functionality can be added to the visualization tool, preferably resulting in a public release.


### Acknowledgment

This work is part of the research programme LINKS, which is financed by the Netherlands Organisation for Scientific Research (NWO), grant 640.004.804. The authors would like to thank Tom Altena for the use of his Gedcom database.

## References


Madeleine Ball. 2012. python-gedcom: Python module for parsing, analyzing, and manipulating GEDCOM files. `https://github.com/madprime/python-gedcom/`.

Gérard Bouchard and Christian Pouyez. 1980. Name variations and computerized record linkage. *Historical Methods: A Journal of Quantitative and Interdisciplinary History*, 13(2):119–125.

Gérard Bouchard. 1992. Current issues and new prospects for computerized record linkage in the province of Québec. *Historical Methods: A Journal of Quantitative and Interdisciplinary History*, 25(2):67–73.

Peter Christen and Ross Gayler. 2008. Towards scalable real-time entity resolution using a similarity-aware inverted index approach. In *Seventh Australasian Data Mining Conference (AusDM 2008)*, volume 87, pages 51–60. ACS.

GEDCOM Team. 1996. The GEDCOM standard release 5.5. Technical report, Family and Church History Department, The Church of Jesus Christ of Latter-day Saints, Salt Lake City.

Paul Johnson. 2013. Gedcom — a module to manipulate Gedcom genealogy files. `http://search.cpan.org/~pjcj/Gedcom-1.18/`.

Michael Kay. 2004. Up-conversion using XSLT 2.0. In *Proceedings of XML: From Syntax to Solutions*. IDEAlliance.

Michael H. Kay. 2006. Positional grouping in XQuery. In *Proceedings of the 3rd International Workshop on XQuery Implementation, Experience and Perspectives (XIME-P)*.

Dallan Quass and Paul Starkey. 2003. Record linkage for genealogical databases. In *KDD-2003 Workshop on Data Cleaning, Record Linkage, and Object Consolidation*, pages 40–42.

Patrick Schone, Chris Cummings, Stuart Davey, Michael Jones, Barry Nay, and Mark Ward. 2012. Comprehensive evaluation of name matching across historic and linguistic boundaries. In *Proceedings of the 12th Annual Family History Technology Workshop*. FamilySearch.

Roxane Segers, Marieke van Erp, and Lourens van der Meij. 2011. Hacking history via event extraction. In *Proceedings of the sixth international conference on Knowledge capture*, K-CAP '11, pages 161–162. ACM.

Matthew Smith and Christophe Giraud-Carrier. 2006. Genealogical implicit affinity network. In *Proceedings of the 6th Annual Family History Technology Workshop*. FamilySearch.

Peter Verthez. 2004. The Gedcom parser library. `http://gedcom-parse.sourceforge.net/`.

D. Randall Wilson. 2001. Graph-based remerging of genealogical databases. In *Proceedings of the 1st Annual Family History Technology Workshop*. FamilySearch.

D. Randall Wilson. 2011. Genealogical record linkage: Features for automated person matching. In *Proceedings of RootsTech 2011*, pages 331–340. FamilySearch.

Ian Winchester. 1970. The linkage of historical records by man and computer: Techniques and problems. *The Journal of Interdisciplinary History*, 1(1):107–124.

Scott Woodfield. 2012. Effective sharing of family history information. In *Proceedings of the 12th Annual Family History Technology Workshop*. FamilySearch.

Ivo Zandhuis. 2005. Towards a genealogical ontology for the semantic web. In *Humanities, Computers and Cultural Heritage: Proceedings of the XVI international conference of the Association for History and Computing*, pages 296–300.

# Semi-automatic Construction of Cross-period Thesaurus

**Chaya Liebeskind, Ido Dagan, Jonathan Schler**
Computer Science Department
Bar-Ilan University
Ramat-Gan, Israel
liebchaya@gmail.com, dagan@cs.biu.ac.il, schler@gmail.com

## Abstract

Cross-period (diachronic) thesaurus construction aims to enable potential users to search for modern terms and obtain semantically related terms from earlier periods in history. This is a complex task not previously addressed computationally. In this paper we introduce a semi-automatic iterative Query Expansion (QE) scheme for supporting cross-period thesaurus construction. We demonstrate the empirical benefit of our scheme for a Jewish cross-period thesaurus and evaluate its impact on recall and on the effectiveness of lexicographer manual effort.

## 1 Introduction and Background

In the last decade, there is a growing interest in applying Natural Language Processing (NLP) methods to historical texts due to the increased availability of these texts in digital form (Sporleder, 2010; Sánchez-Marco et al., 2011; Piotrowski, 2012). The specific linguistic properties of historical texts, such as nonstandard orthography, grammar and abbreviations, pose special challenges for NLP. One of this challenges, which has not been addressed so far, is the problem of bridging the lexical gap between modern and ancient language.

In this paper, we address the interesting task of cross-period thesaurus (a.k.a. diachronic thesaurus) construction. A thesaurus usually contains thousands of entries, denoted here as *target terms*. Each entry includes a list of *related terms*, covering various semantic relations. A cross-period thesaurus aims to enable the potential user to search for a modern term and get related terms from earlier periods. Thus, in a cross-period thesaurus the target terms are modern while their related terms are ancient. In many cases, while the actual modern term (or its synynom) does not appear in earlier historical periods, different aspects of that term were mentioned. For example, in our Jewish historical corpora, the modern term *birth control*, has no equivalent ancient term, However, different contraceptive methods were described in our historical texts that are semantically similar to *birth control*. Thus, a related term is considered similar to the target term when it refers to the same concept.

The goal of our research is to support constructing a high-quality publishable thesaurus, as a cultural resource on its own, alongside being a useful tool for supporting searches in the domain. Since the precision of fully automatically-constructed thesauri is typically low (e.g. (Mihalcea et al., 2006)), we present a semi-automatic setting for supporting thesaurus construction by a domain expert lexicographer. Our recall-oriented setting assumes that manual effort is worthwhile for increasing recall as long as it is being utilized effectively.

Corpus-based thesaurus construction is an active research area (Curran and Moens, 2002; Kilgarriff, 2003; Rychlý and Kilgarriff, 2007; Liebeskind et al., 2012; Zohar et al., 2013). Typically, two statistical approaches for identifying semantic relatedness between words were investigated: first-order (co-occurrence-based) similarity and second-order (distributional) similarity (Lin, 1998; Gasperin et al., 2001; Weeds and Weir, 2003; Kotlerman et al., 2010). In this research, we focus on statistical measures of first-order similarity (see Section 2). These methods were found to be effective for thesaurus construction as standalone methods and as complementary to second-order methods (Peirsman et al., 2008). First-order measures assume that words that frequently occur together are topically related (Schütze and Pedersen, 1997). Thus, co-occurrence provides an appropriate approach to identify highly related terms for the thesaurus entries.

In general, there are two types of historically-relevant corpora: ancient corpora of ancient language, and modern corpora with references and mentions to ancient language (termed here *mixed corpora*). Since in our setting the thesaurus' target terms are modern terms, which do not appear in ancient corpora, co-occurrence methods would be directly applicable only over a mixed corpus. In a preliminary experiment, we applied the Liebeskind et al. (2012) algorithmic scheme, which applies first-order similarity and morphological aspects of corpus-based thesaurus construction, on a mixed corpus of our historical domain. We observed that the target terms had low frequency in this corpus. Since statistical co-occurrence measures have poor performance over low statistics, the experiment's results were not satisfactory. We therefore looked for ways to increase the number of documents in the statistical extraction process, and decided that applying query expansion (QE) techniques might be a viable solution.

We recognized two potential types of sources of lexical expansions for the target terms. The first is lexical resources available over the internet for extracting different types of semantic relations (Shnarch et al., 2009; Bollegala et al., 2011; Hashimoto et al., 2011). The second is lists of related terms extracted from a mixed corpus by a first-order co-occurrence measure. These lists contain both ancient and modern terms. Although only ancient terms will be included in the final thesaurus, modern terms can be utilized for QE to increase thesaurus coverage. Furthermore, expanding the target term with ancient related terms enables the use of ancient-only corpora for co-occurrence extraction.

Following these observations, we present an iterative interactive QE scheme for bootstrapping thesaurus construction. This approach is used to bridge the lexical gap between modern and ancient terminology by means of statistical co-occurrence approaches. We demonstrate the empirical advantage of our scheme over a cross-period Jewish domain and evaluate its impact on recall and on the effectiveness of the lexicographer manual effort.

The remainder of this paper is organized as follows: we start with a description of the statistical thesaurus construction method that we utilize in our scheme. Our main contribution of the iterative scheme is described in Section 3, followed by a case-study in Section 4 and evaluation and summary in Sections 5 and 6.

## 2 Automatic Thesaurus Construction

Automatic thesaurus construction focuses on the process of extracting a ranked list of candidate related terms (termed *candidate terms*) for each given target term. We assume that the top ranked candidates will be further examined (manually) by a lexicographer, who will select the eventual related terms for the thesaurus entry.

Statistical measures of first-order similarity (word co-occurrence), such as *Dice coefficient* (Smadja et al., 1996) and *Pointwise Mutual Information* (PMI) (Church and Hanks, 1990), were commonly used to extract ranked lists of candidate related terms. These measures consider the number of times in which each candidate term co-occurs with the target term, in the same document, relative to their total frequencies in the corpus.

In our setting, we construct a thesaurus for a morphologically rich language (Hebrew). Therefore, we followed the Liebeskind et al. (2012) algorithmic scheme designed for these cases, summarized below. First, our target term is represented in its lemma form. For each target term we retrieve all the corpus documents containing this given target term. Then, we define a set of candidate terms, which are represented in their surface form, that consists of all the terms in all these documents. Next, the Dice co-occurrence score between the target term and each of the candidates is calculated, based on their document-level statistics in the corpus. After sorting the terms based on their scores, the highest rated candidate terms are clustered into lemma-based clusters. Finally, we rank the clusters by summing the co-occurrence scores of their members and the highest rated clusters constitute the candidate terms for the given target term, to be presented to a domain expert.

## 3 Iterative Semi-automatic Scheme for Cross-period Thesaurus Construction

As explained in Section 1, our research focuses on a semi-automatic setting for supporting cross-period thesaurus construction by a lexicographer. In this work, we assume that a list of modern target terms is given as input. Then, we automatically extract a ranked list of candidate related terms for each target term using statistical measures, as detailed in Section 2. Notice that at this first step related terms can be extracted only from the mixed corpora, in which the given (modern) target term may occur. Next, a lexicographer manually selects, from the top ranked candidates, *ancient* related terms for the thesaurus entry as well as terms for QE. The QE terms may be either ancient or modern terms from the candidate list, or terms from a lexical resource. Our iterative QE scheme iterates over the QE terms. In each iteration, a QE term replaces the target term's role in the statistics extraction process. Candidate related terms are extracted for the QE term and the lexicographer judges their relevancy with respect to the original target term. Notice that if the QE term is modern, only the mixed corpora can be utilized. However, if the QE term is ancient, the ancient corpora are also utilized and may contribute additional related terms.

The algorithmic scheme we developed for thesaurus construction is illustrated in Figure 1. Our input is a modern target term. First, we automatically extract candidates by statistical co-occurrence measures, as described in Section 2. Then, a domain-expert annotates the candidates.

The manual selection process includes two decisions on each candidate (either modern or ancient): (i) whether the candidate is related to the target term and should be included in its thesaurus entry, and (ii) whether this candidate can be used as a QE term for the original target term. The second decision provides input to the QE process, which triggers the subsequent iterations. Following the first decision we filter the modern terms and include only ancient ones in the actual thesaurus.

The classification of a candidate term as ancient or modern is done automatically by a simple classification rule: If a term appears in an ancient corpus, then it is necessarily an ancient term; otherwise, it is a modern term (notice that the converse is not true, since an ancient term might appear in modern documents).

In parallel to extracting candidate related terms from the corpus, we extract candidate terms also from our lexical resources, and the domain expert judges their fitness as well. Our iterative process is applied over the expansions list. In each iteration, we take out an expansion term and automatically extract related candidates for it. Then, the annotator selects both ancient related terms for the thesaurus and suitable terms, either modern or ancient, for the expansion list for further iterations.

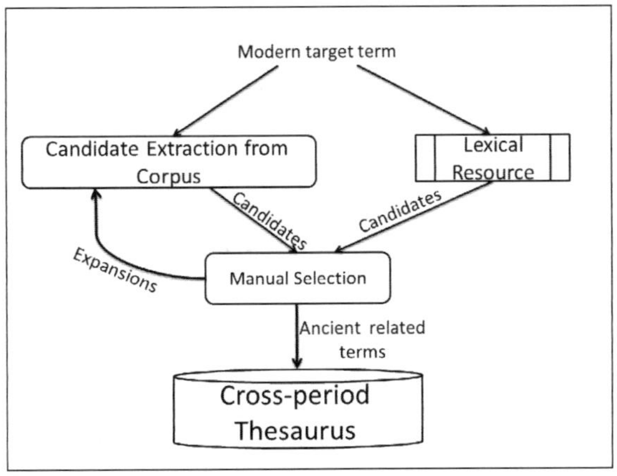


Figure 1: Semi-automatic Algorithmic Scheme

For efficiency, only new candidates that were not judged in pervious iterations are given for judgement. The stopping criterion is when there are no additional expansions in the expansions list.

Since the scheme is recall-oriented, the aim of the annotation process is to maximize the thesaurus coverage. In each iteration, the domain expert annotates the extracted ranked list of candidate terms until $k$ sequential candidates were judged as irrelevant. This stopping criterion for each iteration controls the efforts to increase recall while maintaining a low, but reasonable precision.

In our setting, we extract ancient related terms for modern terms. Therefore, in order to utilize co-occurrence statistics extraction, our scheme requires both ancient and mixed corpora, where the first iteration utilizes only the mixed corpora. Then, our iterative scheme enables subsequent iterations to utilize the ancient corpora as well.

## 4 Case Study: Cross-period Jewish Thesaurus

Our research targets the construction of a cross-period thesaurus for the Responsa project[1]. The corpus includes questions on various daily issues posed to rabbis and their detailed rabbinic answers, collected over fourteen centuries, and was used for previous IR and NLP research (Choueka et al., 1971; Choueka et al., 1987; HaCohen-Kerner et al., 2008; Liebeskind et al., 2012; Zohar et al., 2013).

The Responsa corpus' documents are divided to four periods: the $11^{th}$ century until the end of the $15^{th}$ century, the $16^{th}$ century, the $17^{th}$ through the $19^{th}$ centuries, and the $20^{th}$ century until to-

[1]Corpus kindly provided: http://biu.ac.il/jh/Responsa/

day. We considered the first three periods as our ancient corpora along with the RaMBaM (Hebrew acronym for Rabbi Mosheh Ben Maimon) writings from the $12^{th}$ century. For the mixed corpus we used the corpus' documents from the last period, but due to relatively low volume of modern documents we enriched it with additional modern collections (Tchumin collection [2], ASSIA (a Journal of Jewish Ethics and Halacha), the Medical-Halachic Encyclopedia[3], a collection of questions and answers written by Rabbi Shaul Israeli[4], and the Talmudic Encyclopedia (a Hebrew language encyclopedia that summarizes halachic topics of the Talmud in alphabetical order). Hebrew Wiktionary was used as a lexical resource for synonyms.

For statistics extraction, we applied (Liebeskind et al., 2012) algorithmic scheme using Dice coefficient as our co-occurrence measure (see Section 2). Statistics were calculated over bigrams from corpora consisting of 81993 documents.

## 5 Evaluation

### 5.1 Evaluation Setting

We assessed our iterative algorithmic scheme by evaluating its ability to increase the thesaurus coverage, compared to a similar non-iterative co-occurrence-based thesaurus construction method. In our experiments, we assumed that it is worth spending the lexicographer's time as long as it is productive, thus, all the manual annotations were based on the lexicographer efforts to increase recall until reaching the stopping criterion.

We used Liebeskind et al. (2012) algorithmic scheme as our non-iterative baseline (*Baseline*). For comparison, we ran our iterative scheme, calculated the average number of judgments per target term (88) and set the baseline stopping criterion to be the same number of judgements per target. Thus, we ensured that the number of judgements for our iterative algorithm and for the baseline is equal, and thus coverage increase is due to a better use of lexicographer's effort. For completeness, we present the results of the non-iterative algorithm with the stopping criterion of the iterative algorithm, when reaching $k$ ($k$=*10* was empirically selected in our case) sequential irrelevant candidates (*First-iteration*).

| Method | RT | R | Pro | J |
|---|---|---|---|---|
| *First-iteration* | 50 | 0.31 | 0.038 | 1307 |
| *Baseline* | 63 | 0.39 | 0.024 | 2640 |
| *Iterative* | 151 | 0.94 | 0.057 | 2640 |

Table 1: Results Comparison

To evaluate our scheme's performance, we used several measures: total number of ancient related terms extracted (RT), relative recall (R) and productivity (Pro). Since we do not have any predefined thesaurus, our micro-averaged relative-recall considered the number of ancient related terms from the output of both methods (baseline and iterative) as the full set of related terms. Productivity was measured by dividing the total number of ancient related terms extracted (RT) by the total number of the judgments performed for the method (J).

### 5.2 Results

Table 1 compares the performance of our semi-automatic iterative scheme with that of the baseline over a test set of 30 modern target terms. Our iterative scheme increases the average number of extracted related terms from 2.1 to 5, i.e., increasing recall by 240%. The relative recall of the first-iteration (0.31) is included in the relative recall of both the baseline and our iterative method. Iterating over the first iteration increases recall by 300% (from 50 to 151 terms), while adding more judgements to the non-iterative method increases recall only by 26% (to 63 terms). The productivity of the iterative process is higher even than the productivity of the first iteration, showing that the iterative process optimizes the lexicographer's manual effort.

Table 2 shows examples of thesaurus target terms and their ancient related terms, which were added by our iterative scheme[5]. Since the related terms are ancient Halachic terms, we explain them rather than translate them to English.

We further analyze our scheme by comparing the use of ancient versus modern terms in the iterative process. Although modern related terms were not included in our cross-period thesaurus, in the judgement process the lexicographer judged their

[2] http://www.zomet.org.il/?CategoryID=170

[3] http://medethics.org.il/website/index.php/en/research-2/encyclopedia-of-jewish-medical-ethics

[4] http://www.eretzhemdah.org/data/uploadedfiles/ebooks/14-sfile.pdf

[5] To facilitate readability we use a transliteration of Hebrew using Roman characters; the letters used, in Hebrew lexico-graphic order, are abgdhwzxTiklmns`pcqršt.

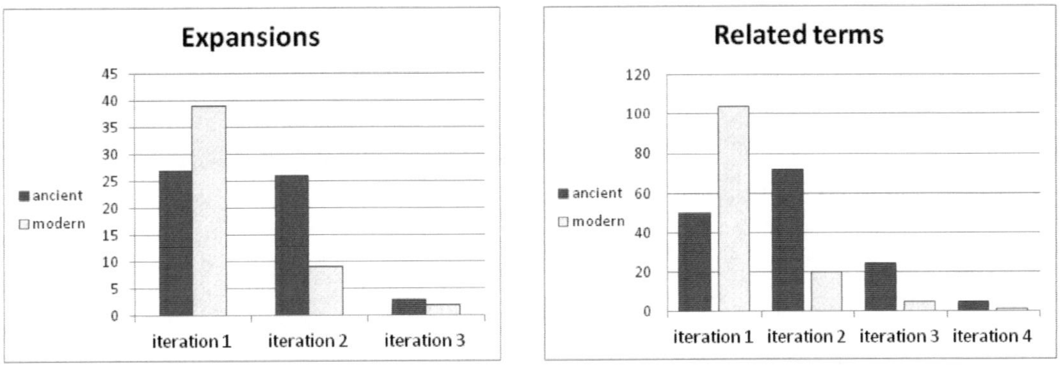


Figure 2: The extraction of ancient terms versus modern terms in the iterative process

| Target term | Related term |
|---|---|
| *zkwiwt iwcrim* (copyright) | *hsgt gbwl* (trespassing) |
| | *iwrd lamnwt xbrw* ([competitively] enter his friend's profession) |
| | *`ni hmhpk bxrrh* (a poor man is deciding whether to buy a cake and another person comes and takes it) |
| *hmtt xsd* (euthanasia) | *rwb gwssin lmith* (most dying people die) |
| | *xii š`h* (living for the moment) |
| *hpsqt hriwn* (abortion) | *xwtkin h`wbr* (killing the fetus) |
| | *hwrg npš* (killing a person) |
| | *rwdp* (pursuer, a fetus endangering its mother's life) |
| *tiknwn hmšpxh* (birth control) | *šlwš nšim mšmšwt bmwk* (three types of women allowed to use cotton diaphragm) |
| | *dš mbpnim wzwrh mbxwc* (withdrawal method) |
| *hprt xwzh* (breach of contract) | *biTwl mqx* (cancelling a purchase) |
| | *dina dgrmi* (indirect damage) |
| | *mqx t`wt* (erroneous bargain) |
| *srwb pqwdh* (insubordination) | *mwrd bmlkwt* (rebel against the sovereign [government]) |
| | *imrh at pik* (to disobey) |
| | *Avner* and *khni Nob* (a biblical story: king Saul ordered to slay Ahimilech together with 85 priests. Avner, the captain of Saul's guard, disobeyed the order.) |

Table 2: Examples for the iterative scheme's contribution

relevancy too. In Figure 2, we report the number of modern related terms in comparison to the number of ancient related terms for each iteration. In parallel, we illustrate the number of ancient expansions in proportion to the number of modern expansions. The x-axis' values denote the iterations, while the y-axis' values denote the number of expansions and related terms respectively. For each iteration, the expansions chart presents the expansions that were extracted while the related terms chart presents the extracted related terms, of which the ancient ones were included in the thesaurus. Since the input for our scheme is a modern target terms, the first iteration extracted more modern related terms than ancient terms and utilized more modern expansions than ancient. However, this proportion changed in the second iteration, probably thanks to the ancient expansions retrieved in the first iteration.

Although there are often mixed results on the effectiveness of QE for information retrieval (Voorhees, 1994; Xu and Croft, 1996), our results show that QE for thesaurus construction in an iterative interactive setting is beneficial for increasing thesaurus' coverage substantially.

## 6 Conclusions and Future Work

We introduced an iterative interactive scheme for cross-period thesaurus construction, utilizing QE techniques. Our semi-automatic algorithm significantly increased thesaurus coverage, while optimizing the lexicographer manual effort. The scheme was investigated for Hebrew, but can be generically applied for other languages.

We plan to further explore the suggested scheme by utilizing additional lexical resources and QE algorithms. We also plan to adopt second-order distributional similarity methods for cross-period thesaurus construction.

## References


D. Bollegala, Y. Matsuo, and M. Ishizuka. 2011. A web search engine-based approach to measure semantic similarity between words. *Knowledge and Data Engineering, IEEE Transactions on*, 23(7):977–990.

Yaacov Choueka, M. Cohen, J. Dueck, Aviezri S. Fraenkel, and M. Slae. 1971. Full text document retrieval: Hebrew legal texts. In *SIGIR*, pages 61–79.

Yaacov Choueka, Aviezri S. Fraenkel, Shmuel T. Klein, and E. Segal. 1987. Improved techniques for processing queries in full-text systems. In *SIGIR*, pages 306–315.

Kenneth Ward Church and Patrick Hanks. 1990. Word association norms, mutual information, and lexicography. *Comput. Linguist.*, 16(1):22–29, March.

James R. Curran and Marc Moens. 2002. Improvements in automatic thesaurus extraction. In *Proceedings of the ACL-02 workshop on Unsupervised lexical acquisition - Volume 9*, ULA '02, pages 59–66, Stroudsburg, PA, USA. Association for Computational Linguistics.

Caroline Gasperin, Pablo Gamallo, Alexandre Agustini, Gabriel Lopes, Vera De Lima, et al. 2001. Using syntactic contexts for measuring word similarity. In *Workshop on Knowledge Acquisition and Categorization, ESSLLI*, Helsinki, Finland.

Yaakov HaCohen-Kerner, Ariel Kass, and Ariel Peretz. 2008. Combined one sense disambiguation of abbreviations. *Proceedings of ACL08: HLT, Short Papers*, pages 61–64.

Chikara Hashimoto, Kentaro Torisawa, Stijn De Saeger, Junichi Kazama, and Sadao Kurohashi. 2011. Extracting paraphrases from definition sentences on the web. In *Proceedings of the 49th Annual Meeting of the Association for Computational Linguistics (ACL)*, pages 1087–1097.

Adam Kilgarriff. 2003. Thesauruses for natural language processing. In *Proceedings of the Joint Conference on Natural Language Processing and Knowledge Engineering*, pages 5–13, Beijing, China.

Lili Kotlerman, Ido Dagan, Idan Szpektor, and Maayan Zhitomirsky-geffet. 2010. Directional distributional similarity for lexical inference. *Nat. Lang. Eng.*, 16(4):359–389, October.

Chaya Liebeskind, Ido Dagan, and Jonathan Schler. 2012. Statistical thesaurus construction for a morphologically rich language. In **SEM 2012: The First Joint Conference on Lexical and Computational Semantics*, pages 59–64, Montréal, Canada, 7-8 June. Association for Computational Linguistics.

Dekang Lin. 1998. Automatic retrieval and clustering of similar words. In *Proceedings of the 36th Annual Meeting of the Association for Computational Linguistics and 17th International Conference on Computational Linguistics - Volume 2*, ACL '98, pages 768–774, Stroudsburg, PA, USA. Association for Computational Linguistics.

Rada Mihalcea, Courtney Corley, and Carlo Strapparava. 2006. Corpus-based and knowledge-based measures of text semantic similarity. In *Proceedings of the 21st national conference on Artificial intelligence - Volume 1*, AAAI'06, pages 775–780. AAAI Press.

Yves Peirsman, Kris Heylen, and Dirk Speelman. 2008. Putting things in order. First and second order context models for the calculation of semantic similarity. In *9es Journées internationales d'Analyse statistique des Données Textuelles (JADT 2008)*. Lyon, France.

Michael Piotrowski. 2012. Natural language processing for historical texts. *Synthesis Lectures on Human Language Technologies*, 5(2):1–157.

Pavel Rychlý and Adam Kilgarriff. 2007. An efficient algorithm for building a distributional thesaurus (and other sketch engine developments). In *Proceedings of the 45th Annual Meeting of the ACL on Interactive Poster and Demonstration Sessions*, ACL '07, pages 41–44, Stroudsburg, PA, USA. Association for Computational Linguistics.

Cristina Sánchez-Marco, Gemma Boleda, and Lluís Padró. 2011. Extending the tool, or how to annotate historical language varieties. In *Proceedings of the 5th ACL-HLT Workshop on Language Technology for Cultural Heritage, Social Sciences, and Humanities*, LaTeCH '11, pages 1–9, Stroudsburg, PA, USA. Association for Computational Linguistics.

Hinrich Schütze and Jan O. Pedersen. 1997. A cooccurrence-based thesaurus and two applications to information retrieval. *Inf. Process. Manage.*, 33(3):307–318, May.

Eyal Shnarch, Libby Barak, and Ido Dagan. 2009. Extracting lexical reference rules from wikipedia. In *Proceedings of the Joint Conference of the 47th Annual Meeting of the ACL and the 4th International Joint Conference on Natural Language Processing of the AFNLP: Volume 1 - Volume 1*, ACL '09, pages 450–458, Stroudsburg, PA, USA. Association for Computational Linguistics.

Frank Smadja, Kathleen R. McKeown, and Vasileios Hatzivassiloglou. 1996. Translating collocations for bilingual lexicons: a statistical approach. *Comput. Linguist.*, 22(1):1–38, March.

Caroline Sporleder. 2010. Natural language processing for cultural heritage domains. *Language and Linguistics Compass*, 4(9):750–768.

Ellen M. Voorhees. 1994. Query expansion using lexical-semantic relations. In *Proceedings of the 17th annual international ACM SIGIR conference on Research and development in information retrieval*, SIGIR '94, pages 61–69, New York, NY, USA. Springer-Verlag New York, Inc.

Julie Weeds and David Weir. 2003. A general framework for distributional similarity. In *Proceedings of the 2003 conference on Empirical methods in natural language processing*, EMNLP '03, pages 81–88, Stroudsburg, PA, USA. Association for Computational Linguistics.

Jinxi Xu and W. Bruce Croft. 1996. Query expansion using local and global document analysis. In *Proceedings of the 19th annual international ACM SIGIR conference on Research and development in information retrieval*, SIGIR '96, pages 4–11, New York, NY, USA. ACM.

Hadas Zohar, Chaya Liebeskind, Jonathan Schler, and Ido Dagan. 2013. Automatic thesaurus construction for cross generation corpus. *Journal on Computing and Cultural Heritage (JOCCH)*, 6(1):4:1–4:19, April.

# Language Technology for Agile Social Media Science

**Simon Wibberley**
Department of Informatics
University of Sussex
sw206@susx.ac.uk

**Jeremy Reffin**
Department of Informatics
University of Sussex
j.p.reffin@susx.ac.uk

**David Weir**
Department of Informatics
University of Sussex
davidw@susx.ac.uk

## Abstract

We present an extension of the DUALIST tool that enables social scientists to engage directly with large Twitter datasets. Our approach supports collaborative construction of classifiers and associated gold standard data sets. The tool can be used to build classifier cascades that decomposes tweet streams, and provide analysis of targeted conversations. A central concern is to provide an environment in which social science researchers can rapidly develop an informed sense of what the datasets look like. The intent is that they develop, not only an informed view as to how the data could be fruitfully analysed, but also how feasible it is to analyse it in that way.

## 1 Introduction

In recent years, automatic social media analysis (SMA) has emerged, not only as a major focus of attention within the academic NLP community, but as an area that is of increasing interest to a variety of business and public sectors organisations. Among the many social media platforms in use today, the one that has received the most attention is Twitter, the second most popular social media network in the world with over 400 million tweets sent each day. The popularity of Twitter as a target of SMA derives from both the public nature of tweets, and the availability of the Twitter API which provides a variety of flexible methods for scraping tweets from the live Twitter stream.

A plethora of social media monitoring platforms now exist, that are mostly concerned with providing product marketing oriented services[1]. For example, brand monitoring services seek to provide companies with an understanding of what is being said about their brands and products, with language processing technology being used to capture relevant comments or conversations and apply some form of sentiment analysis (SA), in order to derive insights into what is being said. This paper forms part of a growing body of work that is attempting to broaden the scope of SMA beyond the realm of product marketing, and into areas of concern to social scientists (Carvalho et al., 2011; Diakopoulos and Shamma, 2010; Gonzalez-Bailon et al., 2010; Marchetti-Bowick and Chambers, 2012; O'Connor et al., 2010; Tumasjan et al., 2011; Tumasjan et al., 2010).

Social media presents an enormous opportunity for the social science research community, constituting a window into what large numbers of people are talking. There are, however, significant obstacles facing social scientists interested in making use of big social media datasets, and it is important for the NLP research community to gain a better understanding as to how language technology can support such explorations.

A key requirement, and the focus of this paper, is agility: the social scientist needs to be able to engage with the data in a way that supports an iterative process, homing in on a way of analysing the data that is likely to produce valuable insight. Given what is typically a rather broad topic as a starting point, there is a need to see what issues related to that topic are being discussed and to what extent. It can be important to get a feeling for the kind of language being used in these discussions, and there is a need to rapidly assess the accuracy of the automated decision making. There is little value in developing an analysis of the data on an approach that relies on the technology making decisions that are so nuanced that the method being used is highly unreliable. As the answers to these questions are being exposed, insights emerge from the data, and it becomes possible for the social scientist to progressively refine the topics that are be-

[1] http://wiki.kenburbary.com/social-media-monitoring-wiki lists 230 Social Media Monitoring Solutions

ing targetted, and ultimately create a way of automatically analysing the data that is likely to be insightful.

Supporting this agile methodology presents severe challenges from an NLP perspective, where the predominant approaches use classifiers that involve supervised machine learning. The need for substantial quantities of training data, and the detrimental impact on performance that results when applying them to "out-of-domain" data mean that exisiting approaches cannot support the agility that is so important when social scientists engage with big social media datasets.

We describe a tool being developed in collaboration with a team of social scientists to support this agile methodology. We have built a framework based on DUALIST, an active learning tool for building classifiers (Settles, 2011; Settles and Zhu, 2012). This framework provides a way for a group of social scientists to collaboratively engage with a stream of tweets, with a goal of constructing a chain (or cascade) of automatic document classification layers that isolate and analyse targeted conversions on Twitter. Section 4 discusses ways in which the design of our framework is intended to support the agile methodology mentioned above, with particular emphasis on the value of DUALIST's active learning approach, and the crucial role of the collaborative gold standard and model building activities. Section 4.3 discusses additional data processing step that have been introduced to increase the frameworks usefulness, and section 5 introduces some projects to which the framework is being applied.

## 2 Related Work

Work that focuses on addressing sociological questions with SMA broadly fall into one of three categories.

- Approaches that employ automatic data analysis without tailoring the analysis to the specifics of the situation e.g. (Tumasjan et al., 2010; Tumasjan et al., 2011; O'Connor et al., 2010; Gonzalez-Bailon et al., 2010; Sang and Bos, 2012; Bollen et al., 2011). This body of research involves little or no manual inspection of the data. An analytical technique is selected *a-priori*, applied to the SM stream, and the results from that analysis are then aligned with a real-world phenomenon in order to draw predictive or correlative conclusions about social media. A typical approach is to predict election outcomes by counting mentions of political parties and/or politicians as 'votes' in various ways. Further content analysis is then overlaid, such as sentiment or mood anlysis, in an attempt to improve performance. However the generic language-analysis techniques that are applied lead to little or no gain, often causing adjustments to target question to something with less strict assessment criteria, such as poll trend instead of election outcome (Tumasjan et al., 2010; Tumasjan et al., 2011; O'Connor et al., 2010; Sang and Bos, 2012). This research has been criticised for applying out-of-domain techniques in a 'black box' fashion, and questions have been raised as to how sensitive the results are to parameters chosen (Gayo-Avello, 2012; Jungherr et al., 2012).

- Approaches that employ manual analysis of the data by researchers with a tailored analytical approach (Bermingham and Smeaton, 2011; Castillo et al., 2011).This approach reflects traditional research methods in the social sciences. Through manual annotation effort, researchers engage closely with the data in a manual but interactive fashion, and this effort enables them to uncover patterns in the data and make inferences as to how SM was being used in the context of the sociocultural phenomena under investigation. This research suffers form either being restricted to fairly small datasets.

- Approaches that employ tailored automatic data analysis, using a supervised machine-learning approach(Carvalho et al., 2011; Papacharissi and de Fatima Oliveira, 2012; Meraz and Papacharissi, 2013; Hopkins and King, 2010). This research infers properties of the SM data using statistics from their bespoke machine learning analysis. Mannual annotation effort is required to train the classifiers and is typically applied in a batch process at the commencement of the investigation.

Our work aims to expand this last category, improving the quality of research by capturing more of the insight-provoking engagement with the data seen in more traditional research.

## 3 DUALIST

Our approach is built around DUALIST (Settles, 2011; Settles and Zhu, 2012), an open-source project designed to enable non-technical analysts to build machine-learning classifiers by annotating documents with just a few minutes of effort.

In Section 4, we discuss various ways in which we have extended DUALIST, including functionality allowing multiple annotators to work in parallel; incorporating functionality to create 'gold-standard' test sets and measure inter-annotator agreement; and supporting on-going performance evaluation against the gold standard during the process of building a classifier. DUALIST provides a graphical interface with which an annotator is able to build a Naïve Bayes' classifier given a collection of unlabelled documents. During the process of building a classifier, the annotator is presented with a selection of documents (in our case tweets) that he/she has an opportunity to label (with one of the class labels), and, for each class, a selection of features (tokens) that the annotator has an opportunity to mark as being strong features for that class.

Active learning is used to select both the documents and the features being presented for annotation. Documents are selected on the basis of those that the current model is most uncertain about (as measured by posterior class entropy), and features are selected for a given class on the basis of those with highest information gain occurring frequently with that class. After a batch of documents and features have been annotated, a revised model is built using both the labelled data and the current model's predictions for the remaining unlabelled data, through the use of the Expectation-Maximization algorithm. This new model is then used as the basis for selecting the set of documents and features that will be presented to the annotator for the next iteration of the model building process. Full details can be found in Settles (2011).

The upshot of this is two-fold: not only can a reasonable model be rapidly created, but the researcher is exposed to an interesting non-uniform sample of the training data. Examples that are relatively easy for the model to classify, i.e. those with low entropy, are ranked lower in the list of unlabelled data awaiting annotation. The effect of this is that the training process facilitates a form of data exploration that exposes the user to the hardest border cases.

## 4 Extending DUALIST for Social Media Science Research

This section describes ways in which we have extended DUALIST to provide an integrated data exploration tool for social scientists. As outlined in the introduction, our vision is that a team of social scientists will be able to use this tool to collaboratively work towards the construction of a cascade of automatic document classification layers that carve up an incoming Twitter data stream in order to pick out one or more targeted 'conversations', and provide an analysis of what is being discussed in each of these 'conversations'. In what follows, we refer to the social scientists as the researchers and the activity during which the researchers are working towards delivering a useful classifier cascade as data engagement.

### 4.1 Facilitating data engagement

When embarking on the process of building one of the classifiers in the cascade, researchers bring preconceptions as to the basis for the classification. It is only when engaging with the data that it becomes possible to develop an adequate classification policy. For example, when looking for tweets that express some attitude about a targeted issue, one needs a policy as to how a tweet that shares a link to an opinion piece on that topic without any further comment should be classified. There are a number of ways in which we support the classification policy development process.

- One of the impacts of the active learning approach adopted in DUALIST is that by presenting tweets that the current model is most unsure of, DUALIST will very rapidly expose issues around how to make decisions on boundary cases.

- We have extended DUALIST to allow multiple researchers to build a classifier concurrently. In addition to reducing the time it takes to build classifiers, this fosters a collaborative approach to classification policy development.

- We have added functionality that allows for the collaborative construction of gold standard data sets. Not only does this provide feedback during the model building process as to when performance begins to plateau, but, as a gold standard is being built, researchers are shown the current inter-annotator agreement score, and are shown examples of tweets where there is disagreement among annotators. This constitutes yet another way in which researchers are confronted with the most problematic examples.

### 4.2 Building classifier cascades

Having considered issues that relate to the construction of an individual classifier, we end this section by briefly considering issues relating to the classifier cascade. The Twitter API provides basic boolean search functionality that is used to scrape the Twitter stream, producing the input to the cascade. A typical strategy is to select query terms for the boolean search with a view to achieving a reasonably high recall of relevant tweets[2]. An effective choice of query terms that actually achieves this is one of the things that is not well understood in advance, but which we expect to emerge during the data engagement phase. Capturing an input stream that contains a sufficiently large proportion of interesting (relevant) tweets is usually achieved at the expense of precision (the proportion of tweets in the stream being scraped that are relevant). As a result, the first task that is typically undertaken during the data engagement phase involves building a relevancy classifier, to be deployed at the top of the classifier cascade, that is designed to filter out irrelevant tweets from the stream of tweets being scraped.

When building the relevancy classifier, the researchers begin to see how well their preconceptions match the reality of the data stream. It is only through the process of building this classifier that the researchers begin to get a feel for the composition of the relevant data stream. This drives the researcher's conception as to how best to divide up the stream into useful sub-streams, and, as a result, provides the first insights into an appropriate cascade architecture. Our experience is that in many cases, classifiers at upper levels of the cascade are involved in decomposing data streams in useful ways, and classifiers that are lower down in the cascade are designed to measure some facet (e.g. sentiment polarity) of the material on some particular sub-stream.

### 4.3 Tools for Data Analysis

As social scientists are starting to engage with real-world data using this framework, it has emerged that certain patterns of downstream data analysis are of particular use.

**Time series analysis.** For many social phenomena, the timing and sequence of social media messages are of critical importance, particularly for a platform such as Twitter. Our framework supports tweet volume analysis across any time frame, allowing researchers to review changes over time in any classifier's input or output tweet flows (classes). This extends the common approach of sentiment tracking over time to tracking over time any attitudinal (or other) response whose essential features can be captured by a classifier of this kind. These class-volume-by-time-interval plots can provide insight into how and when the stream changes in response to external events.

**Link analysis.** It is becoming apparent that link sharing (attaching a URL to a tweet, typically pointing to a media story) is an important aspect of how information propagates through social media, particularly on Twitter. For example, the meaning of a tweet can sometimes only be discerned by inspecting the link to which it points. We are introducing to the framework automatic expansion of shortened URLs and the ability to inspect link URL contents, allowing researchers to interpret tweets more rapidly and accurately. A combination of link analysis with time series analysis is also providing researchers with insights into how mainstream media stories propagate through society and shape opinion in the social media age.

**Language use analysis.** Once a classifier has been initially established, the framework analyses the language employed in the input tweets using an information gain (IG) measure. High IG features are those that have occurrence distributions that closely align the document classification distributions; essentially they are highly indicative of the class. This information is proving useful to social science researchers for three purposes. First, it helps identify the words and phrases people employ to convey a particular attitude or opinion in the domain of interest. Second, it can provide information on how the language employed shifts over time, for example as new topics are introduced or external events occur. Third, it can be used to select candidate keywords with which to augment the stream's boolean scraper query. In this last case, however, we need to augment the analysis; many high IG terms make poor scraper terms because they are poorly selective in the more general case (i.e. outside of the context of the existing query-selected sample). We take a sample using the candidate term alone with the search API and estimate the relevancy precision of the scraped tweet sample by passing the tweets through the first-level relevancy classifier. The precision of the

[2] In many cases it is very hard to estimate recall since there is no way to estimate accurately the volume of relevant tweets in the full Twitter stream.

new candidate term can be compared to the precision of existing terms and a decision made.

## 5 Applications and Extensions

The framework's flexibility enables it to be applied to any task that can be broken down into a series of classification decisions, or indeed where this approach materially assists the social scientist in addressing the issue at hand. In order to explore its application, our framework is being applied to a variety of tasks:

**Identifying patterns of usage.** People use the same language for different purposes; the framework is proving to be a valuable tool for elucidating these usage patterns and for isolating data sets that illustrate these patterns. As an example, the authors (in collaboration with a team of social scientists) are studying the differing ways in which people employ ethnically and racially sensitive language in conversations on-line. The framework has helped to reveal and isolate a number of distinct patterns of usage.

**Tracking changes in opinion over time.** Sentiment classifiers trained in one domain perform poorly when applied to another domain, even when the domains are apparently closely related (Pang and Lee, 2008). Traditionally, this has forced a choice between building bespoke classifiers (at significant cost), or using generic sentiment classifiers (which sacrifice performance). The ability to rapidly construct sentiment classifiers that are specifically tuned to the precise domain can significantly increase classifier performance without imposing major additional costs. Moving beyond sentiment, with these bespoke classifiers it is in principle possible to track over time any form of opinion that is reflected in language. In a second study, the authors are (in collaboration with a team of social scientists) building cascades of bespoke classifiers to investigate shifts in citizens' attitudes over time (as expressed in social media) to a range of political and social issues arising across the European Union.

**Entity disambiguation.** References to individuals are often ambiguous. In the general case, word sense disambiguation is most successfully performed by supervised-learning classifiers (Màrquez et al., 2006), and the low cost of producing classifiers using this framework makes this approach practical for situations where we require repeated high recall, high precision searches of large data sets for a specific entity. As an example, this approach is being employed in the EU attitudinal survey study.

**Repeated complex search.** In situations where a fixed but complex search needs to be performed repeatedly over a relatively long period of time, then a supervised-learning classifier can be expected both to produce the best results and to be cost-effective in terms of the effort required to train it. The authors have employed this approach in a commercial environment (Lyra et al., 2012), and the ability to train classifiers more quickly with this framework reduces the cost still further and makes this a practical approach in a wider range of circumstances.

With regard to extension of the framework, we have identified a number of avenues for expansion and improvement that will significantly increase its usefulness and applicability to real-world scenarios, and we have recently commenced an 18-month research programme to formalise and extend the framework and its associated methodology for use in social science research[3].

## Conclusions and Future Work

We describe an agile analysis framework built around the DUALIST tool designed to support effective exploration of large twitter data sets by social scientists. The functionality of DUALIST has been extended to allow the scraping of tweets through access to the Twitter API, collaborative construction of both gold standard data sets and Naïve Bayes' classifiers, an Information Gain-based method for automatic discovery of new search terms, and support for the construction of classifier cascades. Further extensions currently under development include grouping tweets into threads conversations, and automatic clustering of relevant tweets in order to discover subtopics under discussion.

## Acknowledgments

We are grateful to our collaborators at the Centre for the Analysis of social media, Jamie Bartlett and Carl Miller for valuable contributions to this work. We thank the anonymous reviewers for their helpful comments. This work was partially supported by the Open Society Foundation.

[3]Towards a Social Media Science, funded by the UK ESRC National Centre for Research Methods.

## References


[Bermingham and Smeaton2011] Adam Bermingham and Alan F Smeaton. 2011. On using Twitter to monitor political sentiment and predict election results. In *Proceedings of the Workshop on Sentiment Analysis where AI meets Psychology (SAAIP), IJCNLP 2011*, pages 2–10.

[Bollen et al.2011] Johan Bollen, Alberto Pepe, and Huina Mao. 2011. Modeling public mood and emotion: Twitter sentiment and socio-economic phenomena. In *Proceedings of the Fifth International AAAI Conference on Weblogs and Social Media*, pages 450–453.

[Carvalho et al.2011] Paula Carvalho, Luís Sarmento, Jorge Teixeira, and Mário J. Silva. 2011. Liars and saviors in a sentiment annotated corpus of comments to political debates. In *Proceedings of the 49th Annual Meeting of the Association for Computational Linguistics: Human Language Technologies: short papers - Volume 2*, pages 564–568, Stroudsburg, PA, USA.

[Castillo et al.2011] Carlos Castillo, Marcelo Mendoza, and Barbara Poblete. 2011. Information credibility on Twitter. In *Proceedings of the 20th International Conference on World wide web*, pages 675–684.

[Diakopoulos and Shamma2010] Nicholas A Diakopoulos and David A Shamma. 2010. Characterizing debate performance via aggregated Twitter sentiment. In *Proceedings of the 28th international conference on Human factors in computing systems*, pages 1195–1198.

[Gayo-Avello2012] Daniel Gayo-Avello. 2012. I wanted to predict elections with twitter and all i got was this lousy paper a balanced survey on election prediction using Twitter data. *arXiv preprint arXiv:1204.6441*.

[Gonzalez-Bailon et al.2010] Sandra Gonzalez-Bailon, Rafael E Banchs, and Andreas Kaltenbrunner. 2010. Emotional reactions and the pulse of public opinion: Measuring the impact of political events on the sentiment of online discussions. *arXiv preprint arXiv:1009.4019*.

[Hopkins and King2010] Daniel J. Hopkins and Gary King. 2010. A method of automated nonparametric content analysis for social science. *American Journal of Political Science*, 54(1):229–247.

[Jungherr et al.2012] Andreas Jungherr, Pascal Jürgens, and Harald Schoen. 2012. Why the Pirate Party won the German election of 2009 or the trouble with predictions: A response to Tumasjan, Sprenger, Sander, & Welpe. *Social Science Computer Review*, 30(2):229–234.

[Lyra et al.2012] Matti Lyra, Daoud Clarke, Hamish Morgan, Jeremy Reffin, and David Weir. 2012. Challenges in applying machine learning to media monitoring. In *Proceedings of Thirty-second SGAI International Conference on Artificial Intelligence (AI-2012)*.

[Marchetti-Bowick and Chambers2012] Micol Marchetti-Bowick and Nathanael Chambers. 2012. Learning for microblogs with distant supervision: political forecasting with Twitter. In *Proceedings of the 13th Conference of the European Chapter of the Association for Computational Linguistics*, pages 603–612.

[Màrquez et al.2006] Lluís Màrquez, Gerard Escudero, David Martínez, and German Rigau. 2006. Supervised corpus-based methods for wsd. In Eneko Agirre and Philip Edmonds, editors, *Word Sense Disambiguation*, volume 33 of *Text, Speech and Language Technology*, pages 167–216. Springer Netherlands.

[Meraz and Papacharissi2013] Sharon Meraz and Zizi Papacharissi. 2013. Networked gatekeeping and networked framing on #egypt. *The International Journal of Press/Politics*, 18(2):138–166.

[O'Connor et al.2010] Brendan O'Connor, Ramnath Balasubramanyan, Bryan R Routledge, and Noah A Smith. 2010. From tweets to polls: Linking text sentiment to public opinion time series. In *Proceedings of the International AAAI Conference on Weblogs and Social Media*, pages 122–129.

[Pang and Lee2008] Bo Pang and Lillian Lee. 2008. Opinion mining and sentiment analysis. *Foundations and trends in Information Retrieval*, 2(1-2):1–135.

[Papacharissi and de Fatima Oliveira2012] Zizi Papacharissi and Maria de Fatima Oliveira. 2012. Affective news and networked publics: the rhythms of news storytelling on #egypt. *Journal of Communication*, 62(2):266–282.

[Sang and Bos2012] Erik Tjong Kim Sang and Johan Bos. 2012. Predicting the 2011 dutch senate election results with Twitter. *Proceedings of the European Chapter of the Association for Computational Linguistics 2012*, page 53.

[Settles and Zhu2012] Burr Settles and Xiaojin Zhu. 2012. Behavioral factors in interactive training of text classifiers. In *Proceedings of the 2012 Conference of the North American Chapter of the Association for Computational Linguistics: Human Language Technologies*, pages 563–567.

[Settles2011] Burr Settles. 2011. Closing the loop: Fast, interactive semi-supervised annotation with queries on features and instances. In *Proceedings of the Conference on Empirical Methods in Natural Language Processing*, pages 1467–1478.

[Tumasjan et al.2010] Andranik Tumasjan, Timm O Sprenger, Philipp G Sandner, and Isabell M Welpe. 2010. Predicting elections with Twitter: What 140 characters reveal about political sentiment. In *Proceedings of the fourth international AAAI conference on weblogs and social media*, pages 178–185.

[Tumasjan et al.2011] Andranik Tumasjan, Timm O Sprenger, Philipp G Sandner, and Isabell M Welpe. 2011. Election forecasts with Twitter how 140 characters reflect the political landscape. *Social Science Computer Review*, 29(4):402–418.

# Morphological annotation of Old and Middle Hungarian corpora

**Attila Novák**[1,2] **György Orosz**[2] **Nóra Wenszky**[2]
[1]Research Institute for Linguistics, Hungarian Academy of Sciences
Benczúr u. 33., Budapest, Hungary
[2]MTA-PPKE Natural Language Research Group
Faculty of Information Technology, Pázmány Péter Catholic University
Práter u. 50/a, Budapest, Hungary
{novak.attila,oroszgy}@itk.ppke.hu, wenszkynora@gmail.com

## Abstract

In our paper, we present a computational morphology for Old and Middle Hungarian used in two research projects that aim at creating morphologically annotated corpora of Old and Middle Hungarian. In addition, we present the web-based disambiguation tool used in the semi-automatic disambiguation of the annotations and the structured corpus query tool that has a unique but very useful feature of making corrections to the annotation in the query results possible.

## 1 Introduction

One of the aims of two parallel OTKA projects of the Research Institute for Linguistics of the Hungarian Academy of Sciences[1] is to create morphologically analyzed and searchable corpora of texts from the Old Hungarian and Middle Hungarian period. In the course of the projects, the Humor Hungarian morphological analyzer (Novák, 2003; Prószéky and Novák, 2005) was extended to be capable of analyzing words containing morphological constructions, suffix allomorphs, suffix morphemes, paradigms or stems that were used in Old and Middle Hungarian but no longer exist in present-day Hungarian. In the sections below, we describe how the morphological analyzer was adapted to the task, the problems we encountered and how they were solved. We also present the automatic and the manual disambiguation system used for the morphosyntactic annotation of texts and the corpus manager with the help of which the annotated corpora can be searched and maintained.

[1]*Hungarian historical generative syntax* [OTKA NK78074], and *Morphologically analysed corpus of Old and Middle Hungarian texts representative of informal language use* [OTKA 81189]

## 2 Preprocessing

The overwhelming majority of extant texts from the Old Hungarian period are codices, mainly containing texts translated from Latin. The texts selected for the Corpus of Informal Language Use, however, are much closer to spoken language: minutes taken at court trials, such as witch trials, and letters sent by noblemen and serfs. In the case of the latter corpus, metadata belonging to the texts are also of primary importance, as these make the corpus fit for historical-sociolinguistic research.

### 2.1 Digitization

All the texts selected for our corpora were originally hand-written. However, the basis for the digitized version was always a printed edition of the texts published earlier. The printed texts were scanned and converted to a character stream using OCR. This was not a trivial task, especially in the case of Old Hungarian texts, owing to the extensive use of unusual characters and diacritics. In the lack of an orthographic norm, each text applied a different set of characters; moreover, the printed publications used different fonts. Thus the only way to get acceptable results was to retrain the OCR program[2] for each text from scratch since the out-of-the-box Hungarian language and glyph models of the software did not fit any of our texts. Subsequently, all the automatically recognized documents had to be manually checked and corrected, but even so, this workflow proved to be much faster than attempting to type in the texts.

### 2.2 Normalization

The next step of preprocessing was normalization, i.e. making the texts uniform regarding their orthography and phonology. Normalization, which

[2]We used FineReader, which makes full customization of glyph models possible, including the total exclusion of out-of-the-box models.

was done manually, in our case meant modernization to present-day orthography. Note that this also implies differences in tokenization into individual words between the original and the normalized version. During this process, which also included segmentation of the texts into clauses, certain phonological dialectal variations were neutralized.

Morphological variation, however, was left untouched: no extinct morphemes were replaced by their present day counterparts. We also retained extinct allomorphs unless the variation was purely phonological. In the case of potential irresolvable ambiguity, the ambiguity was preserved as well, even if it was due to the vagueness of the orthography of the era.

An example of this is the non-consistent marking of vowel length. The definite and indefinite 3rd person singular imperfect of the frequently used word *mond* 'say' was *mondá* $\sim$ *monda* respectively, but accents are often missing from the texts. Furthermore, in many texts in the corpus, these two forms were used with a clearly different distribution from their present day counterparts *mondta* $\sim$ *mondott*. Therefore, in many cases, neither the orthography, nor the usage was consistent enough to decide unambiguously how a certain appearance of *monda* should be annotated concerning definiteness.

Another example of inherent ambiguity is a dialectal variant of possessive marking, which is very frequent in these corpora and often neutralizes singular and plural possessed forms. For example, *cselekedetinek* could both mean 'of his/her deed' or 'of his/her deeds', which in many cases cannot be disambiguated based on the context even for human annotators. Such ambiguous cases were annotated as inherently ambiguous regarding number/definiteness etc.

### 2.3 Jakab's databases

Some of the Old Hungarian codices (Jókai (Jakab, 2002), Guary (Jakab and Kiss, 1994), Apor (Jakab and Kiss, 1997), and Festetics (Jakab and Kiss, 2001)) were not digitized using the OCR technique described above, as these were available in the form of historical linguistic databases, created by Jakab László and his colleagues between 1978 and 2002. However, the re-creation of the original texts out of these lexical databases was a difficult task. The first problem was that, in the databases, the locus of word token occurrences only identified codex page, column and line number, but there was no information concerning the order of words within a line. The databases also contain morphological analyses, but they were encoded in a hard-to-read numerical format, which occasionally was incorrect and often incomplete. Furthermore, the categorization was in many respects incompatible with our system. However, finally we managed to re-create the original texts. First the order of words was manually restored and incomplete and erroneous analyses were fixed. Missing lemmas were added to the lexicon of the adapted computational morphology, and the normalized version of the texts was generated using the morphology as a word form generator. Finally, the normalized texts were reanalyzed to get analyses compatible with the annotation scheme applied to the other texts in the corpora.

## 3 The morphological analyzer

The digitized and normalized texts have been analyzed with an extended version of the Humor analyzer for Hungarian. The lexicon of lemmas and the affix inventory of the program have been augmented with items that have disappeared from the language but are present in the historical corpora. Just the affix inventory had to be supplemented with 50 new affixes (not counting their allomorphs).

Certain affixes have not disappeared, but their productivity has diminished compared to the Old Hungarian era. Although words with these morphemes are still present in the language, they are generally lexicalized items, often with a changed meaning. An example of such a suffix is *–At*, which used to be a fully productive nomen actionis suffix. Today, this function belongs to the suffix *–Ás*. The (now lexicalized) words, however, that end in *–At* mark the (tangible) result of an action (i.e. nomen acti) in present-day standard Hungarian, as in *falazat* 'wall' vs. *falazás* 'building a wall'.

One factor that made adaptation of the morphological model difficult was that there are no reliable accounts on the changes of paradigms. Data concerning which affix allomorphs could be attached to which stem allomorphs had to be extracted from the texts themselves. Certain morphological constructions that had already disappeared by the end of the Old Hungarian era were rather rare (such as some participle forms) and often some items in these rare subparadigms have alternative analyses. This made the formal description of these paradigms rather difficult.

However, the most time consuming task was the enlargement of the stem inventory. Beside the addition of a number of new lemmas, the entries of several items already listed in the lexicon of the present-day analyzer had to be modified for our purposes. The causes were various: some roots now belong to another part of speech, or in some constructions they had to be analyzed differently from their present analysis.

Furthermore, the number of pronouns was considerably higher in the examined period than today. The description of their extensive and rather irregular paradigms was really challenging as some forms were underrepresented in the corpora.

Some enhancements of the morphological analyzer made during the corpus annotation projects were also applicable to the morphological description of standard modern Hungarian. One such modification was a new annotation scheme applied to time adverbials that are lexicalized suffixed (or unsuffixed) forms of nouns, like *reggel* 'morning/in the morning' or *nappal* 'daytime/in daytime', quite a few of which can be modified by adjectives when used adverbially, such as *fényes nappal* 'in broad daylight'. This latter fact sheds light on a double nature of these words that could be captured in an annotation of these forms as specially suffixed forms of nouns instead of atomic adverbs, an analysis that is compatible with X-bar theory (Jackendoff, 1977).

## 4 Disambiguation

With the exception of already analyzed sources (i.e. the ones recovered from the Jakab databases), the morphological annotation had to be disambiguated. The ambiguity rate of the output of the extended morphological analyzer on historical texts is higher than that for the standard Humor analyzer for present-day corpora (2.21 vs. 1.92[3] analyses/word with an identical (high) granularity of analyses). This is due to several factors: (i) the historical analyzer is less strict, (ii) there are several formally identical members of the enlarged verbal paradigms including massively ambiguous subparadigms like that of the passive and the factitive,[4] (iii) a lot of inherent ambiguities described above.

The workflow for disambiguation of morphosyntactic annotation was a semi-automatic process: an automatically pre-disambiguated version of each text was checked and corrected manually. For a very short time, we considered using the Jakab databases as a training corpus, but recovering them required so much development and manual labor and the analyses in them lacked so much distinction we wanted to make that we opted for creating the training data completely from scratch instead.

### 4.1 The manual disambiguation interface

To support the process of manual checking and the initial manual disambiguation of the training corpus a web-based interface was created using JavaScript and Ajax where disambiguation and normalization errors can be corrected very effectively. The system presents the document to the user using an interlinear annotation format that is easy and natural to read. An alternative analysis can be chosen from a pop-up menu containing a list of analyses applicable to the word that appears when the mouse cursor is placed over the problematic word. Note that the list only contains grammatically relevant tags and lemmas for the word returned by the morphological analyzer. This is very important, since, due to the agglutinating nature of Hungarian, there are thousands of possible tags (see Figure 1).

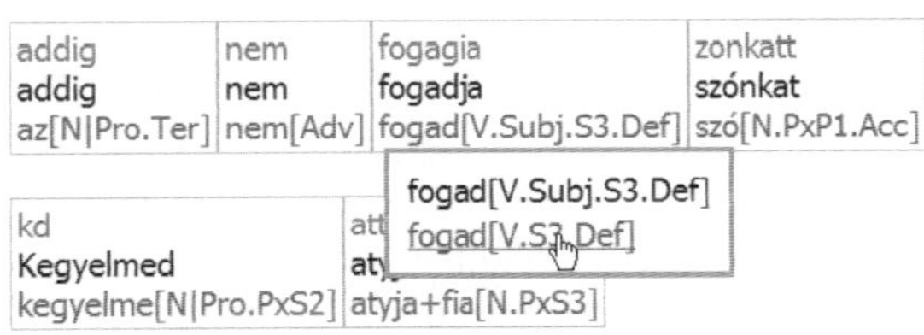


Figure 1: The web-based disambiguation interface

The original and the normalized word forms as well as the analyses can also be edited by clicking them, and an immediate reanalysis by the morphological analyzer running on the web server can be initiated by double clicking the word. We use Ajax technology to update only the part of the page belonging to the given token, so the update is immediate. Afterwards, a new analysis can be selected from the updated pop-up menu.

[3]measured on newswire text

[4]This ambiguity is absent from modern standard Hungarian because the passive is not used any more.

As there is an inherent difference between the original and normalized tokenization, and because, even after thorough proofreading of the normalized version, there may remain tokenization errors in the texts, it is important that tokens and clauses can also be split and joined using the disambiguation interface.

The automatic annotation system was created in a way that makes it possible that details of the annotation scheme be modified in the course of work. One such modification was e.g. the change to the annotation of time adverbs mentioned in Section 3 above. The modified annotation can be applied to texts analyzed and disambiguated prior to the modification relatively easily. This is achieved by the fact that, in the course of reanalysis, the program chooses the analysis most similar to the previously selected analysis (based on a letter trigram similarity measure). Nevertheless, the system highlights all tokens the reanalysis of which resulted in a change of annotation, so that these spots can be easily checked manually. For changes in the annotation scheme where the simple similarity-based heuristic could not be expected to yield an appropriate result (e.g. when we decided to use a more detailed analysis of derived verb forms as before), a more sophisticated method was devised to update the annotations: old analyses were replaced using automatically generated regular expressions.

### 4.2 Automatic disambiguation

While the first few documents were disambiguated completely manually using the web-based tool, we soon started to train and use a tagger for predisambiguation applying the tagger incrementally, trained on an increasing number of disambiguated and checked text. First the HMM-based trigram tagger HunPos (Halácsy et al., 2007) was used. HunPos is not capable of lemmatization, but we used a straightforward method to get a full analysis: we applied reanalysis to the text annotated only by the tags assigned by HunPos using the automatic similarity-based ranking of the analyses. This approach yielded quite good results, but one problem with it was that the similarity-based ranking always prefers shorter lemmas, which was not appropriate for handling the case of a frequent lemma ambiguity for verbs with one of the lemma candidates ending in an *–ik* suffix and the other lacking a suffix (such as *dolgozik* 'work' vs. *(fel)dolgoz* 'process'). Always selecting the *–ik*-less variant is not a good bet in the case of many frequent words in this ambiguity class.

Recently, we replaced HunPos with another HMM-based trigram tagger, PurePos (Orosz and Novák, 2012), that has many nice extra features. It can process morphologically analyzed ambiguous input and/or use an integrated analyzer constraining possible analyses to those proposed by the analyzer or read from the input. This boosts the precision of the tagger dramatically in the case of languages like Hungarian and small training corpora. The fact that PurePos can be fed analyzed input makes it easy to combine with constraint-based tools that can further improve the accuracy of the tagging by handling long distance agreement phenomena not covered by the trigram model or simply removing impossible tag sequences from the search space of the tool.

PurePos can perform lemmatization, even for words unknown to the morphological analyzer (and not annotated on the input) learning a suffix-based lemmatization model from the training corpus along with a similar suffix-based tag guessing model, thus it assigns a full morphological analysis to each token. It is also capable of generating an n-best list of annotations for the input sentence when using beam search instead of the default Viterbi decoding algorithm.

### 4.3 Disambiguation performance

We performed an evaluation of the accuracy of PurePos on an 84000-word manually checked part of the historical corpus using five-fold cross-validation with a training corpus of about 67000 words and a test corpus of about 17000 words in each round. The ratio of words unknown to the MA in this corpus is rather low: 0.32%.

The average accuracy of tagging, lemmatization and full annotation for different versions of the tagger are shown in Table 1. In addition to token accuracy, we also present sentence accuracy values in the table. Note that, in contrast to the usual way of evaluating taggers, these values were calculated excluding the always unambiguous punctuation tokens from the evaluation. The baseline tagger uses no morphological information at all. Its current lemmatization implementation uses suffix guessing in all cases (even for words seen in the training corpus) and selects the most frequent lemma, which is obviously not an ideal solution.

The disambiguator using morphology performs significantly better. Its clause-level accuracy is 81.50%, which means that only every fifth clause contains a tagging error. The tag set we used in the corpus differentiates constructions which are not generally differentiated at the tag level in Hungarian corpora, e.g. deictic pronouns (*ebben* 'in this') vs. deictic pre-determiners (*ebben a házban* 'in this house'). Many of these can only be disambiguated using long-distance dependencies, i.e. information often not available to the trigram tagger. Combination of the tagger with a constraint-based tool (see e.g. Hulden and Francom (2012)) would presumably improve accuracy significantly.

In the rightmost column, we listed a theoretical upper limit of the performance of the current trigram tagger implementation using 5-best output and an ideal oracle that can select the best annotation.

| | | baseline | morph | 5-best+o |
|---|---|---|---|---|
| token | Tag | 90.17% | 96.44% | 98.97% |
| | Lem. | 91.52% | 98.19% | 99.11% |
| | Full | 87.29% | 95.90% | 98.53% |
| clause | Tag | 62.48% | 83.81% | 93.99% |
| | Full | 54.68% | 81.50% | 91.47% |

Table 1: Disambiguation performance of the tagger

## 5 Searching the corpus

The web-based tool we created as a corpus query interface does not only make it possible to search for different grammatical constructions in the texts, but it is also an effective correction tool. Errors discovered in the annotation or the text appearing in the "results" box can immediately be corrected and the corrected text and annotation is recorded in the database. Naturally, this latter functionality of the corpus manager is only available to expert users having the necessary privileges.

A fast and effective way of correcting errors in the annotation is to search for presumably incorrect structures and to correct the truly problematic ones at once. The corrected corpus can be exported after this procedure and the tagger can be retrained on it.

The database used for the corpus manager is based on the Emdros corpus manager (Petersen, 2004). In addition to queries formulated using MQL, the query language of Emdros, either typed in at the query box or assembled using controls of the query interface, advanced users can use a custom-made corpus-specific query language (MEQL), which makes a much more compact formulation of queries possible than MQL. It is e.g. extremely simple to locate a specific locus in the corpus: one simply needs to type in the sequence of words one is looking for. Queries formulated in MEQL are automatically converted to MQL queries by the query processor.

The search engine makes it possible to search inside sentences, clauses, or texts containing grammatical constructions and/or tagged with metadata matching the criteria specified in the query. Units longer than a sentence can also be searched for. The context displayed by default for each hit is the enclosing sentence with focus words highlighted. Clauses may be non-continuous: this is often the case for embedded subordinate clauses, but the corpus also contains many injected parenthetical coordinate clauses and many examples where the topic of a subordinate clause precedes its main clause with the net effect of the subordinate clause being interrupted by the main clause. The query example in Figure 2 shows a sentence containing several clauses with gaps: the clauses enclosed in angle brackets are wedged between the topic and comment part of the clauses which they interrupt. Emdros is capable of representing these interrupted clauses as single linguistic objects with the interrupting clause not being considered part of the interrupted one.

## 6 Conclusion

In our paper, we described the most important steps of the creation of a morphological annotation framework for the analysis of Old and Middle Hungarian extant texts consisting of a morphological analyzer, an automatic disambiguation tool and an intuitive web-based manual disambiguation tool. Certain problems arising during this process were discussed together with their solution. We also presented our corpus manager, which serves both as a structured corpus query tool and as a correction tool.

The morphological analyzer is used for the annotation of the constantly growing Old and Middle Hungarian corpora. Part of these corpora are already searchable by the public. The Old Hun-

Figure 2: The query interface

garian Corpus is available at http://rmk.nytud.hu, while the analyzed part of the Historical Corpus of Informal Language Use can be searched at http://tmk.nytud.hu.

## Acknowledgments

Research reported in this paper was supported by the research project grants OTKA NK78074 and OTKA 81189. In addition, we gratefully acknowledge support by the grants TÁMOP-4.2.1./B-11/2/KMR-2011-002 and TÁMOP-4.2.2./B-10/1-2010-0014. We would also like to thank anonymous reviewers of the paper for their helpful comments and suggestions.

## References

Péter Halácsy, András Kornai, and Csaba Oravecz. 2007. HunPos: an open source trigram tagger. In *Proceedings of the 45th Annual Meeting of the ACL on Interactive Poster and Demonstration Sessions*, ACL '07, pages 209–212, Stroudsburg, PA, USA. Association for Computational Linguistics.

Mans Hulden and Jerid Francom. 2012. Boosting statistical tagger accuracy with simple rule-based grammars. In Nicoletta Calzolari (Conference Chair), Khalid Choukri, Thierry Declerck, Mehmet Uğur Doğan, Bente Maegaard, Joseph Mariani, Jan Odijk, and Stelios Piperidis, editors, *Proceedings of the Eighth International Conference on Language Resources and Evaluation (LREC'12)*, Istanbul, Turkey. European Language Resources Association (ELRA).

Ray Jackendoff. 1977. *X-bar-Syntax: A Study of Phrase Structure*. Linguistic Inquiry Monograph 2. MIT Press, Cambridge, MA.

László Jakab and Antal Kiss. 1994. *A Guary-kódex ábécérendes adattára*. Számítógépes nyelvtörténeti adattár. Debreceni Egyetem, Debrecen.

László Jakab and Antal Kiss. 1997. *Az Apor-kódex ábécérendes adattára*. Számítógépes nyelvtörténeti adattár. Debreceni Egyetem, Debrecen.

László Jakab and Antal Kiss. 2001. *A Festetics-kódex ábécérendes adattára*. Számítógépes nyelvtörténeti adattár. Debreceni Egyetem, Debrecen.

László Jakab. 2002. *A Jókai-kódex mint nyelvi emlék: szótárszerü feldolgozásban*. Számítógépes Nyelvtörténeti Adattár. Debreceni Egyetem, Debrecen.

Attila Novák. 2003. Milyen a jó Humor? [What is good Humor like?]. In *I. Magyar Számítógépes Nyelvészeti Konferencia*, pages 138–144, Szeged. SZTE.

György Orosz and Attila Novák. 2012. PurePos – an open source morphological disambiguator. In *Proceedings of the 9th International Workshop on Natural Language Processing and Cognitive Science.*, Wroclaw, Poland.

Ulrik Petersen. 2004. Emdros — a text database engine for analyzed or annotated text. In *In: Proceedings of COLING 2004. (2004) 1190–1193.*

Gábor Prószéky and Balázs Kis. 1999. A unification-based approach to morpho-syntactic parsing of agglutinative and other (highly) inflectional languages. In *Proceedings of the 37th annual meeting of the Association for Computational Linguistics on Computational Linguistics*, ACL '99, pages 261–268, Stroudsburg, PA, USA. Association for Computational Linguistics.

Gábor Prószéky and Attila Novák. 2005. Computational Morphologies for Small Uralic Languages. In *Inquiries into Words, Constraints and Contexts.*, pages 150–157, Stanford, California.

# Argument extraction for supporting public policy formulation

**Eirini Florou**
Dept of Linguistics, Faculty of Philosophy
University of Athens, Greece
eirini.florou@gmail.coml

**Stasinos Konstantopoulos**
Institute of Informatics and
Telecommunications, NCSR 'Demokritos'
konstant@iit.demokritos.gr

**Antonis Kukurikos** **Pythagoras Karampiperis**
Institute of Informatics and Telecommunications, NCSR 'Demokritos', Athens, Greece
{kukurik,pythk}@iit.demokritos.gr

## Abstract

In this paper we describe an application of language technology to *policy formulation*, where it can support policy makers assess the acceptance of a yet-unpublished policy before the policy enters public consultation. One of the key concepts is that instead of relying on thematic similarity, we extract *arguments* expressed in support or opposition of positions that are general statements that are, themselves, consistent with the policy or not. The focus of this paper in this overall pipeline, is identifying arguments in text: we present and empirically evaluate the hypothesis that verbal *tense* and *mood* are good indicators of arguments that have not been explored in the relevant literature.

## 1 Introduction

The large-scale acquisition, thematic classification, and sentiment analysis of Web content has been extensively applied to brand monitoring, digital reputation management, product development, and a variety of similar applications. More recently, it has also seen application in public policy validation, where the 'brand' to be monitored is a publicized and widely commented government policy.

All these methods typically rely on the *semantic similarity* between a given text or set of terms and Web content; often using domain-specific ontological and terminological resources in order to measure this similarity. This approach, however requires that all parties involved discourse on the same topic; that is to say, that we are seeking the collective opinion of the Web on a topic that has been publicized enough to attract the attention of the Web.

In this paper we present a slightly different approach, where we are looking for *arguments* expressed in support or opposition of opinions with little semantic similarity to our topic of interest. As a rough example, consider how drafting environmental policy can benefit from access to statistics about how people felt about industrial growth at the expense of environmental concerns when other policy in completely different domains was on public consultation: many of the arguments about the relative merits of industrial growth and environmental concerns can retain their structure and be thematically transferred to the new domain, helping draft a policy that best addresses people's concerns.

Of paramount importance for implementing such an approach is the linguistic tools for identifying arguments. In this paper, we first motivate the inclusion of argument extraction inside the larger policy formulation and validation cycle and present the position of an argument extraction tool inside a computational system for supporting this cycle (Section 2). We then proceed to a present the argument extraction literature (Section 3) and our hypothesis that verbal morpho-syntactic features are good discriminators of arguments (Section 4). We close the paper by presenting and discussing empirical results (Section 5) and concluding (Section 6).

## 2 Policy formulation and validation

Our work is carried out in the context of a project that develops computational tools for the early phases of policy making, before policy drafts have been made available for public consultation.[1]

At that stage, the policy's impact on public opinion cannot be estimated by similarity-based searching for relevant Web content, since the policy text has not been announced yet — or even fully authored for that matter. One of the core

[1] Full details about the project have been suppressed to preserve anonymity, but will be included in the camera-ready.

ideas of the project is that in order to assist the policy formulation process, a tool needs to estimate the acceptance of a yet unpublished document based on Web content that is not thematically similar, but is rather supporting or opposing a more general position or maxim that also supports or opposes the policy under formulation.

To make this more concrete, consider a new policy for increasing the penetration of wind power production, setting specific conditions and priorities. The project is developing an authoring environment where specific policy statements are linked to more general statements, such as:

(1) Greenhouse gas emissions should not be a concern at all.

(2) It is desired to reduce greenhouse gas emissions, but this should be balanced against other concerns.

(3) It is desired to reduce greenhouse gas emissions at all costs.

We have, thus, created a formulation of 'relevant content' that includes Examples 1 and 2 below. These are taken from different domains, are commenting policies and laws that are already formulated and made public, and can be used to infer the level of support for the new wind power policy although no textual similarity exists.

(4) In case hard packaging is made compulsory by law, producers will be forced to consume more energy, leading to more greenhouse gas emissions.

(5) Tidal power production does not emit greenhouse gases, but other environmental problems are associated with its widespread deployment.

Leaving aside the ontological conceptualization that achieves this matching, which is reported elsewhere, we will now discuss the language processing pipeline that retrieves and classifies relevant Web content.

Content is acquired via *focused crawling*, using search engine APIs to retrieve public Web pages and social network APIs to retrieve content from social content sharing platforms. Content is searched and filtered (in case of feed-like APIs) based on fairly permissive semantic similarity measures, emphasising a high retrieval rate at the expense of precision. As a second step, clean text is extracted from the raw Web content using the Boilerpipe library (Kohlschütter et al., 2010) in order to remove HTML tags, active components (e.g. JavaScript snippets), and content that is irrelevant to the main content (menus, ad sections, links to other web pages), and also to replace HTML entities with their textual equivalent, e.g., replacing '&' with the character '&'.

The resulting text is tokenized and sentence-splitted and each sentence classified as relevant or not using standard information retrieval methods to assess the semantic similarity of each sentence to the general policy statements. This is based on both general-purpose resources[2] and the domain ontology for the particular policy. Consecutive sentences that are classified as positive are joined into a *segment*.

The main objective of the work described here is the classification of these segments as being representative of a stance that would also support or oppose the policy being formulated, given the premise of the general statements (1)–(3). Our approach is to apply the following criteria:

- That they are semantically similar to the general statements associated with the policy.
- That they are arguments, rather than statements of fact or other types of prose.
- That their polarity towards the general statements is expressed.

In order to be able to assess segments, we thus need a linguistic pipeline that can calculate semantic similarity, identify arguments, and extract their structure (premises/consequences) and polarity (in support or opposition).

The focus of the work described here is identifying arguments, although we also outline how the features we are proposing can also be used in order to classify chunks of text as premises or consequences.

## 3 Related Work

The first approaches of argument extraction were concentrated on building wide-coverage argument

[2]WordNets are publicly available for both English and Greek, that is the language of the experiments reported here. Simpler semantic taxonomies can also be used; the accuracy of the semantic similarity measured here does not have a major bearing on the argument extraction experiments that are the main contribution of this paper.

structure lexicons, originally manually Fitzpatrick and Sager (1980, 1981) and later from electronic versions of conventional dictionaries, since such dictionaries contain morpho-syntactic features Briscoe et al. (1987). More recently, the focus shifted to automatically extracting these lexical resources from corpora Brent (1993) and to hybrid approaches using dictionaries and corpora.

Works using syntactic features to extract topics and holders of opinions are numerous (Bethard et al., 2005). Semantic role analysis has also proven useful: Kim and Hovy (2006) used a FrameNet-based semantic role labeler to determine holder and topic of opinions. Similarly, Choi and Cardie (2006) successfully used a PropBank-based semantic role labeler for opinion holder extraction.

Somasundaran et al. (2008; 2010) argued that semantic role techniques are useful but not completely sufficient for holder and topic identification, and that other linguistic phenomena must be studied as well. In particular, they studied discourse structure and found specific cue phrases that are strong features for use in argument extraction. Discourse markers that are strongly associated with pragmatic functions can be used to predict the class of content, therefore useful features include the presence of a known marker such as 'actually', 'because', 'but'.

Tseronis (2011) describes three main approaches to describing argument markers: Geneva School, Argument within Language Theory and the Pragma-dialectical Approach. According the Geneva School, there are three main types of markers/connective, organisation markers, illocutionary function markers (the relations between acts) and interactive function markers. Argument within Language Theory is a study of individual words and phrases. The words identified are argument connectors: these describe an argumentative function of a text span and change the potential of it either realising or de-realising the span. The Pragma-dialectical Approach looks at the context beyond words and expressions that directly refer to the argument. It attempts to identify words and expressions that refer to any moves in the argument process. Similarly to Marcu and Echihabi (2002), the approach is to create a model of an ideal argument and annotate relevant units.

## 4 Approach and Experimental Setup

As seen above, shallow techniques are typically based on connectives and other discourse markers in order to define shallow argument patterns. What has not been investigated is whether shallow morpho-syntactic features, such as the tense and mood of the verbal constructs in a passage, can also indicate argumentative discourse.

Our hypothesis is that *future* and *conditional* tenses and moods often indicate conjectures and hypotheses which are commonly used in argumentation techniques such as *illustration, justification, rebuttal* where the effects of a position counter to the speaker's argument are analysed. Naturally, such features cannot be the sole basis of argument identification, so we need to experiment regarding their interaction with discourse markers.

To make this more concrete, consider the examples in Section 2: although both are perfectly valid arguments that can help us infer the acceptance or rejection of a policy, in the first one future tense is used to speculate about the effects of a policy; in the second example there is no explicit marker that the effects of large-scale tidal power production are also a conjecture.

Another difficulty is that conditional and future verbal groups are constructed using auxiliary verbs and (in some languages) other auxiliary pointers. Consider, for example, the following PoS-tagged and chunked Greek translation of Example 4:

(6) *[oi* *paragogoi]*$_{np}$
[the-NomPl producers-NounNomPl]
*[tha* *ipochreothoun]*$_{vp}$
[Pointer-Fut force-Perf-3PP]
*[na* *katanalosoun]*$_{vp}$
[Pointer-Subj consume-Inf]
'producers will be forced to consume'

In order to be able to correctly assign *simple future*, information from the future pointer 'tha' needs to be combined with the perfective feature of finite verb form. Conditionals, future perfect, past perfect, and similar tenses or moods like subjuncive also involve the tense of the auxiliary verb, besides the future pointer and the main verb.

We have carried out our experiments in Greek language texts, for which we have developed a JAPE grammar[3] that extract the tense and mood of

[3]JAPE is finite state transducer over GATE annota-

Table 1: Categories of morpho-syntactic features extracted from text segments.

| Label | Description | Features |
|---|---|---|
| DM | Absolute number of occurrences of discourse markers from a given category | 5 numerical features |
| Rel | Relative frequency of each of the 6 tenses and each of the 6 moods | 12 numerical features |
| RCm | Relative frequency of each tense/mood combination (only for those that actually appear). | 9 numerical features |
| Bin | Appearance of each of the 6 tenses and each of the 6 moods | 12 binary features |
| Dom | Most frequent tense, mood, and tense/mood combination | 3 string features |
| | TOTAL | 41 features |

each verb chunk. The grammar uses patterns that combine the features of pointers and auxiliary and main verbs, without enforcing any restrictions on what words (e.g., adverbs) might be interjected in the chunk. That is to say, the chunker is responsible for identifying verb groups and our grammar is restricted to propagating and combining the right features from each of the chunk's constituents to the chunk's own feature structure.

PoS-tagging and chunking annotations have been previously assigned by the ILSP suite of Greek NLP tools (Papageorgiou et al., 2000; Prokopidis et al., 2011), as provided by the relevant ILSP Web Services[4] to get PoS tagged and chunked texts in the GATE XML format.

At a second layer of processing, we create one data instance for each segment (as defined in Section 2 above) and for each such segment we extract features relating to verbal tense/mood and to the appearance of discourse markers. The former are different ways to aggregate the various tenses and moods found in the whole segment, by measuring relative frequencies, recording the appearance of a tense or mood even once, and naming the predominant (most frequent) tense and mood; tense and mood are seen both individually and as tense/mood combinations.

Furthermore, we have defined five absolute frequency features which record the matching against the several patterns and keywords provided for the following five categories of arguments:

- justification, matching patterns such as 'because', 'the reason being', 'due to', etc.
- explanation, matching patterns such as 'in other words', 'for instance', quotesfor this reason(s), etc.
- deduction, 'as a consequence', 'in accordance with the above', 'proving that', etc.
- rebuttal, 'despite', 'however', etc.
- conditionals, 'supposing that', 'in case that', etc.

All features extracted by this process are given on Table 1.

## 5 Results and Discussion

We have used the method described in Section 2 in order to obtain 677 text segments, with a size ranging between 10 and 100 words, with an average of 60 words. Of these, 332 were manually annotated to *not* be arguments; the remaining 345 positive examples were obtained by oversampling the 69 segments in our corpus that we have manually annotated to be arguments.[5]

We have then applied the feature extraction described in Section 4 in order to set up a classification task for J48, the Weka[6] implementation of the C4.5 decision tree learning algorithm (Quinlan, 1992). We have applied a moderate confidence factor of 0.25, noting that experimenting with the confidence factor did not yield any substantially different results.

In order to better understand the feature space, we have run a series of experiments, with quantitative results summarized in Table 2. The first

tions. Please see `http://gate.ac.uk/sale/tao/splitch8.html` The JAPE grammar we have developed will be made available on-line; location cannot be yet disclosed in order to preserve anonymity.

[4]Currently at `http://ilp.ilsp.gr`

[5]The data and relevant scripts for carrying out these experiments are available at `http://users.iit.demokritos.gr/~konstant/dload/arguments.tgz`

[6]Please see `http://www.cs.waikato.ac.nz/ml/weka`

Table 2: Precision and recall for retrieving arguments using different feature mixtures. Please cf. Table 1 for an explanation of the feature labels. The results shown are the 10-fold cross-validation mean.

| Morpho-syntactic features used | With Discourse Markers Prec. | Rec. | $F_{\beta=1}$ | Without Discourse Markers Prec. | Rec. | $F_{\beta=1}$ |
|---|---|---|---|---|---|---|
| All | 75.8% | 71.9% | 73.8% | 75.5% | 70.4% | 72.9% |
| no Dom | 79.8% | 73.3% | **76.4%** | 74.0% | 71.9% | 72.9% |
| no Rel | 74.5% | 72.8% | 73.8% | 73.1% | 69.3% | 71.1% |
| no RCm | 76.3% | 71.0% | 73.6% | 76.8% | 70.1% | 73.3% |
| no Bin | 70.0% | 70.4% | 70.2% | 66.7% | 69.6% | 68.1% |
| Rel | 73.4% | 75.9% | 74.6% | 70.3% | 72.2% | 71.2% |
| Dom | 57.1% | 98.8% | 72.4% | 54.9% | 94.2% | 69.4% |
| RCm | 69.3% | 66.7% | 67.9% | 71.9% | 62.9% | 67.1% |
| Bin | 71.7% | 49.9% | 58.8% | 70.1% | 44.9% | 54.8% |
| None | 67.9% | 20.9% | 31.9% | | — | |

observation is that both morpho-syntactic features and discourse markers are needed, because if either category is omitted results deteriorate. However, not *all* morpho-syntactic features are needed: note how omitting the *Dom*, *Rel*, or *RCm* categories yields identical or improved results. On the other hand, the binary presence feature category *Bin* is significant (cf. 5th row). We cannot, however, claim that only the *Bin* category is sufficient, and, in fact, if one category has to be chosen that would have to be that of relative frequency features (cf. rows 6-9).

## 6 Conclusion

We describe here an application of language technology to *policy formulation*, and, in particular, to using Web content to assess the acceptance of a yet-unpublished policy *before* public consultation. The core of the idea is that classifying Web content as similar to the policy or not does apply, because the policy document has not been made public yet; but that we should rather extract arguments from Web content and assess whether these argue in favour or against general concepts that are (or are not) consistent with the policy being formulated.

As a first step to this end, our paper focuses on the identification of arguments in Greek language content using shallow features. Based on our observation that verb tense appears to be a significant feature that is not exploited by the relevant literature, we have carried out an empirical evaluation of this hypothesis. We have, in particular, demonstrated that the relative frequency of each verb tense/mood and the binary appearance of each verb tense/mood inside a text segment are as discriminative of argumentative text as the (typically used) discourse markers; and that classification is improved by combining discourse marker features with our verbal tense/mood features. For doing this, we developed a regular grammar that combines the PoS tags of the members of a verb chunk in order to assign tense and mood to the chunk. In this manner, our approach depends on PoS taggin and chunking only.

In subsequent steps of our investigation, we are planning to refine our approach to extracting argument structure: it would be interesting to test if argument premises tend to correlate with certain tenses or moods, distinguishing them from from conclusions. Further experiments can also examine if the simultaneous appearance of concrete tenses at the same sentence is an indicator of an argument. Finally, we plan to examine the predicates of an argument, and especially if the head word of each sentence (be it verb or deverbal noun) and its seat at the boundaries of the sentence may contribute to extract an argument or not, especially for impersonal, modal, and auxiliary verbs.

## Acknowledgements

The research leading to these results has received funding from the European Union's Seventh Framework Programme (FP7/2007-2013) under grant agreement no 288513. For more details, please see the NOMAD project's website, `http://www.nomad-project.eu`

## References


Steven Bethard, Hong Yu, Ashley Thornton, Vasileios Hatzivassiloglou, and Dan Jurafsky. 2005. Extracting opinion propositions and opinion holders using syntactic and lexical cues. *In James G. Shanahan, Yan Qu, and Janyce Wiebe, editors, Computing Attitude and Affect in Text: Theory and Applications. Springer.*

Michael Brent. 1993. From grammar to lexicon: unsupervised learning of lexical syntax. In *Computational Linguistics - Special issue on using large corpora: II, Volume 19 Issue 2*, pages 243–262.

Ted Briscoe, Claire Grover, Bran Boguraev, and John. Carroll. 1987. The derivation of a grammatically-indexed lexicon from the longman dictionary of contemporary english. In *Proceeding of ACL '87.*

Yejin Choi and Claire Cardie. 2006. Joint extraction of entities and relations for opinion recognition. In *Proceedings of EMNLP 2006.*

Eileen Fitzpatrick and Naomi Sager. 1980. *The Lexical subclasses of the LSP English Grammar.* Linguistic String Project, New York University.

Eileen Fitzpatrick and Naomi Sager. 1981. The lexical subclasses of the lsp english grammar. In *N. Sager (ed), Natural Language Information Processing, Addison- Wesley, Reading, Ma.*

Soo-Min Kim and Eduard Hovy. 2006. Extracting opinions, opinion holders, and topics expressedin online news media text. In *Proceedings of ACL/COLING Workshop on Sentiment and Subjectivity in Text.*

Christian Kohlschütter, Peter Fankhauser, and Wolfgang Nejdl. 2010. Boilerplate detection using shallow text features. In *Proc. 3rd ACM International Conference on Web Search and Data Mining (WSDM 2010)* New York, USA.

Daniel Marcu and Abdessamad Echihabi. 2002. An unsupervised approach to recognizing discourse relations. In *Proc. ACL '02.*

Haris Papageorgiou, Prokopis Prokopidis, Voula Giouli, and Stelios Piperidis. 2000. A unified POS tagging architecture and its application to Greek. In *Proceedings of the 2nd Language Resources and Evaluation Conference (LREC 2000), Athens, Greece*, pages 1455–1462.

Prokopis Prokopidis, Byron Georgantopoulos, and Haris Papageorgiou. 2011. A suite of NLP tools for Greek. In *Proceedings of the 10th International Conference of Greek Linguistics (ICGL 2011), Komotini, Greece.*

J. Ross Quinlan. 1992. *C4.5: Programs for Machine Learning.* Morgan Kaufmann, San Mateo, CA, USA.

Swapna Somasundaran and Janyce Wiebe. 2010. Recognizing stances in ideological on-line debates. In *Proc. NAACL HLT Workshop on Computational Approaches to Analysis and Generation of Emotion in Text (CAAGET 2010)*

Swapna Somasundaran, Janyce Wiebe, and Joseph Ruppenhofer. 2008. Discourse level opinion interpretation. In *Proceedings of the 22nd International Conference on Computational Linguistics - Volume 1, COLING '08, Stroudsburg, PA, USA. Association for Computational Linguistics.*

Assimakis Tseronis. 2011. From connectives to argumentative markers: A quest for markers of argumentative moves and of related aspects of argumentative discourse. *Argumentation*, 25(4):427–444.

# Towards a Tool for Interactive Concept Building for Large Scale Analysis in the Humanities

**Andre Blessing**[1] **Jonathan Sonntag**[2] **Fritz Kliche**[3]
**Ulrich Heid**[3] **Jonas Kuhn**[1] **Manfred Stede**[2]
[1]Institute for Natural Language Processing
Universitaet Stuttgart, Germany
[2]Institute for Applied Computational Linguistics
University of Potsdam, Germany
[3]Institute for Information Science and Natural Language Processing
University of Hildesheim, Germany

**Abstract**

We develop a pipeline consisting of various text processing tools which is designed to assist political scientists in finding specific, complex concepts within large amounts of text. Our main focus is the interaction between the political scientists and the natural language processing groups to ensure a beneficial assistance for the political scientists and new application challenges for NLP. It is of particular importance to find a "common language" between the different disciplines. Therefore, we use an interactive web-interface which is easily usable by non-experts. It interfaces an active learning algorithm which is complemented by the NLP pipeline to provide a rich feature selection. Political scientists are thus enabled to use their own intuitions to find custom concepts.

## 1 Introduction

In this paper, we give examples of how NLP methods and tools can be used to provide support for complex tasks in political sciences. Many concepts of political science are complex and faceted; they tend to come in different linguistic realizations, often in complex ones; many concepts are not directly identifiable by means of (a small set of) individual lexical items, but require some interpretation.

Many researchers in political sciences either work qualitatively on small amounts of data which they interpret instance-wise, or, if they are interested in quantitative trends, they use comparatively simple tools, such as keyword-based search in corpora or text classification on the basis of terms only; this latter approach may lead to imprecise results due to a rather unspecific search as well as semantically invalid or ambigious search words. On the other hand, large amounts of e.g. news texts are available, also over longer periods of time, such that e.g. tendencies over time can be derived. The corpora we are currently working on contain ca. 700,000 articles from British, Irish, German and Austrian newspapers, as well as (yet unexplored) material in French.

Figure 1 depicts a simple example of a quantitative analysis.[1] The example shows how often two terms, *Friedensmission*('peace operation'), and *Auslandseinsatz*('foreign intervention') are used in the last two decades in newspaper texts about interventions and wars. The long-term goal of the project is to provide similar analysis for complex concepts. An example of a complex concept is the evocation of *collective identities* in political contexts, as indirect in the news. Examples for such *collective identities* are: the Europeans, the French, the Catholics.

The objective of the work we are going to discuss in this paper is to provide NLP methods and tools for assisting political scientists in the exploration of large data sets, with a view to both, a detailed qualitative analysis of text instances, and a quantitative overview of trends over time, at the level of corpora. The examples discussed here have to do with (possibly multiple) collective identities. Typical context of such identities tend to report communication, as direct or as indirect speech. Examples of such contexts are given in 1.

(1) Die Europäer würden die Lücke füllen,
The Europeans would the gap fill,

[1]The figure shows a screenshot of our web-based prototype.

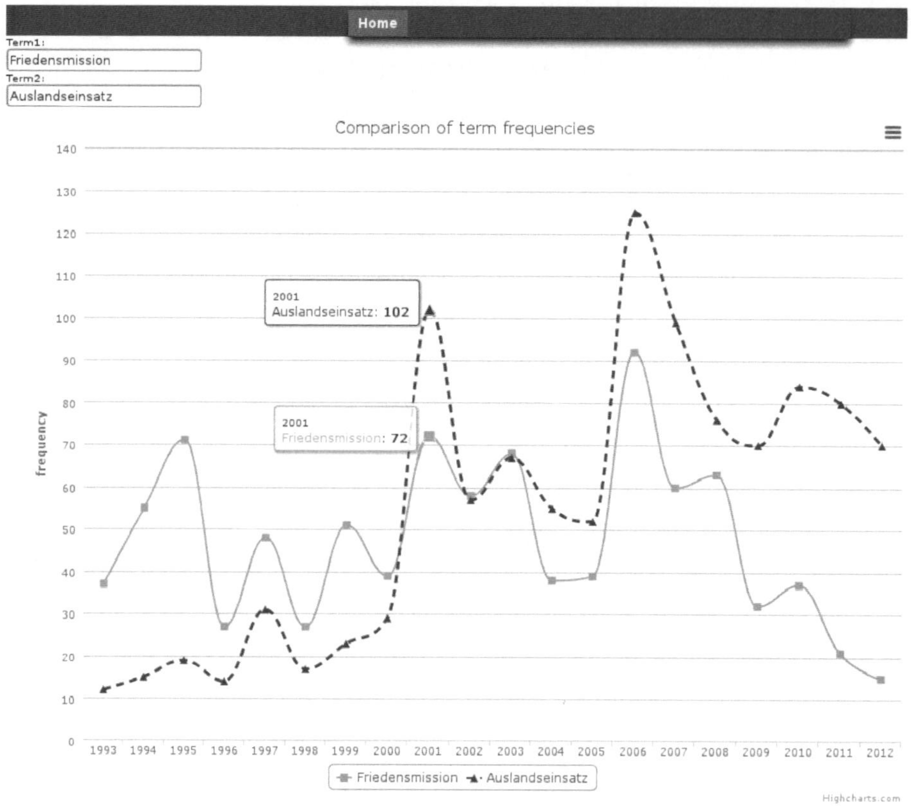


Figure 1: The screenshot of our web-based system shows a simple quantitative analysis of the frequency of two terms in news articles over time. While in the 90s the term Friedensmission (peace operation) was predominant a reverse tendency can be observed since 2001 with Auslandseinsatz (foreign intervention) being now frequently used.

sagte Rühe.
said Rühe.

„The Europeans would fill the gap, Rühe said."

The tool support is meant to be semi-automatic, as the automatic tools propose candidates that need to be validated or refused by the political scientists.

We combine a chain of corpus processing tools with classifier-based tools, e.g. for topic classifiers, commentary/report classifiers, etc., make the tools interoperable to ensure flexible data exchange and multiple usage scenarios, and we embed the tool collection under a web (service) - based user interface.

The remainder of this paper is structured as follows. In section 2, we present an outline of the architecture of our tool collection, and we motivate the architecture. Section 3 presents examples of implemented modules, both from corpus processing and search and retrieval of instances of complex concepts. We also show how our tools are related to the infrastructural standards in use in the CLARIN community. In section 4, we exemplify the intended use of the methods with case studies about steps necessary for identifying evocation: being able to separate reports from comments, and strategies for identifying indirect speech. Section 6 is devoted to a conclusion and to the discussion of future work.

## 2 Project Goals

A collaboration between political scientists and computational linguists necessarily involves finding a common language in order to agree on the precise objectives of a project. For example, social scientists use the term codebook for manual annotations of text, similar to annotation schemes or guidelines in NLP. Both disciplines share methodologies of interactive text analysis which combine term based search, manual annotation and learning-based annotation of large amounts of data. In this section, we give a brief summary of the goals from the perspective of each of the two disciplines, and then describe the text corpus that is used in the project. Section 3 will describe our approach to devising a system architecture that serves to realize the goals.

### 2.1 Social Science Research Issue

Given the complexity of the underlying research issues (cf. Section 1) and the methodological tradition of manual text coding by very well-trained annotators in the social science and particular in political science, our project does not aim at any fully-automatic solution for empirical issues in political science. Instead, the goal is to provide as much assistance to the human text analyst as possible, by means of a workbench that integrates many tasks that otherwise would have to be carried out with different software tools (e.g., corpus preprocessing, KWIC searches, statistics). In our project, the human analyst is concerned specifically with manifestations of collective identities in newspaper texts on issues of war and military interventions: who are the actors in political crisis management or conflict? How is this perspective of responsible actors characterized in different newspapers (with different political orientation; in different countries)? The analyst wants to find documents that contain facets of such constellations, which requires search techniques involving concepts on different levels of abstraction, ranging from specific words or named entities (which may appear with different names in different texts) to event types (which may be realized with different verb-argument configurations). Thus the text corpus should be enriched with information relevant to such queries, and the workbench shall provide a comfortable interface for building such queries. Moreover, various types and (possibly concurrent) layers of human annotations have to complement the automatic analysis, and the manual annotation would benefit from automatic control of codebook[2] compliance and the convergence of coding decisions.

### 2.2 Natural Language Processing Research Issue

Large collections of text provide an excellent opportunity for computational linguists to scale their methods. In the scenario of a project like ours, this becomes especially challenging, because standard automatic analysis components have to be combined with manual annotation or interactive intervention of the human analyst.

In addition to this principled challenge, there may be more mundane issues resulting from processing corpora whose origin stretches over many years. In our case, the data collection phase coincided with a spelling reform in German-speaking countries. Many aspects of spelling changed twice (in 1996 and in 2006), and thus it is the responsibility of the NLP branch of the project to provide an abstraction over such changes and to enable today's users to run a homogeneous search over the texts using only the current spelling. While this might be less important for generic web search applications, it is of great importance for our project, where the overall objective is a combination of quantitative and qualitative text analysis.

In our processing chain, we first need to harmonize the data formats so that the processing tools operate on a common format. Rather than defining these from scratch, we aim at compatibility with the standardization efforts of CLARIN[3] and DARIAH[4], two large language technology infrastructure projects in Europe that in particular target eHumanities applications. One of the objectives is to provide advanced tools to discover, explore, exploit, annotate, analyse or combine textual resources. In the next section we give more details about how we interact which the CLARIN-D infrastructure (Boehlke et al., 2013).

## 3 Architecture

The main goal is to provide a web-based user-interface to the social scientist to avoid any software installation. Figure 2 presents the workflow of the different processing steps in this project. The first part considers format issues that occur if documents from different sources are used. The main challenge is to recognize metadata correctly. Date and source name are two types of metadata which are required for analyses in the social sciences. But also the separation of document content (text) and metadata is important to ensure that only real content is processed with the NLP methods. The results are stored in a repository which uses a relational database as a back-end. All further modules are used to add more annotations to the textual data. First a complex linguistic pro-

[2]or, in NLP terms: annotation scheme.

[3]http://www.clarin.eu/

[4]http://www.dariah.eu/

cessing chain is used to provide state-of-the-art corpus linguistic annotations (see Section 3.2 for details). Then, to ensure that statistics over occurrence counts of words, word combinations and constructions are valid and not blurred by the multiple presence of texts or text passages in the corpus, we filter duplicates. Duplicates can occur if our document set contains the same document twice or if two documents are very similar, e.g. they differ in only one sentence.

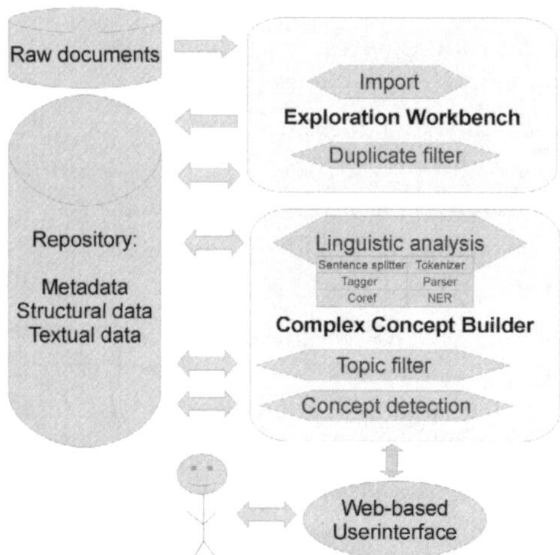


Figure 2: Overview of the complete processing chain.

We split the workflow for the user into two parts: The first part is only used if the user imports new data into the repository. For that he can use the exploration workbench (Section 3.1). Secondly, all steps for analyzing the data are done with the Complex Concept Builder (Section 3.2).

### 3.1 Exploration Workbench

Formal corpus inhomogeneity (e.g. various data formats and inconsistent data structures) are a major issue for researchers working on text corpora. The web-based "Exploration Workbench" allows for the creation of a consistent corpus from various types of data and prepares data for further processing with computational linguistic tools. The workbench can interact with to existing computational linguistic infrastructure (e.g. CLARIN) and provides input for the repository also used by the Complex Concept Builder.

The workbench converts several input formats (TXT, RTF, HTML) to a consistent XML representation. The conversion tools account for different file encodings and convert input files to Unicode (UTF-8). We currently work on newspaper articles wrapped with metadata. Text mining components read out those metadata and identify text content in the documents. Metadata appear at varying positions and in diverse notations, e.g. for dates, indications of authors or newspaper sections. The components account for these variations and convert them to a consistent machine readable format. The extracted metadata are appended to the XML representation. The resulting XML is the starting point for further computational linguistic processing of the source documents.

The workbench contains a tool to identify text duplicates and semi-duplicates via similarity measures of pairs of articles (Kantner et al., 2011). The method is based on a comparison of 5-grams, weighted by significance (tf-idf measure (Salton and Buckley, 1988)). For a pair of documents it yields a value on a "similarity scale" ranging from 0 to 1. Values at medium range (0.4 to 0.8) are considered semi-duplicates.

Data cleaning is important for the data-driven studies. Not only duplicate articles have a negative impact, also articles which are not of interest for the given topic have to be filtered out. There are different approaches to classify articles into a range of predefined topics. In the last years LDA (Blei et al., 2003; Niekler and Jähnichen, 2012) is one of the most successful methods to find topics in articles. But for social scientists the categories typically used in LDA are not sufficient. We follow the idea of Dualist (Settles, 2011; Settles and Zhu, 2012) which is an interactive method for classification. The architecture of Dualist is based on MALLET (McCallum, 2002) which is easily integrable into our architecture. Our goal is to design the correct feature to find relevant articles for a given topic. Word features are not sufficient since we have to model more complex features (cf. Section 2.1).

The workbench is not exclusively geared to the data of the current project. We chose a modular set-up of the tools of the workbench and provide user-modifiable templates for the extraction of various kinds of metadata, in order to keep the workbench adaptable to new data and to develop tools suitable for data beyond the scope of the current corpus.

### 3.2 Complex Concept Builder

A central problem for political scientists who intend to work on large corpora is the linguistic variety in the expression of technical terms and complex concepts. An editorial or a politician cited in a news item can mobilize a collective identity which can be construed from e.g. regional or social affiliation, nationality or religion. A reasonable goal in the context of the search for collective identity evocation contexts is therefore to find all texts which (possibly) contain collective identities. Moreover, while we are training our interactive tools on a corpus on wars and military interventions the same collective identities might be expressed in different ways in a corpus i.e. on the Eurocrisis.

From a computational point of view, many different tools need to be joined to detect interesting texts. An example application could be a case where a political scientist intends to extract newspaper articles that cite a politician who tries to rally support for his political party. In order to detect such text, we need a system to identify direct and indirect speech and a sentiment system to determine the orientation of the statement. These systems in turn need various kinds of preprocessing starting from tokenization over syntactic parsing up to coreference resolution. The Complex Concept Builder is the collection of all these systems with the goal to assist the political scientists.

So far, the Complex Concept Builder implements tokenization (Schmid, 2009), lemmatisation (Schmid, 1995), part-of-speech tagging (Schmid and Laws, 2008), named entity detection (Faruqui and Padó, 2010), syntactical parsing (Bohnet, 2010), coreference analysis for German (Lappin and Leass, 1994; Stuckardt, 2001), relation extraction (Blessing et al., 2012) and sentiment analysis for English (Taboada et al., 2011).

It is important for a researcher of the humanities to be able to adapt existing classification systems according to his own needs. A common procedure in both, NLP and political sciences, is to annotate data. Therefore, one major goal of the project and the Complex Concept Builder is to provide machine learning systems with a wide range of possible features — including high level information like sentiment, text type, relations to other texts, etc. — that can be used by non-experts for semi-automatic annotation and text selection. Active learning is used to provide immediate results that can then be improved continuously. This aspect of the Complex Concept Builder is especially important because new or adapted concepts that may be looked for can be found without further help of natural language processing experts.

### 3.3 Implementation

We decided to use a web-based platform for our system since the social scientist needs no software installation and we are independent of the used operating system. Only a state-of-the-art web-browser is needed. On the server side, we use a tomcat installation that interacts with our UIMA pipeline (Ferrucci and Lally, 2004). A HTML-rendering component designed in the project (and parametrizable) allows for a flexible presentation of the data. A major issue of our work is interaction. To solve this, we use JQuery and AJAX to dynamically interact between client- and server-side.

## 4 Case Study

In this section we explore the interaction between various sub-systems and how they collaborate to find complex political concepts. The following Section 4.1 describes the detection of direct and indirect speech and its evaluation follows in Section 4.2. Section 4.3 is a general exploration of a few selected sub-systems which require, or benefit from direct and indirect speech. Finally, Section 4.4 discusses a specific usage scenario for indirect speech.

### 4.1 Identifying Indirect Speech

The Complex Concept Builder provides analyses on different linguistic levels (currently morphosyntax, dependency syntax, named entities) of annotation. We exploit this knowledge to identify indirect speech along with a mentioned speaker. Our indirect speech recognizer is based on three conditions: i) Consider all sentences that contain at least one word which is tagged as subjunctive (i.e. "*.SUBJ") by the RFTagger. ii) This verb has to be a direct successor of another verb in the dependency tree. iii) This verb needs to have a subject.

Figure 3 depicts the dependency parse tree of sentence 2.

(2) Der Einsatz werde wegen der Risiken für die unbewaffneten Beobachter ausgesetzt, teilte

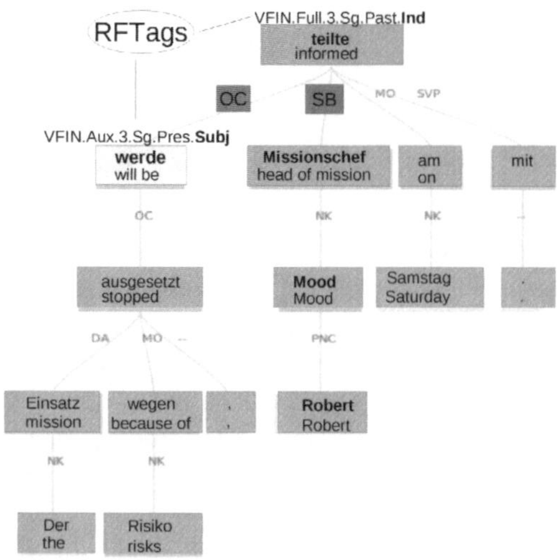


Figure 3: Dependency parse of a sentence that contains indirect speech (see Sentence 2).

Missionschef Robert Mood am Samstag mit.

The mission will be stopped because of the risks to the unarmed observers, informed Head of Mission Robert Mood on Saturday.

The speaker of the indirect speech in Sentence 2 is correctly identified as *Missionschef* (Head of Mission) and the corresponding verb is *teilte mit* (from *mitteilen*) (to inform).

The parsing-based analysis helps to identify the speaker of the citation which is a necessary information for the later interpretation of the citation. As a further advantage, such an approach helps to minimize the need of lexical knowledge for the identification of indirect speech. Our error analysis below will show that in some cases a lexicon can help to avoid false positives. A lexicon of verbs of communication can easily be bootstrapped by using our approach to identify candidates for the list of verbs which then restrict the classifier in order to achieve a higher precision.

## 4.2 Indirect Speech Evaluation

For a first impression, we present a list of sentences which were automatically annotated as positive instances by our indirect speech detector. The sentences were rated by political scientists. Additionally, for each sentence we extracted the *speaker* and the used *verb of speech*. We manually evaluated 200 extracted triples ($sentence$, $speaker$, $verb\ of\ speech$): The precision of our system is: $92.5\%$

Examples 2, 3 and 4 present good candidates which are helpful for further investigations on collective identities. In example 3 Cardinal Lehmann is a representative speaker of the Catholic community which is a collective identity. Our extracted sentences accelerate the search for such candidates which amounts to looking manually for needles in a haystack.

| example | speaker | verb of speech |
|---|---|---|
| (2) | Robert Mood | teilte (told) |
| (3) | Kardinal Karl Lehmann | sagte (said) |
| (4) | Sergej Ordzhonikidse | sagte (said) |
| (5) | Bild (picture) | trüben (tarnish) |
| (6) | sein (be) | sein (be) |

Examples 5 and 6 show problems of our first approach. In this case, the speaker is not a person or an organisation, and the verb is not a verb of speech.

(3) Ein Angriffskrieg jeder Art sei " sittlich verwerflich ", sagte der Vorsitzende der Bischoffskonferenz, Kardinal Karl Lehmann.

Any kind of war of aggression is "morally reprehensible," said the chairman of the Bishops' Conference, Cardinal Karl Lehmann.

(4) Derartige Erklärungen eines Staatschefs seien im Rahmen der internationalen Beziehungen inakzeptabel, sagte der UN-Generaldirektor Sergej Ordzhonikidse gestern in Genf.

Such statements of heads of states are unacceptable in the context of international relations, said UN General Director Sergei Ordzhonikidse in Geneva yesterday.

(5) Würden die Wahlen verschoben, trübte sich das geschönte Bild.

Would the elections be postponed, the embellished image would tarnish.

(6) Dies sei alles andere als einfach, ist aus Offizierskreisen zu hören.

This is anything but simple, is to hear from military circles.

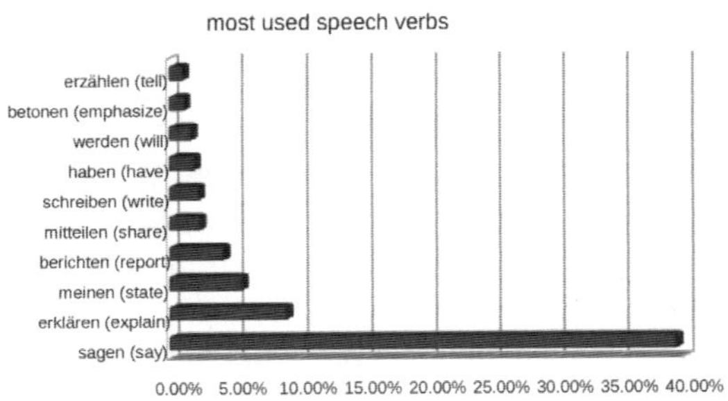


Figure 4: 10 most used verbs (lemma) in indirect speech.

### 4.3 Using Indirect Speech

Other modules benefit from the identification of indirect speech, as can be seen from Sentence 7. The sentiment system assigns a negative polarity of $-2.15$ to the sentence. The nested sentiment sources, as described by (Wiebe et al., 2005), of this sentence require a) a direct speech with the speaker "Mazower" and b) an indirect speech with the speaker "no one" to be found.[5]

(7) "There were serious arguments about what should happen to the Slavs and Poles in eastern Europe," says Mazower, "and how many of them should be sent to the camps and what proportion could be Germanised ... No one ever came out and directly said Hitler had got it wrong, but there was plenty of implied criticism through comparisons with the Roman empire. [...]"[6]

A collective identity evoked in Sentence 7 is "the Germans"— although the term is not explicitly mentioned. This collective identity is described as non-homogeneous in the citation and can be further explored manually by the political scientists.

The following are further applications of the identified indirect speeches a) using the frequency of speeches per text as a feature for classification; e.g. a classification system for news reports/commentaries as described in Section 4.4 b) a project-goal is to find texts in which collective identities are mobilised by entities of political debate (i.e. persons, organisations, etc.); the detection of indirect speech is mandatory for any such analysis.

[5]The reported sentiment value for the whole sentence is applicable only to the direct speech. The indirect speech (i.e. "Hitler had got it wrong") needs a more fine-grained polarity score. Since our Complex Concept Builder is very flexible, it is trivial to score each component separately.

[6]http://www.guardian.co.uk/education/2008/jul /01/academicexperts.highereducationprofile

### 4.4 Commentary/Report Classification

A useful distinction for political scientists dealing with newspaper articles is the distinction between articles that report objectively on events or backgrounds and editorials or press commentaries.

We first extracted opinionated and objective texts from DeReKo corpus (Stede, 2004; Kupietz et al., 2010). Some texts were removed in order to balance the corpus. The balanced corpus contains 2848 documents and has been split into a development and a training and test set. 570 documents were used for the manual creation of features. The remaining 2278 documents were used to train and evaluate classifiers using 10-fold cross-validation with the WEKA machine learning toolkit (Hall et al., 2009) and various classifiers (cf. Table 1).

The challenge is that the newspaper articles from the training and evaluation corpus come from different newspapers and, of course, from different authors. Commentaries in the yellow press tend to have a very different style and vocabulary than commentaries from broadsheet press. Therefore, special attention needs to be paid to the independence of the classifier from different authors and different newspapers. For this reason, we use hand-crafted features tailored to this problem. In return, this means omitting surface-form features (i.e. words themselves).

The support vector machine used the SMO algorithm (Platt and others, 1998) with a polynomial kernel $K(x, y) =< x, y >^{e}$ with $e = 2$. All other algorithms were used with default settings.

| | precision | recall | f-score |
|---|---|---|---|
| SVM | 0.819 | 0.814 | 0.813 |
| Naive Bayes | 0.79 | 0.768 | 0.764 |
| Multilayer Perceptron | 0.796 | 0.795 | 0.794 |

Table 1: Results of a 10-fold cross-validation for various machine learning algorithms.

A qualitative evaluation shows that direct and indirect speech is a problem for the classifier. Opinions voiced via indirect speech should not lead to a classification as 'Commentary', but should be ignored. Additionally, the number of uses of direct and indirect speech by the author can provide insight into the intention of the author. A common way to voice one's own opinion, without having to do so explicitly, is to use indirect speech that the author agrees with. Therefore, the number of direct and indirect speech uses will be added to the classifier. First experiments indicate that the inclusion of direct and indirect speech increase the performance of the classifier.

## 5 Related Work

Many approaches exist to assist social scientists in dealing with large scale data. We discuss some well-known ones and highlight differences to the approach described above.

The Europe Media Monitor (EMM) (Steinberger et al., 2009) analyses large amounts of newspaper articles and assists anyone interested in news. It allows its users to search for specific topics and automatically clusters articles from different sources. This is a key concept of the EMM, because it collects about $100,000$ articles in approximately $50$ languages per day and it is impossible to scan through these by hand. EMM users are EU institutions, national institutions of the EU member states, international organisations and the public (Steinberger et al., 2009).

The topic clusters provide insight into "hot" topics by simply counting the amount of articles per cluster or by measuring the amount of news on a specific topic with regards to its normal amount of news. Articles are also data-mined for geographical information, e.g. to update in which geographical region the article was written and where the topic is located. Social network information is gathered and visualised as well.

Major differences between the EMM and our approach are the user group and the domain of the corpus. The complex concepts political scientists are interested in are much more nuanced than the concepts relevant for topic detection and the construction of social networks. Additionally, the EMM does not allow its users to look for their own concepts and issues, while this interactivity is a central contribution of our approach (cf. Sections 1, 2.1 and 3.2).

The CLARIN-D project also provides a web-based platform to create NLP-chains. It is called WebLicht (Hinrichs et al., 2010), but in its current form, the tool is not immediately usable for social scientists as the separation of metadata and textual data and the encoding of the data is hard for non-experts. Furthermore, WebLicht does not yet support the combination of manual and automatic annotation needed for text exploration in the social science. Our approach is based on the webservices used by WebLicht. But in contrast to WebLicht, we provide two additional components that simplify the integration (exploration workbench) and the interpretation (complex concept builder) of the research data. The former is intended, in the medium term, to be made available in the CLARIN framework.

## 6 Conclusion and Outlook

We developed and implemented a pipeline of various text processing tools which is designed to assist political scientists in finding specific, complex concepts within large amounts of text. Our case studies showed that our approach can provide beneficial assistance for the research of political scientists as well as researcher from other social sciences and the humanities. A future aspect will be to find metrics to evaluate our pipeline. In recently started annotation experiments on topic classification Cohen's kappa coefficient (Carletta, 1996) is mediocre. It may very well be possible that the complex concepts, like multiple collective identities, are intrinsically hard to detect, and the annotations cannot be improved substantially.

The extension of the NLP pipeline will be another major working area in the future. Examples are sentiment analysis for German, adding world knowledge about named entities (e.g. persons and events), identification of relations between entities.

Finally, all these systems need to be evaluated not only in terms of f-score, precision and recall, but also in terms of usability for the political scientists. This also includes a detailed investigation of various political science concepts and if they can be detected automatically or if natural language processing can help the political scientists to detect their concepts semi-automatically. The definition of such evaluation is an open research topic in itself.

## Acknowledgements

The research leading to these results has been done in the project eIdentity which is funded from the Federal Ministry of Education and Research (BMBF) under grant agreement 01UG1234.

## References


David M. Blei, Andrew Y. Ng, and Michael I. Jordan. 2003. Latent dirichlet allocation. *J. Mach. Learn. Res.*, 3:993–1022, March.

Andre Blessing, Jens Stegmann, and Jonas Kuhn. 2012. SOA meets relation extraction: Less may be more in interaction. In *Proceedings of the Workshop on Service-oriented Architectures (SOAs) for the Humanities: Solutions and Impacts, Digital Humanities*, pages 6–11.

Volker Boehlke, Gerhard Heyer, and Peter Wittenburg. 2013. IT-based research infrastructures for the humanities and social sciences - developments, examples, standards, and technology. *it - Information Technology*, 55(1):26–33, February.

Bernd Bohnet. 2010. Top accuracy and fast dependency parsing is not a contradiction. In *Proceedings of the 23rd International Conference on Computational*, pages 89–97.

Jean Carletta. 1996. Assessing agreement on classification tasks: The kappa statistic. *Computational Linguistics*, 22(2):249–254.

Manaal Faruqui and Sebastian Padó. 2010. Training and evaluating a german named entity recognizer with semantic generalization. In *Proceedings of KONVENS 2010*, Saarbrücken, Germany.

D. Ferrucci and A. Lally. 2004. UIMA: an architectural approach to unstructured information processing in the corporate research environment. *Natural Language Engineering*, 10(3-4):327–348.

Mark Hall, Eibe Frank, Geoffrey Holmes, Bernhard Pfahringer, Peter Reutemann, and Ian H Witten. 2009. The weka data mining software: an update. *ACM SIGKDD Explorations Newsletter*, 11(1):10–18.

Erhard W. Hinrichs, Marie Hinrichs, and Thomas Zastrow. 2010. WebLicht: Web-Based LRT Services for German. In *Proceedings of the ACL 2010 System Demonstrations*, pages 25–29.

Cathleen Kantner, Amelie Kutter, Andreas Hildebrandt, and Mark Puettcher. 2011. How to get rid of the noise in the corpus: Cleaning large samples of digital newspaper texts. *International Relations Online Working Paper*, 2, July.

Marc Kupietz, Cyril Belica, Holger Keibel, and Andreas Witt. 2010. The german reference corpus dereko: a primordial sample for linguistic research. In *Proceedings of the 7th conference on international language resources and evaluation (LREC 2010)*, pages 1848–1854.

Shalom Lappin and Herbert J Leass. 1994. An algorithm for pronominal anaphora resolution. *Computational linguistics*, 20(4):535–561.

Andrew Kachites McCallum. 2002. Mallet: A machine learning for language toolkit. http://www.cs.umass.edu/ mccallum/mallet.

Andreas Niekler and Patrick Jähnichen. 2012. Matching results of latent dirichlet allocation for text. In *Proceedings of ICCM 2012, 11th International Conference on Cognitive Modeling*, pages 317–322. Universitätsverlag der TU Berlin.

John Platt et al. 1998. Sequential minimal optimization: A fast algorithm for training support vector machines. *technical report msr-tr-98-14, Microsoft Research.*

Gerard Salton and Christopher Buckley. 1988. Term-weighting approaches in automatic text retrieval. *Information processing & management*, 24(5):513–523.

Helmut Schmid and Florian Laws. 2008. Estimation of conditional probabilities with decision trees and an application to fine-grained POS tagging. In *Proceedings of the 22nd International Conference on Computational Linguistics (Coling 2008)*, pages 777–784, Manchester, UK, August.

Helmut Schmid. 1995. Improvements in part-of-speech tagging with an application to german. In *Proceedings of the ACL SIGDAT-Workshop*, pages 47–50.

Helmut Schmid, 2009. *Corpus Linguistics: An International Handbook*, chapter Tokenizing and Part-of-Speech Tagging. Handbooks of Linguistics and Communication Science. Walter de Gruyter, Berlin.

Burr Settles and Xiaojin Zhu. 2012. Behavioral factors in interactive training of text classifiers. In *Proceedings of the 2012 Conference of the North American Chapter of the Association for Computational Linguistics: Human Language Technologies*, pages 563–567. Association for Computational Linguistics.

Burr Settles. 2011. Closing the loop: Fast, interactive semi-supervised annotation with queries on features and instances. In *Proceedings of the Conference on Empirical Methods in Natural Language Processing*, pages 1467–1478. Association for Computational Linguistics.

Manfred Stede. 2004. The potsdam commentary corpus. In *Proceedings of the 2004 ACL Workshop on Discourse Annotation*, DiscAnnotation '04, pages 96–102, Stroudsburg, PA, USA. Association for Computational Linguistics.

Ralf Steinberger, Bruno Pouliquen, and Erik Van Der Goot. 2009. An introduction to the europe media monitor family of applications. In *Proceedings of the Information Access in a Multilingual World-Proceedings of the SIGIR 2009 Workshop*, pages 1–8.

Roland Stuckardt. 2001. Design and enhanced evaluation of a robust anaphor resolution algorithm. *Computational Linguistics*, 27(4):479–506.

Maite Taboada, Julian Brooke, Milan Tofiloski, Kimberly Voll, and Manfred Stede. 2011. Lexicon-based methods for sentiment analysis. *Computational linguistics*, 37(2):267–307.

Janyce Wiebe, Theresa Wilson, and Claire Cardie. 2005. Annotating expressions of opinions and emotions in language. *Language Resources and Evaluation*, 39(2-3):165–210.

# Learning to Extract Folktale Keywords

**Dolf Trieschnigg, Dong Nguyen and Mariët Theune**
University of Twente
Enschede, The Netherlands
{d.trieschnigg,d.nguyen,m.theune}@utwente.nl

## Abstract

Manually assigned keywords provide a valuable means for accessing large document collections. They can serve as a shallow document summary and enable more efficient retrieval and aggregation of information. In this paper we investigate keywords in the context of the Dutch Folktale Database, a large collection of stories including fairy tales, jokes and urban legends. We carry out a quantitative and qualitative analysis of the keywords in the collection. Up to 80% of the assigned keywords (or a minor variation) appear in the text itself. Human annotators show moderate to substantial agreement in their judgment of keywords. Finally, we evaluate a learning to rank approach to extract and rank keyword candidates. We conclude that this is a promising approach to automate this time intensive task.

## 1 Introduction

Keywords are frequently used as a simple way to provide descriptive metadata about collections of documents. A set of keywords can concisely present the most important aspects of a document and enable quick summaries of multiple documents. The word cloud in Figure 1, for instance, gives a quick impression of the most important topics in a collection of over 40,000 documents (a collection of Dutch folktales).

Keyword assignment or generation is the task of finding the most important, topical keywords or keyphrases to describe a document (Turney, 2000; Frank et al., 1999). Based on keywords, small groups of documents (Hammouda et al., 2005) or large collections of documents (Park et al., 2002) can be summarized. Keyword *extraction* is a restricted case of keyword assignment: the assigned keywords are a selection of the words or phrases appearing in the document itself (Turney, 2000; Frank et al., 1999).

In this paper we look into keyword extraction in the domain of cultural heritage, in particular for extracting keywords from folktale narratives found in the Dutch Folktale Database (more on this collection in section 3). These narratives might require a different approach for extraction than in other domains, such as news stories and scholarly articles (Jiang et al., 2009). Stories in the Dutch Folktale Database are annotated with uncontrolled, free-text, keywords. Because suggesting keywords which do not appear in the text is a considerably harder task to automate and to evaluate, we restrict ourselves to keywords extracted from the text itself.

In the first part of this paper we study the current practice of keyword assignment for this collection. We analyze the assigned keywords in the collection as a whole and present a more fine-grained analysis of a sample of documents. Moreover, we investigate to what extent human annotators agree on suitable keywords extracted from the text. Manually assigning keywords is an expensive and time-consuming process. Automatic assignment would bring down the cost and time to archive material. In the second part of this paper we evaluate a number of automatic keyword extraction methods. We show that a learning to rank approach gives promising results.

The overview of this paper is as follows. We first describe related work in automatic keyword assignment. In section 3 we introduce the Dutch Folktale Database. In section 4 we present an analysis of the keywords currently used in the folktale database. In section 5 we investigate the agreement of human annotators on keyword extraction. In section 6 we present and evaluate an automatic method for extracting and ranking keywords. We end with a discussion and conclusion in section 7.

| Keyword (translation) | Frequency |
|---|---|
| dood (death) | 5,861 |
| man (man) | 4,547 |
| vrouw (woman) | 4,154 |
| sterven (to die) | 3,168 |
| huis (house) | 2,894 |
| spokerij (haunting) | 2,491 |
| duivel (devil) | 2,487 |
| nacht (night) | 2,449 |
| voorteken (omen) | 2,380 |
| voorloop (forerunnings) | 2,372 |
| geld (money) | 2,370 |
| toverij (sorcery) | 2,322 |
| zien (to see) | 2,270 |
| heks (witch) | 2,233 |
| boer (farmer) | 2,189 |
| water (water) | 2,177 |
| angst (fear) | 2,091 |
| hekserij (witchcraft) | 1,911 |
| kind (child) | 1,853 |
| spoken (ghosts) | 1,747 |
| spook (ghost) | 1,742 |
| seks (sex) | 1,659 |

Figure 1: Frequent keywords in the Dutch Folktale Database

## 2 Related Work

Because of space limitations, we limit our discussion of related work to keyword extraction in the context of free-text indexing. Automated *controlled* vocabulary indexing is a fundamentally different task (see for instance Medelyan and Witten (2006) and Plaunt and Norgard (1998)).

Typically, keyword extraction consists of two steps. In the first step candidate keywords are determined and features, such as the frequency or position in the document, are calculated to characterize these keywords. In the second step the candidates are filtered and ranked based on these features. Both unsupervised and supervised algorithms have been used to do this.

### 2.1 Candidate Extraction

Candidate keywords can be extracted in a number of ways. The simplest approach is to treat each single word as a candidate keyword, optionally filtering out stop words or only selecting words with a particular Part-of-Speech (Liu et al., 2009a; Jiang et al., 2009). More sophisticated approaches allow for multi-word keywords, by extracting consecutive words from the text, optionally limited to keywords adhering to specific lexical patterns (Osinski and Weiss, 2005; Hulth, 2003; Rose et al., 2010; Frank et al., 1999; Turney, 2000).

### 2.2 Features to Characterize Keywords

Many features for characterizing candidate keywords have been investigated previously, with varying computational complexities and resource requirements. The simplest features are based on document and collection statistics, for instance the frequency of a potential keyword in the document and the inverse document frequency in the collection (Turney, 2000; Hulth, 2003; Frank et al., 1999). Examples of more complex features are: features based on characteristics of lexical chains, requiring a lexical database with word meanings (Ercan and Cicekli, 2007); features related to frequencies in external document collections and query logs (Bendersky and Croft, 2008; Yih et al., 2006; Liu et al., 2009b; Xu et al., 2010); and a feature to determine the cohesiveness of retrieved documents with that keyword (Bendersky and Croft, 2008).

### 2.3 Unsupervised Methods for Keyword Extraction

Unsupervised methods for keyword extraction typically rely on heuristics to filter and rank the keywords in order of importance. For instance, by ranking the candidates by their importance in the collection – estimated by the inverse document frequency. Another approach is to apply the PageRank algorithm to determine the most important keywords based on their co-occurrence link-structure (Mihalcea and Tarau, 2004). Liu et al. (2009b) employed clustering to extract keywords that cover *all* important topics from the original text. From each topic cluster an exemplar is determined and for each exemplar the best corresponding keyword is determined.

### 2.4 Supervised Methods for Keyword Extraction

Early supervised methods used training data to set the optimal parameters for (unsupervised) systems based on heuristics (Turney, 2000). Other methods approached keyword extraction as a binary classification problem: given a candidate keyword it has to be classified as either a keyword or not. Methods include decision trees (Bendersky and Croft, 2008), Naive Bayes (Frank et al., 1999) and Support Vector Machines (Zhang et al., 2006). Zhang et al. (2008) approached keyword extraction as a labeling problem for which they employed conditional random fields. Recently, keyword extraction has been cast as a ranking problem and learning to rank techniques have been applied to solve it (Jiang et al., 2009). Jiang et al. (2009) concluded that learning to rank approaches performed better than binary classifiers in the context of extracting keywords from scholarly texts and websites. Different variations of learning to rank exist, see (Li, 2011) for an overview.

## 3 The Dutch Folktale Database

The Dutch Folktale Database is a repository of over 40,000 folktales in Dutch, old Dutch, Frisian and a large number of Dutch dialects. The material has been collected in the 19th, 20th and 21th centuries, and consists of stories from various periods, including the Middle Ages and the Renaissance. The collection has both an archival and a research function. It preserves an important part of the oral cultural heritage of the Netherlands and can be used for comparative folk narrative studies. Since 2004 the database is available online[1].

The real value of the database does not only lie the stories themselves, but also in their manually added set of descriptive metadata fields. These fields include, for example, a summary in Dutch, a list of proper names present in the folktales, and a list of keywords. Adding these metadata is a time-consuming and demanding task. In fact, the amount of work involved hampers the growth of the folktale database. A large backlog of digitized folktales is awaiting metadata assignment before they can be archived in the collection. Being able to automatically assign keywords to these documents would be a first step to speed up the archiving process.

## 4 Analysis of Assigned Keywords

In this section we analyze the keywords that have been manually assigned to the stories in the Dutch Folktale Database. First we look at the keywords assigned to the collection as a whole. After that we make a more fine-grained analysis of the keywords assigned to a selection of the documents.

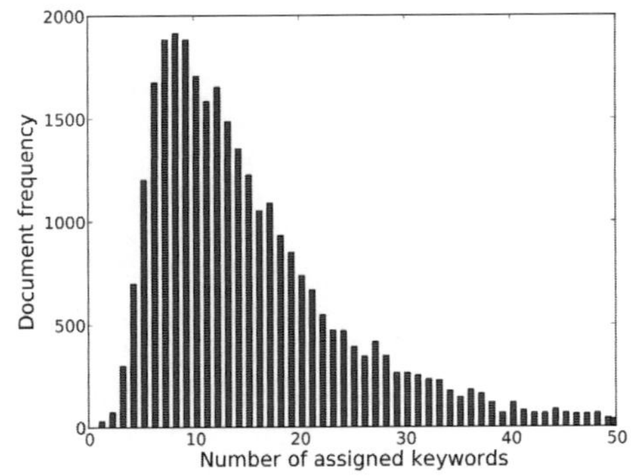


Figure 2: Number of assigned keywords per document

### 4.1 Quantitative Analysis

We analyzed a snapshot from the Dutch Folktale Database (from early 2012) that consists of 41,336 folktales. On average, 15 keywords have been assigned to each of these documents (see Figure 2). The median number of assigned keywords is 10, however. The keywords vocabulary has 43,195 unique keywords, most of which consist of a single word (90%). Figure 1 shows a word cloud of keywords used in the collection; more frequent keyword types appear larger. On the right, it lists the most frequent keyword types (and their translations). The assignment of keywords to documents has a Zipfian distribution: a few keyword types are assigned to many documents, whereas many keyword types are assigned to few documents.

When we limit our collection to stories in Dutch (15,147 documents), we can determine how many of the manually assigned keywords can be found literally in the story text[2]. We define the *keyword coverage* of a document as the fraction of its assigned keywords which is found in the full text or its summary. The average keyword coverage of the Dutch stories is 65%. Figure 3 shows a histogram of the coverage. It shows that most of the documents have a keyword coverage of 0.5 or more.

[1] http://www.verhalenbank.nl, in Dutch only

[2] Stories in other languages or dialects have been assigned Dutch keywords.

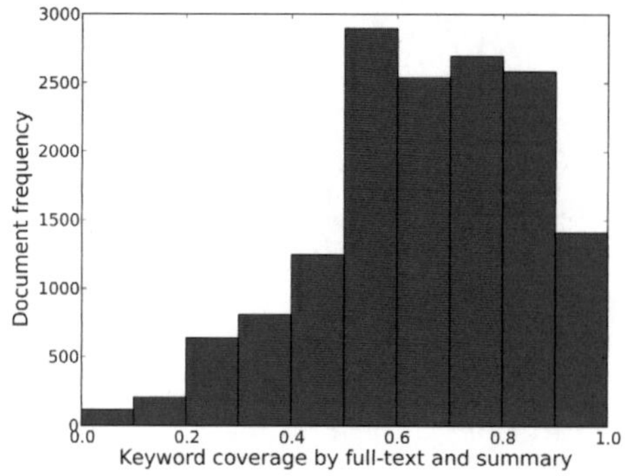


Figure 3: Keyword coverage of folktales in Dutch

### 4.2 Qualitative Analysis

The quantitative analysis does not provide insight into what kind of keywords have been assigned. Therefore, we analyzed a selection of documents more thoroughly. For each of the five largest genres in the collection (fairy tale, traditional legend, joke, urban legend and riddle) we sampled 10 tales and manually classified the keywords assigned to these folktales. A total of almost 1000 keywords was analyzed. Table 1 summarizes the statistics of this analysis. Almost 80% of the keywords appear literally or almost literally in the text. The almost literal appearances include keywords which differ in quantity (plural versus singular form) and verb forms. Verb forms vary in tense (present rather than past tense) and infinitive keywords of separable verbs. An example of the latter is the assignment of the keyword "terugkeren", to return, where "keren" (~ turn) and "terug" (~ back) are used in a sentence. Of the analyzed keywords 5% are synonyms of words appearing the text and 2.3% are hypernyms of words appearing the text (e.g. "wapen", weapon, is used as a keyword with "mes", knife, mentioned in the text). The remaining 13% of the keywords represent abstract topic, event and activity descriptions. For example, the keyword "wegsturen", to send away, when one of the characters explicitly asks someone to leave. Other examples are the keywords "baan", job, and "arbeid", labor, when the story is about an unemployed person.

Based on these numbers we can conclude that based on extraction techniques alone we should be able to reproduce a large portion of the manual keyword assignment. When thesauri are employed to find synonyms and hypernyms, up to 87% of the manually assigned keywords could be found. A much harder task is to obtain the remaining 13% of more abstract keywords, which we will study in future research.

| Classification | Count | Perc. |
|---|---|---|
| Literal | 669 | 67.6% |
| Almost literal | 120 | 12.1% |
| Synonym | 49 | 5.0% |
| Hypernym | 23 | 2.3% |
| Typing error | 2 | 0.2% |
| Other | 126 | 12.7% |
| *Total* | 989 | 100.0% |

Table 1: Keyword types in a set of 1000 folktales

## 5 Evaluating Agreement in Keyword Assignment

The previous analyses raise the question whether the keywords have been consistently assigned: do annotators choose the same keywords when presented with the same text? Moreover, knowing the difficulty of the task for human annotators will give us an indication of the level of performance we may expect from automatic keyword assignment. To determine the agreement between annotators we asked ten annotators to classify the vocabulary of five folktales from different genres. Frog[3] (van den Bosch et al., 2007) was used to extract the vocabulary of lemmas. After carefully reading a folktale, the annotator classified the alphabetically sorted list of lemmas extracted from the text. Each lemma was classified as either: 1) not a relevant keyword – should not be assigned to this document (*non*); 2) a relevant keyword – should be assigned (*rel*); 3) a *highly* relevant keyword – should definitely be assigned (*hrel*). The three levels of relevance were used to see whether annotators have a preference for certain keywords. The pairwise agreement between annotators was measured using Cohen's kappa. Each document was judged twice, totaling a set of 25 documents. Most of the annotators were familiar with the folktale database and its keywords; two were active contributors to the database and thus had previous experience in assigning keywords to folktales.

On average, the annotators judged 79% of the vocabulary as non-relevant as keywords. 9% and 12% of the vocabulary was judged as relevant and highly relevant respectively, but there was a large variation in these percentages: some annotators assigned more highly relevant keywords, others assigned more relevant keywords.

[3] http://ilk.uvt.nl/frog/

| | Cohen's Kappa | | | |
|---|---|---|---|---|
| Classes | Average | $\sigma$ | Min | Max |
| non, rel, hrel | 0.48 | 0.14 | 0.16 | 0.77 |
| non, rel + hrel | 0.62 | 0.16 | 0.25 | 0.92 |
| non + rel, hrel | 0.47 | 0.20 | 0.0 | 0.84 |

Table 2: Classification agreement between annotators. Non: non-relevant, rel: relevant, hrel: highly relevant.

The two experienced annotators showed a consistently higher average agreement in comparison to the other annotators (0.56 and 0.50 for non, rel, hrel; 0.7 and 0.64 for non, rel + hrel; 0.56 and 0.50 for non + rel, hrel). Moreover, they assigned more (relevant and highly relevant) keywords to the documents on average.

Table 2 summarizes the agreement measured between annotators. The first row indicates the agreement when considering agreement over all three classes; the second row indicates the agreement when treating relevant and highly relevant keywords as the same class; the last row shows the agreement in indicating the same highly relevant keywords. The numbers indicate moderate agreement between annotators over all three classes and when considering the choice of highly relevant keywords. Annotators show substantial agreement on deciding between non-relevant and relevant keywords. Table 3 shows the agreement between annotators on keywords with different parts of speech (CGN[4] tagset). Most disagreements are on nouns, adjectives and verbs. Verbs and adjectives show few agreements on relevant and highly relevant keywords. In contrast, on 20% of the nouns annotators agree on their relevance. It appears that the annotators do not agree whether adjectives and verbs should be used as keywords at all. We can give three other reasons why annotators did not agree. First, for longer stories annotators were presented with long lists of candidate keywords. Sometimes relevant keywords might have been simply overlooked. Second, it turned out that some annotators selected some keywords in favor to other keywords (for instance a hyponym rather than a hypernym), where others simply annotated both as relevant. Third, the disagreement can be explained by lack of detailed instructions. The annotators were not told how many (highly) relevant keywords to select or what criteria should be met by the keywords. Such instructions are not available to current annotators of the collection either.

We conclude that annotators typically agree on the keywords from a text, but have a varying notion of highly relevant keywords. The average keywords-based representation strongly condenses the documents vocabulary: a document can be represented by a fifth (21%) of its vocabulary[5]. This value can be used as a cut-off point for methods ranking extracted keywords, discussed hereafter.

## 6 Automatically Extracting Keywords

In the last part of this paper we look into automatically extracting keywords. We compare a learning to rank classifier to baselines based on frequency and reuse in their ability to reproduce keywords found in manually classified folktales.

In all cases we use the same method for extracting keyword candidates. Since most of the manual keywords are single words (90% of the used keyword types in the collection), we simply extract single words as keyword candidates. We use Frog for tokenization and part of speech tagging. Stop words are not removed.

### 6.1 Baseline Systems

We use a basic unsupervised baseline for keyword extraction: the words are ranked according to descending TF-IDF. We refer to this system as *TF-IDF*. TF, *term frequency*, and IDF, *inverse document frequency*, are indicators of the term's local and global importance and are frequently used in information retrieval to indicate the relative importance of a word (Baeza-Yates and Ribeiro-Neto, 2011).

Note that a word appearing once in the collection has the highest IDF score. This would imply that the most uncommon words are also the most important resulting in a bias towards spelling errors, proper names, and other uncommon words. Hence, our second baseline takes into account whether a keyword has been used before in a training set. Again, the candidates are ranked by descending TF-IDF, but now keywords appearing in the training collection are ranked above the keywords not appearing in the collection. We refer to this baseline as *TF-IDF-T*.

[4] Corpus Gesproken Nederlands (Spoken Dutch Corpus), `http://lands.let.kun.nl/cgn/ehome.htm`

[5] Based on the figures that on average 9% of the vocabulary is judged as relevant and 12% as highly relevant

| | Part of speech<br>Number of words | Adjective<br>272 | Adverb<br>257 | Noun<br>646 | Special<br>131 | Numeral<br>53 | Prep.<br>268 | Verb<br>664 |
|---|---|---|---|---|---|---|---|---|
| Agreement | non | 70% | 96% | 40% | 95% | 81% | 99% | 73% |
| | rel | 4% | 0% | 6% | 0% | 0% | 0% | 3% |
| | hrel | 1% | 0% | 14% | 2% | 2% | 0% | 4% |
| Disagreement | non ↔ rel | 15% | 2% | 17% | 2% | 11% | 0% | 12% |
| | non ↔ hrel | 5% | 1% | 8% | 2% | 4% | 1% | 5% |
| | rel ↔ hrel | 5% | 0% | 15% | 0% | 2% | 0% | 4% |

Table 3: Agreement and disagreement of annotators on keywords with different parts of speech. Values are column-wise percentages. Tags with full agreement are not shown.

### 6.2 Learning to Rank Keywords

Following Jiang et al. (2009) we apply a learning to rank technique to rank the list of extracted keywords. We train an SVM to classify the relative ordering of pairs of keywords. Words corresponding to manual keywords should be ranked higher than other words appearing in the document. We use SVM-rank to train a linear ranking SVM (Joachims, 2006). We use the following features.

#### 6.2.1 Word Context

We use the following word context features:
**starts uppercase**: indicates whether the token starts with an uppercase letter (1) or not (0). Since proper names are not used as keywords in the folktale database, this feature is expected to be a negative indicator of a word being a keyword.
**contains space**: indicates whether the token contains a space (Frog extracts some Dutch multiword phrases as a single token). Tokens with spaces are not very common.
**is number**: indicates whether the token consists of only digits. Numbers are expected not to be a keyword.
**contains letters**: indicates whether the token contains at least a single letter. Keywords are expected to contain letters.
**all capital letters**: indicates whether the token consists of only capital letters. Words with only capital letters are not expected to be keywords.
**single letter**: indicates whether the token consists of only one letter. One letter keywords are very uncommon.
**contains punctuation**: indicates whether the token contains punctuation such as apostrophes. Keywords are expected not to contain punctuation.
**part of speech**: indicates the part of speech of the token (each tag is a binary feature). Nouns are expected to be a positive indicator of keywords (Jiang et al., 2009).

#### 6.2.2 Document Context

We use the following document context features:
**tf**: the term frequency indicates the number of appearances of the word divided by the total number of tokens in the document.
**first offset**: indicates the offset of the word's first appearance in the document, normalized by the number of tokens in the document (following Zhang et al. (2008)). Important (key)words are expected to be mentioned early.
**first sentence offset**: indicates the offset of the first sentence in which the token appears, normalized by the number of sentences in the document.
**sentence importance**: indicates the maximum importance of a sentence in which the word appears, as measured by the SumBasic score (Nenkova and Vanderwende, 2005). SumBasic determines the relative importance of sentences solely on word probability distributions in the text.
**dispersion**: indicates the dispersion or scattering of the word in the document. Words which are highly dispersed are expected to be more important. The $DP_{norm}$ is used as a dispersion measure, proposed in Gries (2008).

#### 6.2.3 Collection Context

We use the following features from the collection/training context:
**idf**: the inverse document frequency indicates the collection importance of the word based on frequency: frequent terms in the collection are less important than rare terms in the collection.
**tf.idf**: combines the *tf* and idf features by multiplying them. It indicates a trade-off between local and global word importance.
**is training keyword**: indicates whether the word is used in the training collection as a keyword.
**assignment ratio**: indicates the percentage of documents in which the term is present in the text and in which it is also assigned as a keyword.

### 6.3 Evaluation Method

We evaluate the ranking methods on their ability to reproduce the manual assignment of keywords. Ideally the ranking methods rank these manual keywords highest. We measure the effectiveness of ranking in terms of (mean) average precision (MAP), precision at rank 5 (P@5) and precision at rank R (P@R), similar to Jiang et al. (2009). Note that we use *all* the manually assigned keywords as a ground truth, including words which do not occur in the text itself. This lowers the highest achievable performance, but it will give a better idea of the performance for the real task.

We perform a 10-fold stratified cross-validation with a set of 10,900 documents from the Dutch Folktale Database, all written in modern Dutch.

### 6.4 Results

Table 4 lists the performance of the three tested systems. The *TF-IDF* system performs worst, and is significantly outperformed by the *TF-IDF-T* system, which in turn is significantly outperformed by the *rank-SVM* system. On average, rank-SVM returns 3 relevant keywords in its top 5. The reported mean average precision values are affected by manual keywords which are not present in the text itself. To put these numbers in perspective: if we would put the manual keywords which are in the text in an optimal ranking, i.e. return these keywords first, we would achieve an upper bound mean average precision of 0.5675. Taking into account the likelihood that some of the highly ranked false positives are relevant after all (the annotator might have missed a relevant keyword) and considering the difficulty of the task (given the variation in agreement between manual annotators), we argue that the rank-SVM performs quite well.

Jiang et al. (2009) reported MAPs of 0.288 and 0.503 on the ranking of extracted keyphrases from scholarly articles and tags from websites respectively. Based on these numbers, we could argue that assigning keywords to folktales is harder than reproducing the tags of websites, and slightly easier than reproducing keyphrases from scientific articles. Because of differences in the experimental setup (e.g. size of the training set, features and system used), it is difficult to make strong claims on the difficulty of the task.

| System | MAP | P@5 | P@R |
|---|---|---|---|
| TF-IDF | 0.260 | 0.394 | 0.317 |
| TF-IDF-T | 0.336 | 0.541 | 0.384 |
| rank-SVM | **0.399** | **0.631** | **0.453** |

Table 4: Keyword extraction effectiveness. The differences between systems are statistically significant (paired t-test, $p < 0.001$)

| | | Change in | |
|---|---|---|---|
| Feature | MAP | P@5 | P@R |
| **assignment ratio** | -0.036 | -0.056 | -0.038 |
| **is training keyword** | 0.006 | 0.002 | 0.005 |
| **tf.idf** | -0.004 | -0.010 | -0.002 |
| **part of speech** | -0.003 | -0.007 | 0.000 |
| **dispersion** | -0.001 | -0.001 | 0.000 |
| **idf** | 0.001 | 0.002 | 0.000 |
| **starts uppercase** | 0.000 | 0.000 | -0.001 |
| **first offset** | 0.000 | 0.000 | 0.000 |
| **tf** | 0.000 | 0.000 | 0.000 |
| **contains space** | 0.000 | 0.000 | 0.000 |
| **is number** | 0.000 | 0.000 | 0.000 |
| **all capital letters** | 0.000 | 0.000 | 0.000 |
| **contains punctuation** | 0.000 | 0.000 | 0.000 |
| **contains letters** | 0.000 | 0.000 | 0.000 |
| **sentence importance** | 0.000 | 0.000 | 0.000 |
| **first sentence offset** | 0.000 | 0.000 | 0.000 |
| **single letter** | 0.000 | 0.000 | 0.000 |

Table 5: Differences in performance when leaving out features. The features are ordered by descending difference in MAP.

### 6.5 Feature Ablation

To determine the added value of the individual features we carried out an ablation study. Table 5 lists the changes in performance when leaving out a particular feature (or group of features in case of part of speech). It turns out that many features can be left out without hurting the performance. All the features testing simple word characteristics (such as single letter) do not, or only marginally influence the results. Also taking into account the importance of sentences (sentence importance), or the first appearance of a word (first offset and first sentence offset) does not contribute to the results.

| System | MAP | P@5 | P@R |
|---|---|---|---|
| rank-SVM | 0.399 | 0.631 | 0.453 |
| minimum set | **0.405** | **0.631** | **0.459** |

Table 6: Results using the full set of features and the minimum set of features (assignment ratio, tf.idf, part of speech and dispersion). Differences between systems are statistically significant (t-test, $p < 0.001$).

| Genre (# stories) | MAP | P@5 | P@R |
|---|---|---|---|
| Trad. legend (3783) | **0.439** | **0.662** | **0.494** |
| Joke (2793) | **0.353** | **0.599** | **0.405** |
| Urban legend (1729) | 0.398 | **0.653** | 0.459 |
| Riddle (1067) | 0.391 | **0.573** | **0.415** |
| Fairy tale (558) | 0.404 | **0.670** | **0.477** |
| Pers. narrative (514) | **0.376** | **0.593** | 0.437 |
| Legend (221) | 0.409 | 0.622 | 0.478 |
| None (122) | 0.366 | 0.602 | 0.421 |
| Other (113) | 0.405 | 0.648 | 0.472 |
| *All* (10900) | 0.399 | 0.631 | 0.453 |

Table 7: SVM performance split according to story genre. Values in bold are significantly different from the results on the other genres (independent t-test, p-value $< 0.01$)

These observations suggest that almost identical results can be obtained using only the features assignment ratio, tf.idf, part of speech and dispersion. The results reported in Table 6 confirm this (we do note that these results were obtained by optimizing on the test set).

### 6.6 Performance on Folktale Genres

The folktale database contains stories from different folktale genres, varying from legends to fairy tales and jokes. Table 7 lists the performance measures per story genre. Values in bold indicate significant differences with the stories from the other genres combined. The performance on traditional legends turns out to be significantly better than other genres: this could be explained by the fact that on average these stories are longer and therefore contain more keywords. Similarly, the decrease can be explained for jokes, which are much shorter on average. Another explanation could be that more abstract keywords are used to indicate the type of joke. Interestingly, the riddles, which are even shorter than jokes, do not perform significantly worse than the other genres. Personal narratives also underperformed in comparison to the other genres. We cannot readily explain this, but we suspect it may have something to do with the fact that personal narratives are more varied in content and contain more proper names.

## 7 Discussion and Conclusion

In this work we analyzed keywords in the context of the Dutch Folktale Database. In this database, on average 15 keywords have been assigned to a story, many of which are single keywords which appear literally or almost literally in the text itself. Keyword annotators show moderate to substantial agreement in extracting the same keywords for a story. We showed that a learning to rank method using features based on assignment ratio, tf.idf, part of speech and dispersion can be effectively used to extract and rank keyword candidates. We believe that this system can be used to suggest highly relevant keyword candidates to human annotators to speed up the archiving process.

In our evaluation we aimed to reproduce the manual annotations, but it is unclear whether better performing systems are actually more helpful to the user. In an ad hoc retrieval scenario, in which the user issues a single query and reviews a list of retrieved documents, extracted keywords might be used to boost the early precision of the results. However, a user might not even notice a difference when a different keyword extraction system is used. Moreover, the more abstract keywords which do not appear in the text might be more important for the user experience. In future work we want to get insight in how keywords contribute to the end user experience. Ideally, the evaluation should directly measure how useful the various keywords are for accessing the collection.

In this work we considered only *extracting* keywords from the text we want to annotate. Given the multilingual content of the database this is a limited approach: if the goal of assigning keywords is to obtain a normalized representation of the stories, this approach will require translation of either the source text (before extraction) or the extracted keywords. Even in the monolingual scenario, the extraction of keywords is limited in dealing with differences in style and word use. Writers may use different words or use words in a different way; ideally the representation based on keywords is a normalized representation which closes this semantic gap. In future work we will look into annotation with keywords from multi-lingual thesauri combined with free-text keywords extracted from the text itself. Finally, we want to look into classification of abstract themes and topics.

## Acknowledgments

This research was supported by the Folktales as Classifiable Texts (FACT) project, part of the CATCH programme funded by the Netherlands Organisation for Scientific Research (NWO).

## References


R Baeza-Yates and B. Ribeiro-Neto. 2011. *Modern Information Retrieval*. The Concepts and Technology Behind Search. Addison-Wesley.

M. Bendersky and W.B. Croft. 2008. Discovering key concepts in verbose queries. In *Proceedings of SIGIR 2008*, pages 491–498.

G. Ercan and I. Cicekli. 2007. Using lexical chains for keyword extraction. *Information Processing & Management*, 43(6):1705–1714.

E. Frank, G.W. Paynter, I.H. Witten, C. Gutwin, and C.G. Nevill-Manning. 1999. Domain-specific keyphrase extraction. In *Proceedings of IJCAI-99*, pages 668—673. Morgan Kaufmann Publishers Inc., San Francisco, CA, USA.

Stefan Th. Gries. 2008. Dispersions and adjusted frequencies in corpora. *International Journal of Corpus Linguistics*, 13(4):403–437.

K. Hammouda, D. Matute, and M. Kamel. 2005. Corephrase: Keyphrase extraction for document clustering. *Machine Learning and Data Mining in Pattern Recognition*, pages 265–274.

A. Hulth. 2003. Improved automatic keyword extraction given more linguistic knowledge. In *Proceedings of EMNLP*, volume 10, pages 216–223, Morristown, NJ, USA. Association for Computational Linguistics.

X. Jiang, Y. Hu, and H. Li. 2009. A ranking approach to keyphrase extraction. In *Proceedings of the 32nd international ACM SIGIR conference on Research and development in information retrieval*, pages 756–757. ACM.

T. Joachims. 2006. Training Linear SVMs in Linear Time. In *the 12th ACM SIGKDD international conference*, pages 217–226, New York, NY, USA. ACM.

H. Li. 2011. *Learning to Rank for Information Retrieval and Natural Language Processing*. Synthesis Lectures on Human Language Technology. Morgan & Claypool Publishers.

F. Liu, D. Pennell, F. Liu, and Y. Liu. 2009a. Unsupervised approaches for automatic keyword extraction using meeting transcripts. In *Proceedings of NAACL 2009*, pages 620–628. Association for Computational Linguistics.

Z. Liu, P. Li, Y. Zheng, and M. Sun. 2009b. Clustering to find exemplar terms for keyphrase extraction. In *Proceedings of EMNLP*, pages 257–266. Association for Computational Linguistics.

O Medelyan and Ian H Witten. 2006. Thesaurus based automatic keyphrase indexing. In *JCDL 2006*, pages 296–297. ACM.

R. Mihalcea and P. Tarau. 2004. Textrank: Bringing order into texts. In *Proceedings of EMNLP*, volume 4, pages 404–411. Barcelona, Spain.

A. Nenkova and L. Vanderwende. 2005. The impact of frequency on summarization. *Microsoft Research, Redmond, Washington, Tech. Rep. MSR-TR-2005-101*.

S. Osinski and D. Weiss. 2005. A concept-driven algorithm for clustering search results. *Intelligent Systems, IEEE*, 20(3):48–54.

Y. Park, R.J. Byrd, and B.K. Boguraev. 2002. Automatic glossary extraction: beyond terminology identification. In *Proceedings of COLING 2002*, pages 1–7. Association for Computational Linguistics.

Christian Plaunt and Barbara A Norgard. 1998. An Association Based Method for Automatic Indexing with a Controlled Vocabulary. *Journal of the American Society for Information Science and Technology*, 49(10):888–902.

S. Rose, D. Engel, N. Cramer, and W. Cowley. 2010. Automatic keyword extraction from individual documents. In Michael W. Berry and Jacob Kogan, editors, *Text Mining: Applications and Theory*, pages 3–20. John Wiley & Sons.

P.D. Turney. 2000. Learning algorithms for keyphrase extraction. *Information Retrieval*, 2(4):303–336.

A. van den Bosch, G.J. Busser, W. Daelemans, and S Canisius. 2007. An efficient memory-based morphosyntactic tagger and parser for Dutch. In F. van Eynde, P. Dirix, I. Schuurman, and V. Vandeghinste, editors, *Selected Papers of the 17th Computational Linguistics in the Netherlands Meeting*, pages 99–114, Leuven, Belgium.

S. Xu, S. Yang, and F.C.M. Lau. 2010. Keyword extraction and headline generation using novel word features. *Proceedings of the Twenty-Fourth AAAI Conference on Artificial Intelligence (AAAI-10)*.

W. Yih, J. Goodman, and V.R. Carvalho. 2006. Finding advertising keywords on web pages. In *Proceedings of the 15th international conference on World Wide Web*, pages 213–222. ACM.

K. Zhang, H. Xu, J. Tang, and J. Li. 2006. Keyword extraction using support vector machine. *Advances in Web-Age Information Management*, pages 85–96.

C. Zhang, H. Wang, Y. Liu, D. Wu, Y. Liao, and B. Wang. 2008. Automatic keyword extraction from documents using conditional random fields. *Journal of Computational Information Systems*, 4(3):1169–1180.

# Towards Creating Precision Grammars from Interlinear Glossed Text: Inferring Large-Scale Typological Properties

**Emily M. Bender Michael Wayne Goodman Joshua Crowgey Fei Xia**
Department of Linguistics
University of Washington
Seattle WA 98195-4340
{ebender,goodmami,jcrowgey,fxia}@uw.edu

**Abstract**

We propose to bring together two kinds of linguistic resources—interlinear glossed text (IGT) and a language-independent precision grammar resource—to automatically create precision grammars in the context of language documentation. This paper takes the first steps in that direction by extracting major-constituent word order and case system properties from IGT for a diverse sample of languages.

## 1 Introduction

Hale et al. (1992) predicted that more than 90% of the world's approximately 7,000 languages will become extinct by the year 2100. This is a crisis not only for the field of linguistics—on track to lose the majority of its primary data—but also a crisis for the social sciences more broadly as languages are a key piece of cultural heritage. The field of linguistics has responded with increased efforts to document endangered languages. Language documentation not only captures key linguistic data (both primary data and analytical facts) but also supports language revitalization efforts. It must include both primary data collection (as in Abney and Bird's (2010) universal corpus) and analytical work elucidating the linguistic structures of each language. As such, the outputs of documentary linguistics are dictionaries, descriptive (prose) grammars as well as transcribed and translated texts (Woodbury, 2003).

Traditionally, these outputs were printed artifacts, but the field of documentary linguistics has increasingly realized the benefits of producing digital artifacts as well (Nordhoff and Poggeman, 2012). Bender et al. (2012a) argue that the documentary value of electronic descriptive grammars can be significantly enhanced by pairing them with implemented (machine-readable) precision grammars and grammar-derived treebanks. However, the creation of such precision grammars is time consuming, and the cost of developing them must be brought down if they are to be effectively integrated into language documentation projects.

In this work, we are interested in leveraging existing linguistic resources of two distinct types in order to facilitate the development of precision grammars for language documentation. The first type of linguistic resource is collections of interlinear glossed text (IGT), a typical format for displaying linguistic examples. A sample of IGT from Shona is shown in (1).

| | | | |
|---|---|---|---|
| (1) | Ndakanga | ndakatenga | muchero |
| | ndi-aka-nga | ndi-aka-teng-a | mu-chero |
| | SBJ.1SG-RP-AUX | SBJ.1SG-RP-buy-FV | CL3-fruit |
| | 'I had bought fruit.' [sna] (Toews, 2009:34) | | |

The annotations in IGT result from deep linguistic analysis and represent much effort on the part of field linguists. These rich annotations include the segmentation of the source line into morphemes, the glossing of those individual morphemes, and the translation into a language of broader communication. The IGT format was developed to compactly display this information to other linguists. Here, we propose to repurpose such data in the automatic development of further resources.

The second resource we will be working with is the LinGO Grammar Matrix (Bender et al., 2002; 2010), an open source repository of implemented linguistic analyses. The Grammar Matrix pairs a core grammar, shared across all grammars it creates, with a series of libraries of analyses of cross-linguistically variable phenomena. Users access the system through a web-based questionnaire which elicits linguistic descriptions of languages and then outputs working HPSG (Pollard and Sag, 1994) grammar fragments compatible with DELPH-IN (`www.delph-in.net`) tools based on those descriptions. For present purposes, this system can be viewed as a function which maps simple descriptions of languages to precision grammar fragments. These fragments are relatively modest, yet they relate linguistic strings to semantic representations (and vice versa) and are ready to be built out to broad coverage.

Thus we ask whether the information encoded by documentary linguists in IGT can be leveraged to answer the Grammar Matrix's questionnaire and create a precision grammar fragment automatically. The information required by the Grammar Matrix questionnaire concerns five different aspects of linguistic systems: (i) constituent ordering (including the presence/absence of constituent types), (ii) morphosyntactic systems, (iii) morphosyntactic features, (iv) lexical types and their instances and (v) morphological rules. In this initial work, we target examples of types (i) and (ii): the major constituent word order and the general type of case system in a language. The Grammar Matrix and other related work are described in further in §2. In §3 we present our test data and experimental set-up. §§4–5 describe our methodology and results for the two tasks, respectively, with further discussion and outlook in §§6–7.

## 2 Background and Related Work

### 2.1 The Grammar Matrix

The Grammar Matrix produces precision grammars on the basis of description of languages that include both high-level typological information and more specific detail. Among the former are aspects (i)–(iii) listed in §1. The third of these (morphosyntactic features) concerns the type and range of grammaticized information that a language marks in its morphology and/or syntax. This includes person/number systems (e.g., is there an inclusive/exclusive distinction in non-singular first person forms?), the range of aspectual distinctions a language marks, and the range of cases (if any) in a language, inter alia. The answers to these questions in turn cause the system to provide relevant features that the user can reference in providing the more specific information elicited by the questionnaire ((iv) and (v) above), viz., the definition of both lexical types (e.g., first person dual exclusive pronouns) and morphological rules (e.g., nominative case marking on nouns).

The information input by the user to the Grammar Matrix questionnaire is stored in a file called a 'choices file'. The choices file is used both in the dynamic definition of the html pages (so that the features available for lexical definitions depend on earlier choices) and as the input to the customization script that actually produces the grammar fragments to spec. The customization system distinguishes between choices files which are complete and consistent (and can be used to create working grammar fragments) and those which do not yet have answers to required questions or give answers which are inconsistent according to the underlying grammatical theory. The ultimate goal of the present project is to be able to automatically create complete and consistent choices files on the basis of IGT, and in fact to create complete and consistent choices files which take maximal advantage of the analyses stored in the Grammar Matrix customization system, answering not only the minimal set of questions required but in fact all which are relevant and possible to answer based on the information in the IGT.

Creating such complete and consistent choices files is a long-term project, with different approches required for the different types of questions outlined in §1. Bender et al. (2012b) take some initial steps towards answering the questions which define lexical rules. We envision answering the questions regarding morphosyntactic features through an analysis of the grams that appear on the gloss line, with reference to the GOLD ontology (Farrar and Langendoen, 2003). The implementation of such systems in such a way that they are robust to potentially noisy data will undoubtedly be non-trivial. The contribution of this paper is the development of systems to handle one example each of the questions of types (i) and (ii), namely detecting major constituent word order and the underlying case system. For the first, we build directly on the work of Lewis and Xia (2008) (see §2.2). Our experiment can be viewed as an attempt to reproduce their results in the context of the specific view of word order possibilities developed in the Grammar Matrix. The second question (that of case systems) is in some ways more subtle, requiring not only analysis of IGT instances in isolation and aggregation of the results, but also identification of particular kinds of IGT instances and comparison across them.

### 2.2 RiPLes

The RiPLes project has two intertwined goals. The first goal is to create a framework that allows the rapid development of resources for resource-poor languages (RPLs), which is accomplished by

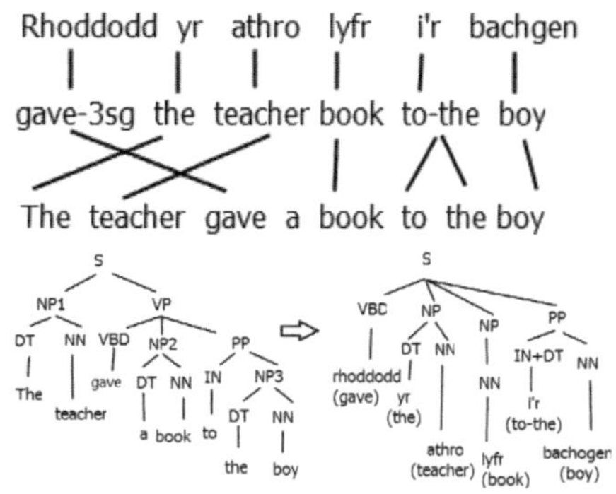


Figure 1: Welsh IGT with alignment and projected syntactic structure

bootstrapping NLP tools with initial seeds created by projecting syntactic information from resource-rich languages to RPLs through IGT. Projecting syntactic structures has two steps. First, the words in the language line and the translation line are aligned via the gloss line. Second, the translation line is parsed by a parser for the resource-rich language and the parse tree is then projected to the language line using word alignment and some heuristics as illustrated in Figure 1 (adapted from Xia and Lewis (2009)).[1] Previous work has applied these projected trees to enhance the performance of statistical parsers (Georgi et al., 2012). Though the projected trees are noisy, they contain enough information for those tasks.

The second goal of RiPLes is to use the automatically created resources to perform cross-lingual study on a large number of languages to discover linguistic knowledge. For instance, Lewis and Xia (2008) showed that IGT data enriched with the projected syntactic structure could be used to determine the word order property of a language with a high accuracy (see §4). Naseem et al. (2012) use this type of information (in their case, drawn from the WALS database (Haspelmath et al., 2008)) to improve multilingual dependency parsing. Here, we build on this aspect of RiPLes and begin to extend it towards the wider range of linguistic phenomena and more detailed classification within phenomena required by the Grammar Matrix questionnaire.

### 2.3 Other Related Work

Our work is also situated with respect to attempts to automatically characterize typological properties of languages, including Daumé III and Campbell's (2007) Bayesian approach to discovering typological implications and Georgi et al.'s (2010) work on predicting (unknown) typological properties by clustering languages based on known properties. Both projects use the typological database WALS (Haspelmath et al., 2008), which has information about 192 different typological properties and about 2,678 different languages (though the matrix is very sparse). This approach is complementary to ours, and it remains an interesting question whether our results could be improved by bringing in information about other typological properties of the language (either extracted from the IGT or looked up in a typological database).

Another strand of related work concerns the collection and curation of IGT, including the ODIN project (Lewis, 2006; Xia and Lewis, 2008), which harvests IGT from linguistics publications available over the web and TypeCraft (Beermann and Mihaylov, 2009), which facilitates the collaborative development of IGT annotations. TerraLing/SSWL[2] (Syntactic Structures of the World's Languages) has begun a database which combines both typological properties and IGT illustrating those properties, contributed by linguists.

Finally, Beerman and Hellan (2011) represents another approach to inducing grammars from IGT, by bringing the hand-built linguistic knowledge sources closer together: On the one hand, their cross-linguistic grammar resource (TypeGram) includes a mechanism for mapping from strings specifying verb valence and valence-altering lexical rules to sets of grammar constraints. On the other hand, their IGT authoring environment (TypeCraft) provides support for annotating examples with those strings. The approach advocated here attempts to bridge the gap between IGT and grammar specification algorithmically, instead.

## 3 Development and Test Data

Our long-term goal is to produce working grammar fragments from IGT produced in documentary linguistics projects. However, in order to evaluate the performance of approaches to answering the high-level questions in the Grammar Matrix questionnaire, we need both IGT and gold-standard answers for a reasonably-sized sample of languages. We have constructed development and test data for this purpose on the basis of work done

[1]The details of the algorithm and experimental results were reported in (Xia and Lewis, 2007).

[2]`http://sswl.railsplayground.net/`, accessed 4/25/13

| Sets of languages | DEV1 (n=10) | DEV2 (n=10) | TEST (n=11) |
|---|---|---|---|
| Range of testsuite sizes | 16–359 | 11–229 | 48–216 |
| Median testsuite size | 91 | 87 | 76 |
| Language families | Indo-European (4), Niger-Congo (2), Afro-Asiatic, Japanese, Nadahup, Sino-Tibetan | Indo-European (3), Dravidian (2), Algic, Creole, Niger-Congo, Quechuan, Salishan | Indo-European (2), Afro-Asiatic, Austro-Asiatic, Austronesian, Arauan, Carib, Karvelian, N. Caucasian, Tai-Kadai, Isolate |

Table 1: Language families and testsuites sizes (in number of grammatical examples)

by students in a class that uses the Grammar Matrix (Bender, 2007). In this class, students work with descriptive resources for languages they are typically not familiar with to create testsuites (curated collections of grammatical and ungrammatical examples) and Grammar Matrix choices files. Later on in the class, the students extend the grammar fragments output by the customization system to handle a broader fragment of the language. Accordingly, the testsuites cover phenomena which go beyond the customization system.

Testsuites for grammars, especially in their early stages of development, require examples that are simple (isolating the phenomena illustrated by the examples to the extent possible), built out of a small vocabulary, and include both grammatical and ungrammatical examples (Lehmann et al., 1996). The examples included in descriptive resources often don't fit these requirements exactly. As a result, the data we are working with include examples invented by the students on the basis of the descriptive statements in their resources.[3]

In total, we have testsuites and associated choices files for 31 languages, spanning 17 language families (plus one creole and one language isolate). The most well-represented family is Indo-European, with nine languages. We used 20 languages, in two dev sets, for algorithm development (including manual error analysis), and saved 11 languages as a held-out test set to verify the generalizability of our approach. Table 1 lists the language families and the range of testsuite sizes for each of these sets of languages.

## 4 Inferring Word Order

Lewis and Xia (2008) show how IGT from ODIN (Lewis, 2006) can be used to determine, with high accuracy, the word order properties of a language. They identify 14 typological parameters related to word order for which WALS (Haspelmath et al., 2008) or other typological resources provide information. The parameter most closely relevant to the present work is Order of Words in a Sentence (Dryer, 2011). For this parameter, Lewis and Xia tested their method in 97 languages and found that their system had 99% accuracy provided the IGT collections had at least 40 instances per language.

The Grammar Matrix's word order questions differ somewhat from the typological classification that Lewis and Xia (2008) were using. Answering the Grammar Matrix questionnaire amounts to more than making a descriptive statement about a language. The Grammar Matrix customization system translates collections of such descriptive statements into working grammar fragments. In the case of word order, this most directly effects the number and nature of phrase structure rules included in the output grammar, but can also interact with other aspects of the grammar (e.g., the treatment of argument optionality). More broadly, specifying the word order system of a grammar determines both grammaticality (accepting some strings, ruling out others) and, for the fixed word orders at least, aspects of the mapping of syntactic to semantic arguments.

Lewis and Xia (2008), like Dryer (2011), gave the six fixed orders of S, O and V plus "no dominant order". In contrast, the Grammar Matrix distinguishes Free (pragmatically constrained), V-final, V-initial, and V2 orders, in addition to the six fixed orders. It is important to note that the relationship between the word order type of a language and the actual orders attested in sentences can be somewhat indirect. For a fixed word order language, we would expect the order declared as its type to be the most common in running text, but not the only type available. English, for example, is an SVO language, but several constructions allow for other orders, including subject-auxiliary inversion, so-called topicalization, and others:

(2) Did Kim leave?

(3) The book, Kim forgot.

In a language with more word order flexibility in general, there may still be a preferred word order

[3]Such examples are flagged in the testsuites' meta-data.

which is the most common due to pragmatic or other constraints. Users of the Grammar Matrix are advised to choose one of the fixed word orders if the deviations from that order can generally be accounted for by specific syntactic constructions, and a freer word order otherwise.

The relationship between the correct word order choice for the Grammar Matrix customization system and the distribution of actual token word orders in our development and test data is affected by another factor, related to Lewis and Xia's 'IGT bias' which we dub 'testsuite bias'. The collections of IGT we are using were constructed as testsuites for grammar engineering projects and thus comprise examples selected or constructed to illustrate specific grammatical properties in a testing regime where one example is enough to represent each sentence type of interest. Therefore, they do not represent a natural distribution of word order types. For example, the testsuite authors may show the full range of possible word orders in the word order section of the testsuite and then default to one particular choice for other portions (those illustrating e.g., case systems or negation).

### 4.1 Methodology

Our first stpes mirror the RiPLes approach, parsing parse the English translation of each sentence and projecting the parsed structure onto the source language line. Functional tags, such as SBJ and OBJ, are added to the NP nodes on the English side based on our knowledge of English word order and then carried over to the source language side during the projection of parse trees. The trees are then searched for any of ten patterns: SOV, SVO, OSV, OVS, VSO, VOS, SV, VS, OV, and VO. The six ternary patterns match when both verbal arguments are present in the same clause. The four binary patterns are for intransitive sentences or those with dropped arguments. These ten patterns make up the *observed word orders*.

Given our relatively limited data set (each language is one data point), we present an initial approach to determining *underlying word order* based on heuristics informed by general linguistic knowledge. We compare the distribution of observed word orders to distributions we expect to see for canonical examples of underlying word orders. We accomplish this by first deconstructing the ternary observed-word-orders into binary patterns (the four above plus SO and OS). This gives us three axes: one for the tendency to exhibit VS or SV order, another for VO or OV order, and another for OS or SO order. By counting the observed word orders in the IGT examples, we can place the language in this three-dimensional space. Figure 4.1 depicts this space with the positions of canonical word orders.[4] The canonical word order positions are those found under homogeneous observations. For example, the canonical position for SOV order is when 100% of the sentences exhibit SO, OV, and SV orders; and the canonical position for Free word order is when each observed order occurs with equal frequency to its opposite order (on the same axis; e.g. VO and OV). We select the underlying word order by finding which canonical word order position has the shortest Euclidean distance to the observed word order position.

When a language is selected as Free word order, we employ a secondary heuristic to decide if it is actually V2 word order. The V2 order cannot be easily recognized only with the binary word orders, so it is not given a unique point in the three-dimensional space. Rather, we try to recognize it by comparing the ternary orders. A Free-order language is reclassified as V2 if SVO and OVS occur more frequently than SOV and OSV.[5]

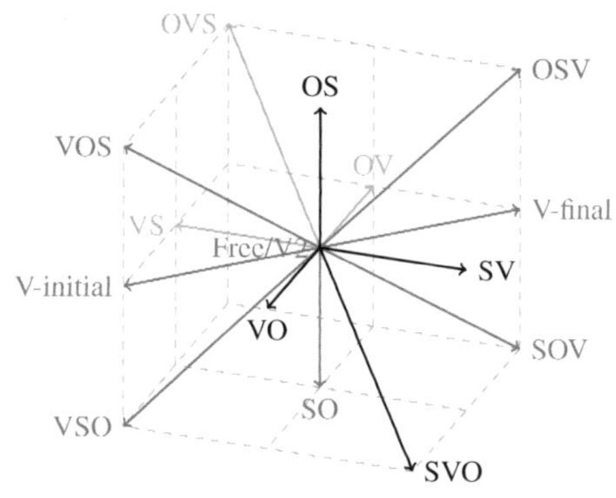


Figure 2: Three axes of basic word order and the positions of canonical word orders.

### 4.2 Results

Table 2 shows the results we obtained for our dev and test sets. For comparison, we use a most-

[4]Of the eight vertices of this cube, six represent canonical word orders the other two impossible combinations: The vertex for (SV, VO, OS) (e.g.) has S both before and after O.

[5]The VOS and VSO patterns are excluded from this comparison, since they can go either way—there may be unaligned constituents (i.e. not a S, O, or V) before the verb which are ignored by our system.

frequent-type baseline, selecting SOV for all languages, based on Dryer's (2011) survey. We get high accuracy for DEV1, low accuracy for DEV2, and moderate accuracy for TEST, but all are significantly higher than the baseline.

| Dataset | Inferred WO | Baseline |
|---|---|---|
| DEV1 | 0.900 | 0.200 |
| DEV2 | 0.500 | 0.100 |
| TEST | 0.727 | 0.091 |

Table 2: Accuracy of word-order inference

Hand analysis of the errors in the dev sets show that some languages fall victim to the testsuite bias, such as Russian, Quechua, and Tamil. All of these languages have Free word order, but our system infers SVO for Russian and SOV for Quechua and Tamil, because the authors of the testsuites used one order significantly more than the others. Similarly, the Free word order language Nishnaabemwin is inferred as V2 because there are more SVO and OVS patterns given than others. We also see errors due to misalignment from RiPLes' syntactic projection. The VSO language Welsh is inferred as SVO because the near-ubiquitous sentence-initial auxiliary doesn't align to the main verb of the English translation.

## 5 Inferring Case Systems

Case refers to linguistic phenomena in which the form of a noun phrase (NP) varies depending on the function of the NP in a sentence (Blake, 2001). The Grammar Matrix's case library (Drellishak, 2009) focuses on case marking of core arguments of verbs. Specifying a grammar for case involves both choosing the high-level case system to be modeled as well as associating verb types with case frames and defining the lexical items or lexical rules which mark the case on the NPs. Here, we focus on the high-level case system question as it is logically prior, and in some ways more interesting than the lexical details: Answering this question requires identifying case frames of verbs in particular examples and then comparing across those examples, as described below.

The high-level case system of a language concerns the alignment of case marking between transitive and intransitive clauses. The three elements in question are the subjects of intransitives (dubbed S), the subjects (or agent-like arguments) of transitives (dubbed A) and the objects (or patient-like arguments) of intransitives

| Case system | Case grams present: NOM ∨ ACC | ERG ∨ ABS |
|---|---|---|
| none | | |
| nom-acc | ✓ | |
| erg-abs | | ✓ |
| split-erg (conditioned on V) | ✓ | ✓ |

Table 3: GRAM case system assignment rules

(O). Among languages which make use of case, the most common alignment type is a nominative-accusative system (Comrie 2011a,b). In this type, S takes the same kind of marking as A.[6] The Grammar Matrix case library provides nine options, including none, nominative-accusative, ergative-absolutive (S marked like O), tripartite (S, A and O all distinct) and several more intricate types. For example, in a language with one type of split case system the alignment is nominative-accusative in non-past tense clauses, but ergative-absolutive in past tense ones.

As with major constituent word order, the constraints implementing a case system in a grammar serve to model both grammaticality and the mapping between syntactic and semantic arguments. Here too, the distribution of tokens may be something other than a pure expression of the case alignment type. Sources of noise in the distribution include: argument optionality (e.g., transitives with one or more covert arguments), argument frames other than simple intransitives or transitives, and quirky case (verbs that use a non-standard case frame for their arguments, such as the German verb *helfen* which selects a dative argument, though the language's general system is nominative-accusative (Drellishak, 2009)).

### 5.1 Methodology

We explore two possible methodologies for inferring case systems, one relatively naïve and one more elaborate, and compare them to a most-frequent-type baseline. Method 1, called GRAM, considers only the gloss line of the IGT and assumes that it complies with the Leipzig Glossing Rules (Bickel et al., 2008). These rules not only prescribe formatting aspects of IGT but also provide a set of licensed 'grams', or tags for grammatical properties that appear in the gloss line. GRAM scans for the grams associated with case, and assigns case systems according to Table 3.

This methodology is simple to implement and

[6] English's residual case system is of this type.

expected to work well given Leipzig-compliant IGT. However, since it does not model the function of case, it is dependent on the IGT authors' choice of gram symbols, and may be confused by either alternative case names (e.g., SBJ and OBJ for nominative and accusative or LOC for ergative in languages where it is homophonous with the locative case) or by other grams which collide with the case name-space (such as NOM for nominalizer). It also only handles four of the nine case systems (albeit the most frequent ones).

Method 2, called SAO, is more theoretically motivated, builds on the RiPLes approach used in inferring word order, and is designed to be robust to idiosyncratic glossing conventions. In this methodology, we first identify the S, A and O arguments by projecting the information from the parse of the English translation (including the function tags) to the source sentence (and its glosses). We discard all items which do not appear to be simple transitive or intransitive clauses with all arguments overt, and then collect all grams for each argument type (from all words within in the NP, including head nouns as well as determiners and adjectives). While there are many grammatical features that can be marked on NPs (such as number, definiteness, honorifics, etc.), the only ones that should correlate strongly with grammatical function are case-marking grams. Furthermore, in any given NP, while case may be multiply marked, we only expect one type of case gram to appear. We thus assume that the most frequent gram for each argument type is a case marker (if there are any) and assign the case system according to the following rules, where $S_g$, $O_g$ and $A_g$ denote the most frequent grams associated with these argument positions, respectively:

- Nominative-accusative: $S_g$=$A_g$, $S_g$≠$O_g$
- Ergative-absolutive: $S_g$=$O_g$, $S_g$≠$A_g$
- No case: $S_g$=$A_g$=$O_g$, or $S_g$≠$A_g$≠$O_g$ and $S_g$, $A_g$, $O_g$ also present on each of the other argument types
- Tripartite: $S_g$≠$A_g$≠$O_g$, and $S_g$, $A_g$, $O_g$ (virtually) absent from the other argument types
- Split-S: $S_g$≠$A_g$≠$O_g$, and $A_g$ and $O_g$ are both present in the list for the S argument type

Here, we're using Split-S to stand in for both Split-S and Fluid-S. These are both systems where some S arguments are marked like A, and some like O. In Split-S, which is taken depends on the verb. In Fluid-S, it depends on the interpretation of the verb. These could be distinguished by looking for intransitive verbs that appear more than once in the data and checking whether their S arguments all have consistently A or O marking.

This system is agnostic as to the spelling of the case grams. By relying on more analysis of the IGT than GRAM, it also introduces new kinds of brittleness. Recognizing the difference between grams being present and (virtually) absent makes the system susceptible to noise.

### 5.2 Results

Table 4 shows the results for the inference of case-marking systems. Currently GRAM performs best, but both methods generally perform better than the baseline. The better performance of GRAM is expected, given the small size and generally Leipzig-compliant glossing of our data sets. In future work, we plan to incorporate data from ODIN, which is likely less consistently annotated but more voluminous, and we expect SAO to be more robust than GRAM to this kind of data.

| Dataset | GRAM | SAO | Baseline |
|---|---|---|---|
| DEV1 | 0.900 | 0.700 | 0.400 |
| DEV2 | 0.900 | 0.500 | 0.500 |
| TEST | 0.545 | 0.545 | 0.455 |

Table 4: Accuracy of case-marking inference

We find that GRAM is sometimes able to do well when RiPLes gives alignment errors. For example, Old Japanese is a NOM-ACC language, but the case-marking grams (associated to postpositions) are not aligned to the NP arguments, so SAO is not able to judge their distribution. On the other hand, SAO prevails when non-standard grams are used, such as the NOM-ACC language Hupdeh, which is annotated with SUBJ and OBJ grams. This complementarity suggests scope for system combination, which we leave to future work.

## 6 Discussion and Future Work

Our initial results are promising, but also show remaining room for improvement. Error analysis suggests two main directions to pursue:

**Overcoming testsuite bias** In both the word order and case system tasks, we see the effect of testsuite bias on our system results. The testsuites for freer word order languages can be artificially dominated by a particular word order that the testsuite author found convenient. Further, the restricted vocabulary used in testsuites, combined with a general preference for animates as subjects, leads to stems and certain grams potentially being misidentified as case markers.

We believe that these aspects of testsuite bias are not typical of our true target input data, viz., the larger collections of IGT created by field projects. On the other hand, there may be other aspects of testsuites which are simplifying the problem and to which our current methods are overfitted. To address these issues, we intend to look to larger datasets in future work, both IGT collections from field projects and IGT from ODIN. For the field projects, we will need to construct choices files. For ODIN, we can search for data from the languages we already have choices files for.

As we move from testsuites to test corpora (e.g., narratives collected in documentary linguistics projects), we expect to find different distributions of word order types. Our current methodology for extracting word order is based on idealized locations in our word order space for each strict word order type. Working with naturally occurring corpora it should be possible to gain a more empirically based understanding of the relationship between underlying word order and sentence type distributions. It will be particularly interesting to see how stable these relationships are across languages with the same underlying word order type but from different language families and/or with differences in other typological characteristics.

**Better handling of unaligned words** The other main source of error is words that remain unaligned in the projected syntactic structure and thus only loosely incorporated into the syntax trees. This includes items like case marking adpositions in Japanese, which are unaligned because there is no corresponding word in English, and auxiliaries in Welsh, which are unaligned when the English translation doesn't happen to use an auxiliary. In the former case, our SAO method for case system extraction doesn't include the case grams in the set of grams for each NP. In the latter, the word order inference system is unable to pick up on the VSO order represented as Aux+S+[VP]. Simply fixing the attachment of the auxiliaries will not be enough in this case, as the word order inference algorithm will need to be extended to handle auxiliaries, but fixing the alignment is the first step. Alignment problems are also the main reason our initial attempts to extract information about the order of determiners and nouns haven't yet been able to beat the most-frequent-type baseline.

Better handling of these unaligned words is a non-trivial task, and will require bringing in sources of knowledge other than the structure of the English translation. The information we have to leverage in this regard comes mainly from the gloss line and from general linguistic/typological knowledge which can be added to the algorithm. That is, there are types of grams which are canonically associated with verbal projections and types of grams canonically associated with nominal projections. When these grams occur on unaligned elements, we can hypothesize that the elements are auxiliaries and case-marking adpositions respectively. Further typological considerations will motivate heuristics for modifying tree structures based on these classifications.

Other directions for future work include extending this methodology to other aspects of grammatical description, including additional high-level systems (e.g., argument optionality), discovering the range of morphosyntactic features active in a language, and describing and populating lexical types (e.g., common nouns with a particular gender). Once we are able to answer enough of the questionnaire that the customization system is able to output a grammar, interesting options for detailed evaluation will become available. In particular, we will be able to parse the IGT (including held-out examples) with the resulting grammar, and then compare the resulting semantic representations to those produced by parsing the English translations with tools that produce comparable semantic representations for English (using the English Resource Grammar (Flickinger, 2000)).

## 7 Conclusions and Future Work

In this paper we have presented an approach to combining two types of linguistic resources—IGT, as produced by documentary linguists and a cross-linguistic grammar resource supporting precision parsing and generation—to create language-specific resources which can help enrich language documentation and support language revitalization efforts. In addition to presenting the broad vision of the project, we have reported initial results in two case studies as a proof-of-concept. Though there is still a ways to go, we find these initial results a promising indication of the approach's ability to assist in the preservation of the key type of cultural heritage that is linguistic systems.

## Acknowledgments

We are grateful to the students in Ling 567 at the University of Washington who created the testsuites and choices files used as development and test data in this work and to the three anonymous reviewers for helpful comments and discussion.

This material is based upon work supported by the National Science Foundation under Grant No. BCS-1160274. Any opinions, findings, and conclusions or recommendations expressed in this material are those of the author(s) and do not necessarily reflect the views of the National Science Foundation.

## References

Steven Abney and Steven Bird. 2010. The human language project: building a universal corpus of the world's languages. In *Proceedings of the 48th Annual Meeting of the Association for Computational Linguistics*, ACL '10, pages 88–97, Stroudsburg, PA, USA. Association for Computational Linguistics.

Dorothee Beerman and Lars Hellan. 2011. Inducing grammar from IGT. In *Proceedings of the 5th Language and Technology Conference: Human Language Technologies as a Challenge for Computer Science and Linguistics (LTC 2011)*.

Dorothee Beermann and Pavel Mihaylov. 2009. TypeCraft: Linguistic data and knowledge sharing, open access and linguistic methodology. Paper presented at the Workshop on Small Tools in Cross-linguistic Research, University of Utrecht. The Netherlands.

Emily M. Bender, Dan Flickinger, and Stephan Oepen. 2002. The grammar matrix: An open-source starter-kit for the rapid development of cross-linguistically consistent broad-coverage precision grammars. In John Carroll, Nelleke Oostdijk, and Richard Sutcliffe, editors, *Proceedings of the Workshop on Grammar Engineering and Evaluation at the 19th International Conference on Computational Linguistics*, pages 8–14, Taipei, Taiwan.

Emily M. Bender, Scott Drellishak, Antske Fokkens, Laurie Poulson, and Safiyyah Saleem. 2010. Grammar customization. *Research on Language & Computation*, pages 1–50. 10.1007/s11168-010-9070-1.

Emily M. Bender, Sumukh Ghodke, Timothy Baldwin, and Rebecca Dridan. 2012a. From database to treebank: Enhancing hypertext grammars with grammar engineering and treebank search. In Sebastian Nordhoff and Karl-Ludwig G. Poggeman, editors, *Electronic Grammaticography*, pages 179–206. University of Hawaii Press, Honolulu.

Emily M. Bender, David Wax, and Michael Wayne Goodman. 2012b. From IGT to precision grammar: French verbal morphology. In *LSA Annual Meeting Extended Abstracts 2012*.

Emily M. Bender. 2007. Combining research and pedagogy in the development of a crosslinguistic grammar resource. In Tracy Holloway King and Emily M. Bender, editors, *Proceedings of the GEAF 2007 Workshop*, Stanford, CA. CSLI Publications.

Balthasar Bickel, Bernard Comrie, and Martin Haspelmath. 2008. The Leipzig glossing rules: Conventions for interlinear morpheme-by-morpheme glosses. Max Planck Institute for Evolutionary Anthropology and Department of Linguistics, University of Leipzig.

Barry J. Blake. 2001. *Case*. Cambridge University Press, Cambridge, second edition.

Bernard Comrie. 2011a. Alignment of case marking of full noun phrases. In Matthew S. Dryer and Martin Haspelmath, editors, *The World Atlas of Language Structures Online*. Max Planck Digital Library, Munich.

Bernard Comrie. 2011b. Alignment of case marking of pronouns. In Matthew S. Dryer and Martin Haspelmath, editors, *The World Atlas of Language Structures Online*. Max Planck Digital Library, Munich.

Hal Daumé III and Lyle Campbell. 2007. A Bayesian model for discovering typological implications. In *Proceedings of the 45th Annual Meeting of the Association of Computational Linguistics*, pages 65–72, Prague, Czech Republic, June. Association for Computational Linguistics.

Scott Drellishak. 2009. *Widespread But Not Universal: Improving the Typological Coverage of the Grammar Matrix*. Ph.D. thesis, University of Washington.

Matthew S. Dryer. 2011. Order of subject, object and verb. In Matthew S. Dryer and Martin Haspelmath, editors, *The World Atlas of Language Structures Online*. Max Planck Digital Library, Munich.

Scott Farrar and Terry Langendoen. 2003. A linguistic ontology for the semantic web. *Glot International*, 7:97–100.

Dan Flickinger. 2000. On building a more efficient grammar by exploiting types. *Natural Language Engineering*, 6 (1) (Special Issue on Efficient Processing with HPSG):15 – 28.

Ryan Georgi, Fei Xia, and William Lewis. 2010. Comparing language similarity across genetic and typologically-based groupings. In *Proceedings of the 23rd International Conference on Computational Linguistics (Coling 2010)*, pages 385–393, Beijing, China, August. Coling 2010 Organizing Committee.

Ryan Georgi, Fei Xia, and William Lewis. 2012. Improving dependency parsing with interlinear glossed text and syntactic projection. In *Proceedings of COLING 2012: Posters*, pages 371–380, Mumbai, India, December.

Ken Hale, Michael Krauss, Lucille J. Watahomigie, Akira Y. Yamamoto, Colette Craig, LaVerne Masayesva Jeanne, and Nora C. England. 1992. Endangered languages. *Language*, 68(1):pp. 1–42.

Martin Haspelmath, Matthew S. Dryer, David Gil, and Bernard Comrie, editors. 2008. *The World Atlas of Language Structures Online*. Max Planck Digital Library, Munich. http://wals.info.

Sabine Lehmann, Stephan Oepen, Sylvie Regnier-Prost, Klaus Netter, Veronika Lux, Judith Klein, Kirsten Falkedal, Frederik Fouvry, Dominique Estival, Eva Dauphin, Hervè Compagnion, Judith Baur, Lorna Balkan, and Doug Arnold. 1996. TSNLP: Test suites for natural language processing. In *Proceedings of the 16th conference on Computational linguistics - Volume 2*, COLING '96, pages 711–716, Stroudsburg, PA, USA. Association for Computational Linguistics.

William D. Lewis and Fei Xia. 2008. Automatically identifying computationally relevant typological features. In *Proceedings of the Third International Joint Conference on Natural Language Processing*, pages 685–690, Hyderabad, India.

William D. Lewis. 2006. ODIN: A model for adapting and enriching legacy infrastructure. In *Proceedings of the e-Humanities Workshop, Held in cooperation with e-Science*, Amsterdam.

Tahira Naseem, Regina Barzilay, and Amir Globerson. 2012. Selective sharing for multilingual dependency parsing. In *Proceedings of the 50th Annual Meeting of the Association for Computational Linguistics (Volume 1: Long Papers)*, pages 629–637, Jeju Island, Korea, July. Association for Computational Linguistics.

Sebastian Nordhoff and Karl-Ludwig G. Poggeman, editors. 2012. *Electronic Grammaticography*. University of Hawaii Press, Honolulu.

Carl Pollard and Ivan A. Sag. 1994. *Head-Driven Phrase Structure Grammar*. Studies in Contemporary Linguistics. The University of Chicago Press and CSLI Publications, Chicago, IL and Stanford, CA.

Carmela Toews. 2009. The expression of tense and aspect in Shona. *Selected Proceedings of the 39th Annual Converence on African Linguistics*, pages 32–41.

Tony Woodbury. 2003. Defining documentary linguistics. *Language documentation and description*, 1(1):35.

Fei Xia and William D. Lewis. 2007. Multilingual structural projection across interlinear text. In *Proc. of the Conference on Human Language Technologies (HLT/NAACL 2007)*, pages 452–459, Rochester, New York.

Fei Xia and William D. Lewis. 2008. Repurposing theoretical linguistic data for tool development and search. In *Proceedings of the Third International Joint Conference on Natural Language Processing*, pages 529–536, Hyderabad, India.

Fei Xia and William Lewis. 2009. Applying NLP technologies to the collection and enrichment of language data on the web to aid linguistic research. In *Proceedings of the EACL 2009 Workshop on Language Technology and Resources for Cultural Heritage, Social Sciences, Humanities, and Education (LaTeCH – SHELT&R 2009)*, pages 51–59, Athens, Greece, March. Association for Computational Linguistics.

# Using Comparable Collections of Historical Texts for Building a Diachronic Dictionary for Spelling Normalization

**Marilisa Amoia**
Saarland University
m.amoia1@mx.uni-saarland.de

**Jose Manuel Martinez**
Saarland University
j.martinez@mx.uni-saarland.de

**Abstract**

In this paper, we argue that comparable collections of historical written resources can help overcoming typical challenges posed by heritage texts enhancing spelling normalization, POS-tagging and subsequent diachronic linguistic analyses. Thus, we present a comparable corpus of historical German recipes and show how such a comparable text collection together with the application of innovative MT inspired strategies allow us (i) to address the word form normalization problem and (ii) to automatically generate a diachronic dictionary of spelling variants. Such a diachronic dictionary can be used both for spelling normalization and for extracting new "translation" (word formation/change) rules for diachronic spelling variants. Moreover, our approach can be applied virtually to any diachronic collection of texts regardless of the time span they represent. A first evaluation shows that our approach compares well with state-of-art approaches.

## 1 Introduction

The study of heritage documents has been one of the regular sources of knowledge in the Humanities, specially in history-related disciplines. The last years have witnessed an increased interest in approaches combining NLP and corpus-based techniques in the Humanities (Piotrowski, 2012) as they can provide new insights and/or a more consistent and reliable account of findings.

Until recently, research efforts have been focused on building diachronic corpora (e.g. Old Bailey Online project (Hitchcock et al., 2012) and its follow-up, the Old Bailey Corpus (Huber, 2007), the Bonn Corpus of Early New High German (Diel et al., 2002) or the GerManC (Scheible et al., 2011b) for German and many others). Such resources are generally annotated with shallow metadata (e.g. year of publication, author, geographical location) for allowing fast retrieval. However, the annotation of richer linguistic and semantic information still poses a series of challenges that have to be overcome, such as (i) the noise introduced by deviant linguistic data (spelling/orthography variation, lack of sentence boundaries, etc.) typical of this kind of material, due to the lack of standardized writing conventions in terms of words and punctuation and hence (ii) the higher error rates obtained when applying standard NLP methods.

Further, standardization of spelling variation in historical texts can be broken down at least into two subproblems:

1. the old word forms often differ from the modern orthography of the same items. Consider, for instance, the diachronic variants of the third person singular of present tense of the verb *werden* in German (which means 'become' as full verb, or is used as auxiliary verb to build the future): wirt, wirdt, wirdet vs wird; (Piotrowski, 2012) and

2. the denomination of certain objects may result completely different from that used in the modern language due to historical reasons (e.g. adoption of foreign language terms, semantic shift). Consider, as an example, the German historical/modern variants of the word *lemon* (e.g. *Limonie*/Zitrone) or of the word *woman* (e.g. *Weib*/Frau).

Previous approaches to spelling normalization of historical texts have focused on the first subproblem. Two main strategies that have been applied:

- a rule based strategy, in which the translation of historical variants into modern forms is performed on the ground of manually written or semi-automatically gathered rules (cf. (Pilz et al., 2008), (Bollmann et al., 2011));

- a string similarity strategy, in which a semi-automatic attempt is made to link historical variants with modern dictionary entries following string similarity (cf. (Giusti et al., 2007), (Kunstmann and Stein, 2007), (Dipper, 2010), (Hendrickx and Marquilhas, 2011), (Gotscharek et al., 2011)) or phonetic conflation strategies (cf. (Koolen et al., 2006), (Jurish, 2008) ).

These approaches have the disadvantage of ending up relying on a time-specific dictionary of variants, e.g. they can cope with variants realized in texts stemming from the same period of time for which they have been created but may result inappropriate for texts belonging to other time spans.

Moreover, to our knowledge, there is currently no approach to spelling normalization that can address successfully the second subproblem stated above – the recognition of paraphrastic variations realized as completely different strings or consisting of semantic shifts.

As it has been often noted, the problem of standardizing diachronic variants can be understood as a translation operation, where instead of translating between two different languages, translation takes place between two diachronic varieties of the same language. Inspired by experiments done for interlinguistic translation (Rapp et al., 2012), the idea is to use diachronic comparable corpora to automatically produce a dictionary of diachronic spelling variants even including semantic shifts, regardless of the historical variants at stake.

In short, we first build a comparable historical corpus made up of recipe repertoires published in the German language during the Early Modern Age along with a contemporary comparable corpus. Second, we address the problem of recognizing and translating different variants by relaying on MT techniques based on string similarity as well as on semantic similarity measures. Finally, we automatically extract a diachronic dictionary of spelling and semantic variants which also provides a canonical form.

This paper is organized as follows. Section 2 presents the comparable corpus of German recipes. Section 3 describes the approach used for generating the dictionary of diachronic spelling variants. Section 4 shows the results of a preliminary evaluation. Finally, in Section 5 we conclude by discussing some final remarks.

## 2 The Historical Comparable Corpus of German Recipes

The text collection encoded in our corpus spans two hundred years and includes samples from 14 cook books written in German between 1569 and 1729. The core of the recipe corpus was compiled as part of a PhD work in the field of Translation Studies (cf. (Wurm, 2007)). This corpus has been aligned resulting into two comparable corpora:

- a historical comparable dataset aligned at recipe level providing multiple versions of the same dish across the time span of the core corpus;
- a contemporary comparable dataset providing contemporary German versions for each recipe.

In order to produce the historical comparable component we proceeded in the following way:

- first, we classified the core recipes by main ingredient and cooking method (e.g. chicken, roast). These two parameters form the criteria to consider the recipes aligned, then;
- we collected as many as possible diachronic versions/variants of the same recipe by also searching online resources providing collections of historical texts.

The historical component of the corpus (core and comparable) contains a total of 430 recipes and about 45.000 tokens. This dataset constitutes the object of study for subsequent research, providing a representative sample of German during the Early Modern Age in this specific domain. Moreover, language and genre evolution can be traced thanks to its comparable nature.

Regarding the compilation of the contemporary German comparable corpus, we collected a set of recipes belonging to the same register but representing contemporary German language. These recipes were collected from Internet sources and filtered by geographical criteria (only the ones categorized as belonging to the cuisine of German speaking regions were selected). The corpus contains around 1500 recipes and over 500.000 tokens, which have been also aligned with their

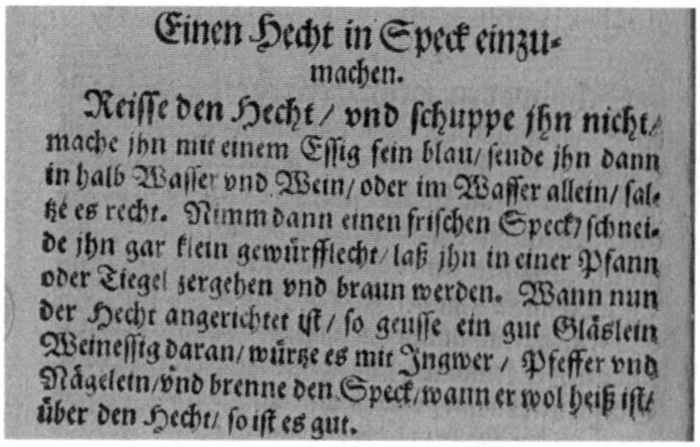

Einen Hecht in Speck einzu-
machen.
Reiſſe den Hecht / vnd ſchuppe jhn nicht/
mache jhn mit einem Eſſig fein blau/ ſeude jhn dann
in halb Waſſer vnd Wein/ oder im Waſſer allein/ ſal-
tze es recht. Nimm dann einen friſchen Speck/ ſchnei-
de jhn gar klein gewürfflecht/ laß jhn in einer Pfann
oder Tiegel zergehen vnd braun werden. Wann nun
der Hecht angerichtet iſt / ſo geuſſe ein gut Gläslein
Weineſſig daran/ würtze es mit Jngwer / Pfeffer vnd
Nägelein/ vnd brenne den Speck/ wann er wol heiß iſt/
über den Hecht/ ſo iſt es gut.

Figure 1: A text excerpt from Wecker 1679.

comparable historical counterparts according to the same parameters explained above. This subset allows not only to compare historical recipes with their modern versions but also to use them as a reference corpus to extract standard word forms.

### 2.1 Digitization Strategy

The corpus has been manually transcribed. The transcription can be regarded as a diplomatic one, since it tries to preserve as many features of the original as possible. Some standardization has been performed at punctuation and hyphenation level but no spellchecking or word separation has been carried out. The corpus is encoded in UTF-8 and we have used a TEI-compatible XML format to store both text and metadata.

### 2.2 Annotations

The corpus currently includes some shallow semantic annotation describing text structure (e.g. recipe, title, and body) and providing a basic classification of recipes based on the main ingredient and recipe type. The figure 2 below shows an example of semantic annotation.

```
<recipe id="26" author="Deckhardt" year="1611"
language="german" ingredient="Erdbeere"
cookingMethod="Mus">
<title> Ein Erdbeermuhs zumachen. < /title>
<body> <seg type="newline">
Nimb Erdbeer
</seg>
<seg type="newline"/ >
treibe es durch mit Weine
</seg>
<seg type="newline">
thue Zucker darein
</seg>
<seg type="newline">
darnach man es gerne süsse haben wil
</seg>
...
< /body>
< /recipe>
```

Figure 2: Comparable diachronic corpus: an example of annotation.

## 3 Building a Diachronic Dictionary of Spelling Variants

Our spelling normalization strategy aims at solving both subproblems discussed in the Introduction. In order to extract the mapping between diachronic variants by also capturing paraphrases and semantic shifts, we apply two different strategies one based on string similarity and the other based on semantic similarity measures.

Our workflow can be summarized as follows:

1. In a first step, we relay on clustering techniques based on string similarity measures to identify a set of diachronic variations of the same word form. In this phase, clustering corresponds to the extraction of "similar strings".

2. In the second step, we address the problem of finding semantic variants, i.e. those variants that are not realized as similar strings by applying paraphrase recognition techniques to identify different denominations of the same object.

3. Finally, we integrate the results of both phases and generate a dictionary of diachronic variants, that is used to extract the normalized spelling for each word in the corpus. We assume that the normalized word form corresponds to the most modern variant found in the dictionary.

### 3.1 String Similarity

In the first step, we extract comparable recipes from different decades and from the corpus of modern recipes. Then we apply clustering techniques to find spelling variations. The fact that we use comparable texts for clustering, should reduces the errors as all tokens come from similar terminological fields.

We apply agglomerative hierarchical clustering as implemented in the R statistical programming environment with the *average* agglomeration method. As a string similarity measure, we use the standard Levenshtein edit distance as implemented in the R package *Biostrings*. In order to build the dictionary, we select clusters that have a string similarity greater than 65%. Figure 3 shows an example of diachronic dictionary entries generated with this approach.

| | |
|---|---|
| Hühner: | Hüner_1574, Hünern_1574, hüner_1574, Hünner_1611 |
| und: | vnd_1569, vnnd_1569, vnd_1679, und_1698 |
| magsts: | magst_1574, magstu_1602, magst_1679 |
| lasst: | lassen_1679, lassets_1682, lässets_1715 |
| Muscatenblüh: | Muscatblü_1569, Muscatenblüh_1715 |

Figure 3: Diachronic Dictionary.

For each list of diachronic variants gathered at this point, we extracted the most recent variant and used it as normalized form.

### 3.2 Semantic similarity

In order to cluster paraphrastic variants and semantic shifts, we apply a slightly modified version of Lin's algorithm (Lin, 1998) based on the assumption that words sharing similar contexts should have similar semantics. Contrary to Lin, in our approach we do not perform any dependency analysis of the corpus data and compute semantic similarity between strings simply in terms of the mutual information of trigrams.

The semantic similarity strategy we implemented can be summarized as follows:

- We start by generating a list of trigrams from the corpus.
- We assign to each pair of tokens in the corpus a value for their mutual information.
- We assign to each pair of tokens in the corpus a value for their similarity.
- For each token in the corpus, we extract the N most similar tokens and take the most modern one as the normalized form.

The mutual information $I$ for a pair of tokens $t1$ and $t2$ is defined as:

$$I(t1, t2) = log\frac{\|t1,*,t2\|\|*,*,*\|}{\|t1,*,*\|\|*,*,t2\|}, \text{ with}$$

$\| \ t1, *, t2 \ \|$ the frequency of the occurrence of the trigram *t1,*,t2* in the corpus, $\| \ *, *, * \ \|$ the total number of trigrams in the corpus, $\| \ t1, *, * \ \|$ the number of trigrams with $t1$ as first token and $\| \ *, *, t2 \ \|$ the number of trigrams with $t2$ as last token.

Semantic similarity between tokens is defined in terms of their mutual information:

$$sim(t1, t2) = \frac{\sum_{T_{t1} \cap T_{t2}} I(t1,*)+I(t2,*)}{\sum I(t1,*)+\sum I(w2,*)},$$

with $T_{t1} = \{(v, w) : I(t1.w) > 0\}$ and $T_{t2} = \{(v, w) : I(t2.w) > 0\}$, the sets of token pairs that form trigrams with t1 or t2 as first element and such that they have positive mutual information values.

## 4 Evaluation

In order to evaluate the performance of our normalization strategy, we extracted a subset of recipes from the corpus for testing purposes. This subcorpus includes 32 comparable recipes on how to roast a chicken that have been written in a time period ranging from 1569 to 1800 reaching a size of 7103 words (about 8% of whole corpus). We take as reference the results yielded by TreeTagger[1] (Schmid, 1994), the state-of-art POS-tagger for German, regarding lemmatization and POS-tagging.

First, we tagged the subcorpus on the non-normalized word forms. The performance of POS-tagging, in this case, is around 80%, which is higher than the one observed in similar experiments (cf. (Scheible et al., 2011a)) on other historical corpora of German. We believe the reason for this is the relative syntactic simplicity of recipe texts in comparison to other kind of texts (dramas, sermons, letters, scientific or legal texts).

The tagger's poor performance is due to the existence of lexical items unknown to the system (around 27%), on the one hand, and the high inconsistency of the spelling, on the other hand. Our strategy to circumvent this problem consists of providing a modern word form to all historical word variants that we obtained from the previously discussed diachronic dictionary. We expected, that after the two normalization steps discussed in Section 3, the performance of the tagging process should improve.

[1]The TreeTagger was trained on the TüBa-D/Z treebank. Its performance is about 97.4% on newspaper texts and 78% on texts containing unknown words.

| Strategy | Lemma | POS |
|---|---|---|
| no-norm | 73% | 80% |
| string-similarity | 81% | 81.4% |
| semantic similarity | 82.5% | 82% |

Table 1: Evaluation Results.

Therefore, we repeated the experiment, first, on the test subcorpus normalized by using the diachronic dictionary generated with first normalization strategy, i.e. the one based on string similarity measure and, second, on the normalized version obtained after using the second strategy based on semantic similarity.

Table 1 summarizes the results of a preliminary evaluation of our strategy.

After string similarity normalization, the tagger was able to identify all lemmas except for 1358 tokens (19% of unknown tokens). While POS-tagging improved to 81.4%.

The semantic similarity step improved the performance of lemmatization and POS reaching 82.5% and 82% respectively.

Despite the fact that our experiments refer to very few data and to a restricted domain, we believe they are promising and show that our strategy, the integration of string similarity and semantic similarity measures can lead to a high quality automatic spelling normalization and outperform state-of-art approaches.

## 5 Conclusion

In this paper we have presented a comparable corpus of historical German recipes and shown that such comparable resources can help removing sources of noise typical of these text types that hinder standard NLP manipulation of such material. The old German recipes corpus is, to our knowledge, one of the first attempts[2] to build a comparable historical corpus of German. The corpus is accessible through a web interface and allows sophisticated queries according to different levels of annotation: 1) historical word forms; 2) modern normalized forms; 3) lemmas on top of normalized forms; 4) part-of-speech, and, last but not least; 5) semantics, namely main ingredient and cooking method. Further, we describe an innovative strategy for word form normalization that integrate string similarity measure with semantic similarity thereby being able to cope not only with formal spelling variations but also with paraphrastic variations and semantic shift. Moreover, this method can be applied to any comparable diachronic corpus, regardless of the time span at stake. A preliminary evaluation has shown that such a strategy may outperform state-of-art approaches.

[2]We are aware of only one similar project (Bartsch et al., 2011) aimed at building a comparable corpus of German texts for three main periods Old High, Middle High and Early New High German. However, those corpora are not yet available.

## References


Nina Bartsch, Stefanie Dipper, Birgit Herbers, Sarah Kwekkeboom, Klaus-Peter Wegera, Lars Eschke, Thomas Klein, and Elke Weber. 2011. Annotiertes Referenzkorpus Mittelhochdeutsch (1050-1350). Poster session at the 33rd annual meeting of the German Linguistic Society (DGfS-2011) (Abstract, Poster) .

Marcel Bollmann, Florian Petran, and Stefanie Dipper. 2011. Applying Rule-Based Normalization to Different Types of Historical Texts — An Evaluation. In *Proceedings of the 5th Language & Technology Conference: Human Language Technologies as a Challenge for Computer Science and Linguistics*, Poznań, November.

Marcel Diel, Bernhard Fisseni, Winfried Lenders, and Hans-Christian Schmitz. 2002. XML-Kodierung des Bonner Frühneuhochdeutschkorpus. IKP-Arbeitsbericht NF 02, Bonn .

Stefanie Dipper. 2010. Pos-tagging of historical language data: First experiments. In *Semantic Approaches in Natural Language Processing. Proceedings of the 10th Conference on Natural Language Processing (KONVENS-10)*, pages 117–121, Saarbrücken.

Rafael Giusti, Arnaldo Candido Jr, Marcelo Muniz, Lívia Cucatto, and Sandra Aluísio. 2007. Automatic Detection of Spelling Variation in Historical Corpus : An Application to Build a Brazilian Portuguese Spelling Variants Dictionary. In *Proceedings of the Corpus Linguistics Conference*, pages 1–20.

A. Gotscharek, U. Reffle, C. Ringlstetter, K. U. Schulz, and A. Neumann. 2011. Towards information retrieval on historical document collections: the role of matching procedures and special lexica. *IJDAR*, 14(2):159–171.

Iris Hendrickx and Rita Marquilhas. 2011. From old texts to modern spellings: an experiment in automatic normalisation. *Journal for Language Technology and Computational Linguistics*, 26(2):65–76.

Tim Hitchcock, Robert Shoemaker, Clive Emsley, Sharon Howard, and Jamie McLaughliin. 2012. The Old Bailey Proceedings Online, 1674-1913 (version 7.0).

Magnus Huber. 2007. The Old Bailey Proceedings, 1674-1834. Evaluating and annotating a corpus of 18th- and 19th-century spoken English. In

Meurman-Solin. Anneli and Arja Nurmi, editors, *Annotating Variation and Change*, volume 1. Research Unit for Variation, Contacts and Change in English (VARIENG), University of Helsinki, Helsinki.

Bryan Jurish. 2008. Finding canonical forms for historical German text. In Angelika Storrer, Alexander Geyken, Alexander Siebert, and Kay-Michael Würzner, editors, *Text Resources and Lexical Knowledge. Selected Papers from the 9th Conference on Natural Language Processing KONVENS 2008*, pages 27–38. Mouton de Gruyter, Berlin / New York.

Marijn Koolen, Frans Adriaans, Jaap Kamps, and Maarten de Rijke. 2006. A cross-language approach to historic document retrieval. In Mounia Lalmas, Andy MacFarlane, Stefan Rueger, Anastasios Tombros, Theodora Tsikrika, Alexei Yavlinsky, editor, *Advances in Information Retrieval*, volume 3936, pages 407–419. Lecture Notes in Computer Science, Berlin/Heidelberg: Springer.

Pierre Kunstmann and Achum Stein. 2007. Le Nouveau Corpus d'Amsterdam. In Pierre Kunstmann Achim Stein, editor, *Le Nouveau Corpus d'Amsterdam. Actes de l'atelier de Lauterbad, 23-26 février 2006*, pages 9–27. Stuttgart, Germany: Steiner.

Vladimir I. Levenshtein. 1965. Binary codes capable of correcting deletions, insertions, and reversals. *Doklady Akademii Nauk SSSR*, 163(4):845–848.

Dekang Lin. 1998. Automatic retrieval and clustering of similar words.

Thomas Pilz, Andrea Ernst-Gerlach, Sebastian Kempken, Paul Rayson, and Dawn Archer. 2008. The Identification of Spelling Variants in English and German Historical Texts: Manual or Automatic? *Literary and Linguistic Computing*, 23(1):65–72, April.

Michael Piotrowski. 2012. *Natural Language Processing for Historical Texts*, volume 5. Morgan & Claypool Publishers, September.

Reinhard Rapp, Serge Sharoff, and Bogdan Babych. 2012. Identifying word translations from comparable documents without a seed lexicon. In *LREC*, pages 460–466.

Silke Scheible, Richard J. Whitt, Martin Durrell, and Paul Bennett. 2011a. Evaluating an f-the-shelfS-tagger on Early Modern German text. In *Proceedings of the 5th ACL-HLT Workshop on Language Technology for Cultural Heritage, Social Sciences, and Humanities*, number June, pages 19–23, Portland, Oregon. Association for Computational Linguistics.

Silke Scheible, Richard J. Whitt, Martin Durrell, and Paul Bennett. 2011b. A gold standard corpus of early modern german. In *Linguistic Annotation Workshop*, pages 124–128.

Helmut Schmid. 1994. Probabilistic part-of-speech tagging using decision trees. In *Proceedings of International Conference on New Methods in Language Processing*, Manchester, UK.

Andrea Wurm. 2007. *Translatorische Wirkung: ein Beitrag zum Verständnis von Übersetzungsgeschichte als Kulturgeschichte am Beispiel deutscher Übersetzungen französischer Kochbücher in der Frühen Neuzeit*. Ph.D. thesis, Universität des Saarlandes, Saarbrücken.

# Integration of the Thesaurus for the Social Sciences (TheSoz) in an Information Extraction System

**Thierry Declerck**
DFKI GmbH, LT-Lab
Stuhsatzenhausweg, 3
D-66123 Saarbrücken, Germany
declerck@dfki.de

## Abstract

We present current work dealing with the integration of a multilingual thesaurus for social sciences in a NLP framework for supporting Knowledge-Driven Information Extraction in the field of social sciences. We describe the various steps that lead to a running IE system: lexicalization of the labels of the thesaurus and semi-automatic generation of domain specific IE grammars, with their subsequent implementation in a finite state engine. Finally, we outline the actual field of application of the IE system: analysis of social media for recognition of relevant topics in the context of elections.

## 1 Introduction

Within a running research project dealing with the automatic linguistic and semantic processing of social media[1], we are working on a use case concerned with the analysis of tweets exchanged in the context of approaching election events. Besides the detection of Named Entities (name of politicians, political parties, locations, etc.) and associated opinions, we are also interested in identifying and classifying the topics people are addressing in their messages.

There are for sure topics that are very particular to a specific election, but there are also more generic and recurrent topics, some of them being of special interest to social scientists. In order to be able to detect such topics in various types of text, we have been searching for knowledge sources in the field of social and political sciences that can be used for the corresponding (both manual and automatic) semantic annotation of text. Our best candidate is for the time being the Thesaurus for the Social Sciences (TheSoz), developed by the GESIS institute at the Leibniz Institute for the Social Sciences[2]. This resource is available in the SKOS format[3], and therefore adapted to the Linked Data framework[4]. In this short paper we present first in some details the thesaurus, before describing the steps that allow us to integrate the (multilingual) language data it includes into a NLP tools suite, for the goal of supporting Knowledge-Driven analysis of texts in the field of social sciences, with a focus on micro-blogs.

## 2 The Thesaurus for the Social Sciences (TheSoz)

The thesaurus for social sciences is a knowledge source under continuous development (we are currently using version 0.92). The list of keywords used in TheSoz contains about 12,000 entries, of which more than 8,000 are descriptors (or "authorized keywords").

It is encoded in RDF and SKOS. While the main conceptual elements of the thesaurus are encoded in the core syntax of SKOS, the resource makes also use of the SKOS-XL properties[5] for including labels containing natural language expressions (authorized keywords, which act as domain terms) that are attached to the conceptual elements., using the "prefLabel" and "altLabel" annotation properties, allowing thus to describe main terms and their variants. The natural language expressions corresponding to the labels are encoding using the SKOS-XL annotation property "literalForm".

---

[1] The TrendMiner project, www.trendminer-project.eu, co-funded by the European Commission with Grant No. 287863.

[2] http://www.gesis.org/en/services/research/thesauri-und-klassifikationen/social-science-thesaurus/

[3] See http://www.w3.org/TR/skos-primer/ for a concise introduction to SKOS.

[4] http://linkeddata.org/

[5] See http://www.w3.org/TR/skos-reference/skos-xl.html

In order to give a (human readable) idea of the content of the thesaurus[6], we extracted with a Perl script the main elements from the SKOS code and present those in a tabular fashion, an example of which is given below, displaying also the terms in the languages covered by TheSoz (English, French and German):

**concept id "10034303"**

*term "10034303"*

- prefLabel id "10034303"
- lang=de "Abbrecher"
- lang=en "drop-out"
- lang=fr "drop-out"
- altLabel id "10034307"
- lang=de "Studienabbrecher"
- lang=en "university drop-out"
- lang=fr "étudiant qui abandonne ses études"

*notation „3.2.00"*

- lang=de „Schule und Beruf (berufliche Qualifikationselemente im Bereich der schulischen Ausbildung)"
- lang=en "School and Occupation (Elements of Occupational Qualification in School Education)"
- lang=fr « École et profession (éléments de qualification professionnelle dans le domaine de l'enseignement scolaire) »

*broader notation „3.2"*

- lang=de „Beruf und Qualifikation"
- lang=en „Occupation and Qualification"
- lang=fr « profession et qualification »

*broader notation „3"*

- lang=de „Interdiszipinäre Anwendungsbereiche der Sozialwissenschaften"
- lang=en "Interdisciplinary Application Areas of Social Sciences"
- lang=fr « domaines interdisciplinaires d'application des sciences sociales »

In the example above the reader can see how the English preferred label "drop-out" is associated with the concept "School and Occupation", which is itself a subclass of the concept "Occupation and Qualification", classified itself as a field of the broader concept "Interdisciplinary Application Areas of Social Sciences". All the language material contained in the labels or used for naming the "notations" can be re-used for detecting and semantically annotating the related topics in running texts.

## 3 TheSoz as Linked Data

The encoding of TheSoz in SKOS is an important asset, since it allows linking the data to other knowledge sources, like for example DBpedia[7] in the Linked Data framework, and so to complement information contained in TheSoz, which remains at the terminological level, and is thus not giving detailed information about the included multilingual terms for the described concepts and the relations between those.

So for example TheSoz mentions the main political parties in Germany, Austria and other countries, but not their actual leader, their actual role (in the government or in the opposition) or weight in the current legislation period. TheSoz also lists the names of important persons, like "Merkel, A." or "Brandt, W.", but no biographical indication or relation to political parties or institutions are given. As such TheSoz is providing for a light-weight ontological basis, with multilingual labels, which allows detecting in text mentions of topics or entities relevant to the social scientists.

The linking of concepts and associated terms to more elaborated knowledge sources, like DBpedia, is thus necessary in order to implement a full Knowledge Driven Information Extraction (KDIE) system in the field of social sciences. So for example the TheSoz sub-term "university" in "university drop-out" can be completed by information in the DBpedia entry for "university", stating among others that "university" is *rdfs domain* of "numberOfPostgraduateStudents" and that it is a *subClassOf* "EducationalInstitution. "http://schema.org/EducationalOrganization" is given as an *equivalenceClass* of the DBpedia entry for "EducationalInstitution". From the schema.org entry we can make use of additional relations associated to "EducationalInstitution", like for example a relation to more specific types, such as "CollegeOrUniversity", "ElementarySchool", "HighSchool", "MiddleSchool", "Preschool", "School". We can this way expand the terminological base of TheSoz by accessing the labels of the classes and concepts of other knowledge sources referred to by explicit semantic relations like *owl:equivalentClass*, *owl:sameAs* or *skos:exactMatch*.

As the reader can see from the name of the mentioned ontology classes above, natural language expressions associated to elements of knowledge sources can have different surface forms as the one we saw in the examples of "literalForms" of TheSoz. Beyond the utilization of the annotation properties, such as rdfs:label,

---

[6] Online visualizations and access are available at http://lod.gesis.org/thesoz/

[7] See http://dbpedia.org/About. And in fact, 5024 TheSoz concepts are linked to DBpedia via SKOS "exact matches".

skosxl:prefLabel" or skosxl:literalForm, dedicated to ease the understanding by human users, several other syntax elements of knowledge representation systems, such as the RDF URI references, like rdf:ID, rdf:about, or rdf:resource, may contain instead of numerical codes natural language expressions, often using the CamelCase notation. Fu et al. (2012) describes NLP tasks and applications using natural language expressions contained in such RDF URI references. In our work, we focus on natural language expressions contained in the annotation properties rdfs:label, sxkos:label (skosxl:prefLabel and others) and skosxl:literalForm, which typically include textual material to be consumed by human readers, and which can be normally directly processed by NLP tools, without requiring prior transformation processes of the textual material.

## 4 Integration of TheSoz in a NLP Framework

Before applying the (possibly extended) terminological material of TheSoz for supporting the semantic annotation of running texts, it has to be submitted to pre-processing steps, in order to ensure as a minimum a possible matching to morpho-syntactic variations of (elements of) the terms that are to be expected in external text. For this, we need to lexicalize the labels of the thesaurus, transforming the terms to linguistic data that can be used for matching linguistically processed text. A first sketch of this approach has been described in (Declerck & Lendvai, 2010) and a more elaborated methodology, encoding the linguistic data in RDF is presented in (McCrae et al, 2012).

And for ensuring a linking of linguistic data in text to the conceptual elements of the thesaurus (or other knowledge sources), the development of an information extraction grammar is needed. We present in section 3.2 below an automatized approach for this.

For both steps we are using the NooJ platform[8], whose finite states engine supports the flexible implementation of lexicons, morphological, syntactic and semantic grammars.

### 4.1 Lexicalization

The lexicalization step consists in submitting all the language material included in the knowledge source to a lexical and a syntactic analyzer, which in our case are lexicons and grammars implemented in NooJ.

The results of such a processing can be encoded in the lexicon-ontology model *lemon* (McCrae et al, 2012), which declaratively represents textual and linguistic information of ontologies as additional RDF resource linked to the original concepts associated to the labels. The *lemon* model decomposes multi-word expressions to individual words and represents the results in a phrase structure, which can be shared by multiple lexical entries. Furthermore, dependency relations between decomposed phrase constituents can be modeled. A simplified example of the *lemon* representation of the NooJ parsed term "university drop-out" is shown below:

```
:university_drop-out [lemon:writtenRep "univer-
sity drop-out"@en]
lemon:sense [lemon:reference ontol-
ogy:TheSoz10034307];
lemon:decomposition ( :university_comp
:drop-out_comp ) ;
lemon:phraseRoot [ lemon:constituent :NP ;
lemon:edge [lemon:constituent :NP ;
lemon:edge [lemon:constituent :NN ;
lemon:leaf university_comp ] ;
lemon:edge [lemon:constituent :NN ;
lemon:leaf drop-out_comp ] ];
].
```

For the sake of simplicity we do not display the *lemon* representation of additional analysis provided by NooJ (for example the one, which is decomposing "drop-out" in two lemmas). It is enough to mention that *lemon* also supports the representation of preferred and alternative labels. This is important if one wants to consider all possible (linguistically annotated) term variants for improving the matching of TheSoz terms to terminological variants in text, going thus beyond the matching of terms to purely morpho-syntactic variations. So for example, in TheSoz "drop-out" is the prefLabel, while "university drop-out" is marked as altLabel of the same concept. Such term variants can also be "imported" in our lexicalization step from other source. Or one can import additional lexical material, so for example the corresponding WordNet synonyms or glosses. In the next future we also plan to "tap" the BabelNet[9] resource, which is providing links to WordNet, Wikipedia and DBpedia (and more is planed), for extending the terminological

[8] http://www.nooj4nlp.net/pages/nooj.html

[9] See http://lcl.uniroma1.it/babelnet/ or (Navigli & Ponzetto, 2012).

base of the (lexicalized) TheSoz labels, also with terms in languages not covered by TheSoz for now.

### 4.2 Automatic Generation of Domain specific IE grammars

On the basis of the lexicalization step described in section 3.1, we wrote a Perl program that generates IE grammars in the NooJ finite state engine. This procedure is done in 5 steps.

1) Using the Term ID of TheSoz as names for NooJ recognition rules.
   *term10034307 =*
2) Using the corresponding lexicalised labels as the expressions to be recognized by the NooJ rule (abstract representation):
   *term10034307 = [lemma=„university" cat=„N"] [lemma=„drop-out" cat=„N"] ;*
3) Adding possible term variants to the rule) [10]:
   *term10034307 = ([lemma=„university" cat=„N"] [lemma=„drop-out" cat=„N"] | :var10034307) ;*

   *var10034307 = [lemma=„university" cat=„N"] [lemma=„drop" cat=„V"] [lemma=„out" cat=„P"] ;*
4) Linking the linguistically annotated prefLabel and the altLabel(s) to the corresponding Concept ID, as the basis of the semantic organization of the lexical material in NooJ:
   *concept10034303 = (term10034303 | term10034307) ;*
5) Defining the annotation generation procedure of the NooJ rules: Successful application of the rule *concept10034303* can generate the following annotation:
   *CLASS= TheSoz_ID="10034303"*
   *altLabel_ID="10034307"*
   *altLabel ="universtiy drop-out@en"*
   *SuperClass=TheSoz_ID_3.2*
   *SuperClassLabel = „Occupation and Qualification"*
   *altLabel_Translation = „Studienabbrecher@de"*
   etc.[11] )

This procedure has been fully implemented, using Perl scripts. The addition of term variants (in red color in the example above, point 3) can be done manually or automatically. We are also currently adding information about the context of such terms to be expected in running texts, like for example the agent of the event "drop-out", and further modifications, like date, location and reasons.

At the moment we are able to semantically disambiguate in text for example the two senses of the TheSoz term "drop-out": one in the sense of "university drop-out" and the one in the sense of "resignation from occupation". The generated NooJ grammars are currently being tested for a use case dealing with the elections in Austria.

## 5 Use Case

Our actual focus is the elections in Austria. Our aim is to detect which topics are of have been discussed in the social media, and how this relates to election results obtained by candidates and parties.

As such we cannot report yet on evaluation results, both at the technological and usability level, since an evaluation study is still to be performed. We will be using collection of polls for measuring the accuracy of the detection of topics and the related popularity of parties/politicians detected in social media.

The use case partner involved in the project has been designing an annotation schema and is performing a semi-automatic annotation of selected tweets and blogs, which we will use as gold standard.

A fully operational system is expected to work for the national elections in Austria to be held on the 28th September of 2013.

## 6 Future Work

Besides the evaluation work sketched in the former section, the next steps in our work will consist in aggregating information from other

[10] In this simplified example we do just include as a term variant the decomposition of the noun "drop-out" in two lemmas, extending thus the lexical coverage of the original label. The final rule (not displayed here for the sake of simplicity) is also stating that the sub-term "university" doesn't have to immediately precede the sub-term "drop", accounting thus also for alternative word order.

[11] An example text is: "Mar 29, 2012 – Record numbers of students quit *university courses* last year as the higher education *drop-out* rate soared above 30000 for the first time…"

knowledge source, not only from DBpedia but also from a recently developed political ontology, which has been designed in the context of our project.

We have also already conducted experiments in relating the linguistically annotated terms of TheSoz with terms available in other thesauri, like for example GEMET[12]. As GEMET is containing labels in 33 languages, this linking will allow us to find more multilingual equivalents of terms in TheSoz, at least for the concepts of TheSoz that can be associated with concepts in GEMET.

Another line of investigation will consist in adapting the work on correcting and complementing the labels used in TheSoz, following the reports described in (Declerck & Gromann, 2012), where correcting and completive patterns have been applied to the labels of multilingual taxonomies dealing with the description of industry activity fields of companies listed in various stock exchanges. Improving the terminological quality of labels seems to be a good strategy for improving knowledge-driven information extraction.

Following the approaches to cross-lingual harmonization of taxonomy labels described in (Declerck & Gromann, 2012; Gromann & Declerck, 2013), we notice that in many multilingual knowledge sources (Thesauri, Taxonomies or Ontologies), the content of multilingual labels is not parallelized. In one of our example within the TheSoz, displayed in Section 2, we had the following concept with the labels in three languages:

```
term "10034303"
  concept id "10034303"
    ...
    altLabel id "10034307"
    altLabel de "Studienabbrecher"
    altLabel en "university drop-out"
    altLabel fr "étudiant qui abandonne ses études"
    ....
```

As the reader can see, only the French label is containing explicitly the fact the entity "performing" the drop-out is a student. Although the super-classes make clear that "university drop-out" is in the field of "School and Occupation", none of the metadata or labels, other as the French "altLabel" is mentioning that a student is involved in this field. The German label can lead to the reading that a person is involved, if adequate lexical semantics resources are used. The English label does not mention at all that an agent is involved: it just names the event. The French and German labels are about abandoning "studies" while the English label is about abandoning "university".

As suggested by Gromann & Declerck (2013), we can add (either manually or by automated process) to the English alternative labels the translations of the French label (in this particular case, the one with the richest contextual information), like "a student, who is dropping out his studies". This is important since it improves the matching of the concepts of TheSoz to running texts.

## 7 Conclusion

We have described actual work in integrating multilingual knowledge sources in the field of social sciences into a NLP task, consisting in identifying relevant topics of discussion in social media. As it is still too early to report on results (due to the internal calendar of the project), we could only present for the time being the current state of implementation, which consisted in first lexicalizing the labels of the knowledge source "TheSoz", freely available – in the SKOS format. On the basis of the lexicalized labels, and their relation to conceptual element of the knowledge source, we implemented an automatic generation of knowledge-driven IE grammars, which have been realized as finite state transducers in the NooJ platform. Those resulting IE grammars are to be deployed in the context of a use case dealing with the detection of topics addressed in social media on approaching elections.

**Acknowledgments**

The work presented in this paper has been supported by the TrendMiner project, co-funded by the European Commission with Grant No. 287863.
The author is thanking the reviewers for their very helpful comments, which led to substantial changes brought to the final version of the paper.
The author is also thanking Dagmar Gromann (Vienna University of Economics and Business). Intensive discussions with her on related topics have been heavily inspiring the work described in this paper.

[12] GEMET stands for "GEneral Multilingual Environmental Thesaurus". See also http://www.eionet.europa.eu/gemet/

## References


Declerck, T., Lendvai, P. 2010. Towards a standardized linguistic annotation of the textual content of labels in Knowledge Representation Systems. In: *Proceedings of the seventh international conference on Language Resources and Evaluation*, Valetta, Malta, ELRA.

Fu, B., Brennan, R., O'Sullivan, D.: A Con_gurable Translation-Based Cross-Lingual Ontology Mapping System to Adjust Mapping Outcomes. Journal of Web Semantics, Vol. 15, pp.15_36 (2012)

Declerck, T., Gromann, D. 2012. Towards the Generation of Semantically Enriched Multilingual Components of Ontology Labels. In: *Proceedings of the 3rd Multilingual Semantic Web Workshop.*

Ell, B., Vrandecic, D., Simperl, E. 2011. Labels in the Web of Data. In Aroyo, L., Welty, C., Alani, H., Taylor, J., Bernstein, A. (eds.): *Proceedings of the 10th international conference on the semantic web* - Volume Part I (ISWC'11), Vol. Part I. Springer-Verlag, Berlin, Heidelberg, pp.162_176.

Fu, B., Brennan, R., O'Sullivan, D.: A Configurable Translation-Based Cross-Lingual Ontology Mapping System to Adjust Mapping Outcomes. Journal of Web Semantics, Vol. 15, pp.15_36 (2012)

Garcia, J., Montiel-Ponsoda, E., Cimiano, P., Gómez-Pérez, A., Buitelaar, P., Mc- Crae, J. 2012. *Challenges for the Multilingual Web of Data.* Web Semantics: Science, Services and Agents on the World Wide Web, Vol. 11, pp.63-71.

Gromann, D., Declerck, T. 2013. Cross-Lingual Correcting and Completive Patterns for Multilingual Ontology Labels. In Buitelaar, P. and Cimiano, P. (eds) *Multilingual Semantic Web*, Springer-Verlag (to appear)

McCrae, J., Aguado-de-Cea, G., Buitelaar, P., Cimiano, P., Declerck, T., Gómez-Pérez, A., Gracia, J., Hollink, L., Montiel-Ponsoda, E., Spohr, D., Wunner, T. 2012. *Interchanging lexical resources on the SemanticWeb.* Journal of Language Resources and Evaluation, pp.1_19.

Navigli, N., Ponzetto, S.P.. 2012. *BabelNet: The Automatic Construction, Evaluation and Application of a Wide-Coverage Multilingual Semantic Network.* Artificial Intelligence, 193, Elsevier, pp. 217-250.

Silberztein, Max. 2003. *NooJ manual.* Available at the WEB site http://www.nooj4nlp.net (200 pages)

Wimalasuriya, D. C., Dou, D. 2012. *Ontology-based information extraction: an introduction and a survey of current approaches.* Journal of Information Science, Vol. 36, No. 3, pp.306-_323.

Zapilko, B., Johann Schaible, Philipp Mayr, Brigitte Mathiak. 2012. *TheSoz. A SKOS Representation of the Thesaurus for the Social Sciences.* Semantic-Web Journal.

# The (Un)faithful Machine Translator

**Ruth Jones**
Dept. of French and Francophone Studies
University of California Los Angeles

**Ann Irvine**
Center for Language and Speech Processing
Johns Hopkins University

## Abstract

Applying machine translation (MT) to literary texts involves the same domain shift challenges that arise for any sublanguage (e.g. medical or scientific). However, it also introduces additional challenges. One focus in the discussion of translation theory in the humanities has been on the human translator's role in staying faithful to an original text versus adapting it to make it more familiar to readers. In contrast to other domains, one objective in literary translation is to preserve the *experience* of reading a text when moving to the target language. We use existing MT systems to translate samples of French literature into English. We then use qualitative analysis grounded in translation theory and real example outputs in order to address what makes literary translation particularly hard and the potential role of the machine in it.

## 1 Introduction

The question of how to translate, especially when the source text is valued for its perceived literary merit, has been the focus of a discussion that is nearly as old as written text itself. A key debate is whether the translator should (1) adapt the source language text as it is translated into the target language to make it familiar and understandable to the reader, or (2) stay as faithful as possible to the original. Schleiermacher (2012) calls the former a *free* translation and the latter *faithful*. The former has also been referred to as *domesticating* the text, or *bringing the text to the reader*, in contrast to *foreignizing* the text, or *bringing the reader to the text* (Venuti, 2008; Berman, 1992).

Consider the French phrase *enculer les mouches*. Staying as faithful to the original French as possible, the first word, *enculer* translates as the infinitive for the French word for anal penetration, while the second is the more banal *flies*. Google translate gives *to fuck flies*. However, idiomatically, it is, despite the strongly sexual first term, a not uncommon way to say *to nitpick*. This translation makes the text more understandable, at the cost of staying faithful to the meanings of the individual words of the original text. Stylistic elements such as metaphor, alliteration, metonymy, and rhyme likewise require the translator to make interpretive choices beyond the literal meaning of the original, bringing the original text to the reader of the translation even at the expense of losing some of the literal meaning of the source.

Often multiple equally faithful translations of a word or phrase exist, and the translator must choose one based on context, either local or more broad. For example, the French *il neige* can be translated as *it snows* or *it is snowing*.[1] In English, *it is snowing* suggests the narrative present, while *it snows* suggests a habitual occurrence.

Like human translators, a statistical machine translation (SMT) system may produce translations that are relatively free or faithful and must constantly make translation choices in decoding. For SMT, choices are dependent on what is observed in training and language modeling data and their frequencies. When systems are trained on datasets that are similar to a test text, they are more likely to make reasonable translation choices. Additionally, if a model, either a priori or automatically, knows something about what the output should look like (e.g. poetry should rhyme or have rhythm), features could encourage free translations to take a certain form.

How much a translation sounds like an original text in its target language and how much it preserves elements of its source language, which make it sound foreign, is in part an ethical choice made by the human translator. Still, even experienced human translators have difficulty recogniz-

[1]There is no present progressive tense in French.

ing when they are being faithful and when their cultural experiences have influenced a translation. Current SMT models have no awareness of this and no ability to make specific choices to balance the two tendencies in the same output. Our work shines a light on SMT from the perspective of translation theory based on a qualitative analysis of two translated samples of French literature, one prose and one poetry. We compare SMT and human translations to address the following:

- What types of translation choices does the machine make, compared with humans?
- Is there evidence for the need to encourage a machine to translate more freely?
- Can SMT translate non-ethnocentrically?

## 2 Background

### 2.1 Translation Theory

Schleiermacher (2012) raises the issue of a translation's approximation of its source language vs. its fluency or resemblance to an original work in its target language, referring to translations "that are faithful or free." Berman (1992), alternatively, outlined the need for an ethics and an analytics of translation. For Berman, the translator has an imperative to avoid "freedom" where it brings with it a tendency to alter the foreign text by making it resemble a work of literature created in the target language through adjustments to the original on the levels of style, idiom, and content (both lexical and explicative). His is an argument for what Venuti (2008) calls "foreignization" in translation, preserving the distance between the language of the original text and the language of the translation by creating a translation that is perceptibly different from an original work in the target language. He opposes this to domestication, which instead privileges fluency and readability.

Venuti (2008) uses a similar critique to address the relative visibility or invisibility of the translator. For Venuti, part of the domestication of the translated text comes in the form of the invisibility of its translator in the finished (marketed) product. Compare, for instance, Venuti's example of the translator's invisibility in the 2002 Penguin translation of the Anna Karenina, advertised with praise for the "transparency" of its translation without naming the translators, to Seamus Heany's 2000 translation of Beowulf, which includes both original and translated texts side-by-side and features the poet/translator's name prominently on the cover. In the first case, the reader is asked to forget that she is not, in fact, reading Tolstoy in his own words, while, in the second, Heany's text is open to constant comparison with its original.

### 2.2 MT of Non-Standard Language

Prior work applying SMT to non-standard language focuses primarily on domain adaptation. In that task, an MT system trained on, for example, newswire, is used to translate text in a different domain, such as science. Much of this work has focused on up-weighting subsets of the training or language modeling data that are most similar to the new domain (Matsoukas et al., 2009; Foster et al., 2010; Ananthakrishnan et al., 2011; Niehues and Waibel, 2010; Foster and Kuhn, 2007; Tiedemann, 2010; Lavergne et al., 2011).

Other work has focused on literary texts (Reddy and Knight, 2011; Kao and Jurafsky, 2012; Roque, 2012). Most relevant is Greene et al. (2010), which presents a model for translating Italian poetry into English. That work focuses on preserving meaning as well as rhythm and is an interesting first attempt at integrating models of poetry ("how to say") and storyline ("what to say") generation. In many cases, it is hard to do both well at once; simultaneously maintaining the meaning and rhythm of a poem is challenging.

## 3 Experiments

### 3.1 Data and Setup

We analyze translations of two samples of French literature, one prose and one poem (Figures 1-2). The prose selection is a sample of the twentieth century novel L'Étranger by Albert Camus (Camus, 1955). We use the Camus and Ward (1989) English translation as a reference. The poetry selection is a sample of the twentieth century poem "Jardin" by Yves Bonnefoy (Bonnefoy, 1968), from the collection *Début et fin de la neige*, translated in Bonnefoy et al. (2012). We selected the passages because they use fairly simple language and have modern and well-known authors.

We translate the two literary selections using two SMT systems. First, we train a phrase-based MT model using the Hansard data.[2] The corpus contains over 8 million parallel lines of text and is one of the largest freely available parallel corpora for any language pair. It contains proceedings of the Canadian parliament. Recent work has

[2] http://www.parl.gc.ca

shown that newswire corpora, the other common bitext domain, is not very different from the parliamentary domain. Thus, a model trained on the Hansard data reflects the status of a typical modern SMT system trained on freely available data. We use the Moses SMT framework (Koehn et al., 2007), GIZA++ automatic word alignments (Och and Ney, 2003), and the batch version of MIRA for tuning (Cherry and Foster, 2012). For comparison, we also present and analyze translations by Google translate.[3]

In addition to our detailed manual analysis, we automatically evaluated outputs using case-insensitive BLEU and a single reference. The Moses system achieve a slightly higher BLEU score than Google (16.62 vs. 11.25) on the Bonnefoy selection and the opposite is true for the Camus selection (26.03 vs. 30.05). However, because the selections are small, we don't interpret these results as particularly meaningful.

### 3.2 Analysis

Figures 1 and 2 show the outputs. Focusing on the differences between the machine and human translations with respect to the originals reveals places where the human translators' choices diverged from the translations considered probable by the two SMT models. Close reading of the source text and human translation suggests possible reasons for the translator's choices. The probabilities that the SMT model assigns to the human translations relative to those assigned to the observed MT output highlights the need for probabilistic translation models that are specific to the domain of the particular texts or for literary translation more generally. While differences occurred based on a variety of factors, for the sake of brevity, we only consider lexical variation and the question of time as an aspect of translation. We take examples from Camus' prose and Bonnefoy's poem while keeping in mind the possibility of a definable difference in domain between the two.

Ward's translation puts the plain language of Camus' text into a clear and conversational English, a stylistic choice for fluency and domestication of the French. The focus in this passage is on the speaker, actively calming himself after the departure of the warden, and the "re" of "retrouvé" appears as "again." The machine translations, looking at the words in the absence of Camus' protagonist, give "found," eliminating the "re." Ward translates "se calmer" exactly, "to calm (down)." In contrast, the machine versions give "found (the) calm." It is not the passive aspect of Camus' phrase that is problematic ("finding calm" as opposed to "calming down"); rather, it is the return implied by the "re" that gives pause. Ward's translation gives a plainer, more informal style than the translations offered by the SMT systems, choosing to preserve the repetition of "re" (in "retrouvé") with "again" rather than the core meaning of "found" in "trouvé."

**L'étranger - Albert Camus**

lui parti, j' ai retrouvé le calme.
j' étais épuisé et je me suis jeté sur ma couchette.
je crois que j' ai dormi parce que je me suis réveillé avec des étoiles sur le visage.
des bruits de campagne montaient jusqu' à moi.
des odeurs de nuit , de terre et de sel rafraîchissaient mes tempes.
la merveilleuse paix de cet été endormi entrait en moi comme une marée.
a ce moment, et à la limite de la nuit, des sirènes ont hurlé.
elles annonçaient des départs pour un monde qui maintenant m' était à jamais indifférent.
pour la première fois depuis bien longtemps j' ai pensé à maman.

**Hansard SMT**

his party, i found the calm.
i was exhausted and i had on my sleeper.
i think i slept because i woke up with stars on your face.
the campaign noise up to me.
the smell of night of land and salt rafraîchissaient my tempes.
the great peace of this summer asleep came into me as a tide.
has this time, and the limit of the night of sirens screamed and yelled.
they announced departures for a world that now was never indifferent.
for the first time in a long time i thought about mom.

**Google SMT**

he was gone, i found calm.
i was exhausted and i threw myself on my bunk.
i think i slept because i woke up with stars on her face.
noises campaign amounted to me.
the smell of night, earth and salt refreshed my temples.
heavenly peace this summer sleeping entered me like a tide.
at that time, and the limit of the night, sirens screamed .
they announced departures for a world that now was never indifferent to me.
for the first time in ages i thought mom.

**The Stranger, translation by Matthew Ward**

with him gone , i was able to calm down again.
i was exhausted and threw myself on my bunk.
i must have fallen asleep, because i woke up with the stars in my face.
sounds of the countryside were drifting in.
smells of night, earth, and salt air were cooling my temples.
the wondrous peace of that sleeping summer flowed through me like a tide.
then, in the dark hour before dawn, sirens blasted.
they were announcing departures for a world that now and forever meant nothing to me.
for the first time in a long time i thought about maman.

Figure 1: The Stranger by Albert Camus

Later in the passage (line 3), the phrase "je

[3]translate.google.com

| **Début et fin de la neige, Yves Bonnefoy, « Le jardin »** |
|---|
| il neige.<br>sous les flocons la porte<br>ouvre enfin au jardin<br>de plus que le monde.<br>j' avance. mais se prend<br>mon écharpe à du fer<br>rouillé, et se déchire<br>en moi l' étoffe du songe.<br>il neige.<br>sous les flocons la porte ouvre enfin au jardin de plus que le monde.<br>j' avance.<br>mais se prend mon écharpe à du fer rouillé, et se déchire en moi l' étoffe du songe. |

| **Hansard SMT** |
|---|
| it snows.<br>under the snowflakes the door<br>opens finally au jardin<br>more than the world.<br>but is my point.<br>my scarf to iron<br>rusty tears,<br>i think in character.<br>it snows.<br>under the cornflakes and opens the door au jardin de more than the world.<br>my point.<br>but does my scarf to iron rusty, that tears character in me thinking. |

| **Google SMT** |
|---|
| it snows.<br>flakes under the door<br>finally opens to the garden<br>over the world.<br>i advance. but takes<br>my scarf with iron<br>rusty, and tears<br>in me the stuff of dreams.<br>it snows.<br>finally, in the snow the door opens to the garden over the world.<br>i advance.<br>but take my scarf of rusty iron, and tears in me the stuff of dreams. |

| **Beginning and End of the Snow, Emily Grolsholz, "The Garden"** |
|---|
| it's snowing.<br>beneath the snowflakes the gate<br>opens at last on the garden<br>of more than the world.<br>i enter. but my scarf<br>catches on rusty iron,<br>and it tears apart in me<br>the fabric of the dream.<br>it's snowing.<br>beneath the snowflakes the gate opens at last on the garden of more than the world.<br>i enter.<br>but my scarf catches on rusty iron, and it tears apart in me the fabric of the dream. |

Figure 2: The Garden by Yves Bonnefoy

me suis réveillé avec des étoiles sur le visage" is translated as "I woke up with the stars in my face" in Ward's translation, whereas the Hansard and Google translations drop the indefinite article and assume a second person in the scene, giving "i woke up with stars on {your, her} face." Later, the phrase "des bruits de campagne" (line 4) also provides a source of linguistic confusion. It is "sounds of the countryside" in Ward, but "the campaign noise" and "noises campaign" in Hansard and Google, respectively. Ward's translations make two distinct choices for the indefinite article "des," converting it to a definite article (the) in the first instance while dropping it in the second. Both examples again show Ward working the text into plain-spoken English prose by choosing the specific "the stars" over the general "stars" for "des étoiles" and the more conventional construction sounds of the coutryside over countryside sounds, which would preserve the unfamiliar (as shown by the difficulty of both MT systems in translating this phrase) construction of "des bruits de campagne." The discrepancies between the human and MT versions of Camus' text suggest that the MT systems might, at the least, be able to identify the difficulties of translating certain stylistic elements of the French.

The translations of Bonnefoy's poem reveal slightly different concerns. The translations of "étoffe" exemplify a lexical choice problem. Grolsholz's choice of "fabric" has a lower translation probability in the SMT models than "stuff" (Google translation). Both meanings are possible, but while "stuff" is more common, the source text suggests an association between "écharpe" (scarf) and "étoffe" (stuff/fabric) that comes to the fore in Grolsholz's translation. Taken with similar choices ("gate" for "door", also "snowflakes" for "flocons," earlier in the poem), Grolsholz's translation reveals a preference for specificity over probability that goes beyond rhythmic consistency to effect the translated poem's recreation of the images present in the original.

Temporality also appears as a difference between Grolsholz's and the machine translations. Specifically, Grolscholz translates "il neige" (line 1) as "it is snowing." Neither SMT model selected the present progressive. Their translation, "it snows" has a distinctly high probability in the Hansard model, as the parliamentary proceedings deal most often with general conditions when discussing weather (i.e. "it snows in the prairies"). While this is an adequate translation of the French phrase, Grolsholz's choice of the progressive anchors the poem in a narrative present that is absent in the general expression "it snows." This moment is key to understanding the poem in the context of the larger collection, as it gives the poet a defined position in time that anchors the poem's imagery.

The fact that neither MT system made this choice suggests a difference between literary and nonliterary texts in terms of how each treats time and the experience of duration. Temporality functions in subtly different ways in French and English. It is important to narrative and literary text and is particularly difficult for the MT system.

## 4 Discussion

Defining the type and degree of domestication that a literary translation should take is difficult to express, even to a human. We can say that Ward's translation, with its conversational style and choice of sense and style over language play, is more domestic than Grolsholz's, which tries to reflect the syntax of the original. Indeed, if we look back to Venuti's complaint about the translation of Anna Karenina, Grolsholz is certainly the more visible of the two translators, each of her translations being accompanied by its original on the facing page. From a technical standpoint, we may want a translation to take into consideration the narrative of a text in order to describe events in the narrative present (e.g. choosing "it is snowing" over "it snows"). However, defining the scope of the relevant narrative context is difficult and may vary substantially from text to text.

From the ethical perspective of the foreign/domestic debate, deciding how much the narrative context needs to be explicated or altered to be understandable in the translation is dependent on variables including the translator's stance on this issue, the author's wishes (if the author is living) and the publisher's requirements. Even once they have been determined, specifying such preferences precisely enough for a computational model to follow is even harder. For example, we could model a general preference for specific translations of nouns over more probable translations (e.g. 'snowflakes' instead of 'flakes'), but translation rules are typically very noisy and an SMT system would likely be tempted by garbage translation rules (e.g. in the Hansard system, 'flocons' translates as 'cornflakes' with higher probability than 'snow', 'flakes', or 'snowflakes'). In short, part of the human translator's job is knowing when to make exceptions to convention for the sake of the reader's experience of the translated text, and the question of the exception is difficult for the machine to account for.

Even if the type and degree to which a text should be domesticated could be accurately modeled, some types of free/fluent/flexible translations will be easier for a machine to produce than others. For example, idioms may be easy to integrate; if they are observed in training data, then a machine can easily produce them. This, however, requires in-domain training data, and domain is somewhat of a moving target in literature due to extremely high variability. In contrast to the ease of memorizing static idioms, computationally choosing correct, relevant, and appropriately specific translations of individual nouns (e.g. 'porte' as 'gate' instead of 'door') is difficult.

We end our discussion on a note about *visibility*. Introducing an SMT system into debates surrounding literary translation by human translators would seem to cause the translator to disappear entirely. Indeed, according to Cronin (2012), "machine translation services would appear to render invisible the labour of translation..." However, for Venuti, visibility is crucial to the ethics of balancing domestication and foreignization to create non-ethnocentric translations in that it reminds the reader to be attentive to the translation and to the translator as creative labourer. As a level of domestication is to be expected in fluent translations, Venuti's argument for visibility is also an argument for a disruption to the reader's experience that reinserts the distance of the foreignizing translation in a different way, suggesting that fluency, which hides the act of translation, might be ethical under conditions of visibility. Difficulties encountered by an SMT system can constitute a kind of visibility, because they expose problems in the translation, which often come in the form of disfluencies. However, these systems cannot consider translation in terms of domestication and foreignization; the SMT objective is to use patterns observed in training data example translations to produce something that has the same meaning as the source text and looks like the target language. There is a constant tradeoff between fluency and faithfulness. Although SMT can deal with fluency, it cannot handle ideas of domestic and foreign. Therefore, if we accept that domesticating and foreignization is key to distinguishing visibility, then the relationship between visibility and invisibility for the human translator and the machine translator must be different. And this divergence, in turn, means that current approaches to SMT could not ensure non-ethnocentric translations.

## References


Sankaranarayanan Ananthakrishnan, Rohit Prasad, and Prem Natarajan. 2011. On-line language model biasing for statistical machine translation. In *Proceedings of the Conference of the Association for Computational Linguistics (ACL)*.

Antoine Berman. 1992. *The Experience of the Foreign: Culture and Translation in Romantic Germany*. State University of New York Press, New York. Trans. by S. Heyvaert.

Y. Bonnefoy, E. Grosholz, and F. Ostovani. 2012. *Beginning and End of the Snow / Debut Et Fin de la Neige: Followed by Where the Arrow Falls / Suivi de La Ou Retombe la Fleche*. Rowman & Littlefield Publishers, Incorporated.

Yves Bonnefoy. 1968. *Selected poems*. Cape editions. Cape.

A. Camus and M. Ward. 1989. *The Stranger*. Everyman's library. Knopf Doubleday Publishing Group.

A. Camus. 1955. *L'étranger*. Appleton-Century-Crofts.

Colin Cherry and George Foster. 2012. Batch tuning strategies for statistical machine translation. In *Proceedings of the Conference of the North American Chapter of the Association for Computational Linguistics (NAACL)*.

Michael Cronin. 2012. *The Translation Age: Translation, Technology, and the new Instrumentalism*. The Translation Studies Reader, Third Editions. Routledge, New York.

George Foster and Roland Kuhn. 2007. Mixture-model adaptation for smt. In *Proceedings of the Workshop on Statistical Machine Translation (WMT)*.

George Foster, Cyril Goutte, and Roland Kuhn. 2010. Discriminative instance weighting for domain adaptation in statistical machine translation. In *Proceedings of the Conference on Empirical Methods in Natural Language Processing (EMNLP)*.

Erica Greene, Tugba Bodrumlu, and Kevin Knight. 2010. Automatic analysis of rhythmic poetry with applications to generation and translation. In *Proceedings of the Conference on Empirical Methods in Natural Language Processing (EMNLP)*.

Justine Kao and Dan Jurafsky. 2012. A computational analysis of style, affect, and imagery in contemporary poetry. In *NAACL Workshop on Computational Linguistics for Literature*.

Philipp Koehn, Hieu Hoang, Alexandra Birch, Chris Callison-Burch, Marcello Federico, Nicola Bertoldi, Brooke Cowan, Wade Shen, Christine Moran, Richard Zens, Chris Dyer, Ondrej Bojar, Alexandra Constantin, and Evan Herbst. 2007. Moses: Open source toolkit for statistical machine translation. In *Proceedings of the Conference of the Association for Computational Linguistics (ACL)*.

T. Lavergne, A. Allauzen, H. Le, and F. Yvon. 2011. LIMSI's experiments in domain adaptation for IWSLT11. In *Proceedings of the International Workshop on Spoken Language Translation (IWSLT)*.

Spyros Matsoukas, Antti-Veikko I. Rosti, and Bing Zhang. 2009. Discriminative corpus weight estimation for machine translation. In *Proceedings of the Conference on Empirical Methods in Natural Language Processing (EMNLP)*.

Jan Niehues and Alex Waibel. 2010. Domain adaptation in statistical machine translation using factored translation models. In *Proceedings of the European Association for Machine Translation (EAMT)*.

Franz Josef Och and Hermann Ney. 2003. A systematic comparison of various statistical alignment models. *Comput. Linguist.*, 29(1):19–51, March.

Sravana Reddy and Kevin Knight. 2011. Unsupervised discovery of rhyme schemes. In *Proceedings of the Conference of the Association for Computational Linguistics (ACL)*.

Antonio Roque. 2012. Towards a computational approach to literary text analysis. In *NAACL Workshop on Computational Linguistics for Literature*.

Fredreich Schleiermacher. 2012. *On different methods of translating*. The Translation Studies Reader, Third Editions. Routledge, New York. Trans. by Susan Bernofsky.

Jörg Tiedemann. 2010. To cache or not to cache? experiments with adaptive models in statistical machine translation. In *Proceedings of the ACL Workshop on Statistical Machine Translation and Metrics (MATR)*.

Lawrence Venuti. 2008. *The Translator's Invisibility: A History of Translation*. Routledge, New York.

# Temporal classification for historical Romanian texts

**Alina Maria Ciobanu**
**Liviu P. Dinu**
**Octavia-Maria Șulea**
Faculty of Mathematics and Computer Science
Center for Computational Linguistics
University of Bucharest
alinamaria.ciobanu@yahoo.com
ldinu@fmi.unibuc.ro
mary.octavia@gmail.com

**Anca Dinu**
Faculty of Foreign Languages
University of Bucharest
anca_d_dinu@yahoo.com

**Vlad Niculae**
University of Wolverhampton
vlad@vene.ro

**Abstract**

In this paper we look at a task at border of natural language processing, historical linguistics and the study of language development, namely that of identifying the time when a text was written. We use machine learning classification using lexical, word ending and dictionary-based features, with linear support vector machines and random forests. We find that lexical features are the most helpful.

## 1 Introduction

Text dating, or determination of the time period when it was written, proves to be a useful component in NLP systems that can deal with such diachronistically dynamic inputs (Mourão et al., 2008). Besides this, the models that can perform such classification can shine light on less than obvious changes of certain features.

The knowledge captured in such systems can prove useful in transferring modern language resources and tools to historical domains (Meyer, 2011). Automatic translation systems between and across language stages, as in the corpus introduced by (Magaz, 2006), can benefit from the identification of feature variation over time.

In this paper we study the problem of supervised temporal text classification across genres and authors. The problem turns out to be solvable to a very high degree of accuracy.

## 2 Related Work

The influence of the temporal effects in automatic document classification is analyzed in (Mourão et al., 2008) and (Salles et al., 2010). The authors state that a major challenge in building text classification models may be the change which occurs in the characteristics of the documents and their classes over time (Mourão et al., 2008). Therefore, in order to overcome the difficulties which arise in automatic classification when dealing with documents dating from different epochs, identifying and accounting for document characteristics changing over time (such as class frequency, relationships between terms and classes and the similarity among classes over time (Mourão et al., 2008)) is essential and can lead to a more accurate discrimination between classes.

In (Dalli and Wilks, 2006) a method for classification of texts and documents based on their predicted time of creation is successfully applied, proving that accounting for word frequencies and their variation over time is accurate. In (Kumar et al., 2012) the authors argue as well for the capability of this method, of using words alone, to determine the epoch in which a text was written or the time period a document refers to.

The effectiveness of using models for individuals partitions in a timeline with the purpose of predicting probabilities over the timeline for new documents is investigated in (Kumar et al., 2011) and (Kanhabua and Nørvåg, 2009). This approach, based on the divergence between the language model of the test document and those of the timeline partitions, was successfully employed in predicting publication dates and in searching for web pages and web documents.

In (de Jong et al., 2005) the authors raise the problem of access to historical collections of documents, which may be difficult due to the different historical and modern variants of the text, the less standardized spelling, words ambiguities and other language changes. Thus, the linking of current word forms with their historical equivalents and accurate dating of texts can help reduce the temporal effects in this regard.

Recently, in (Mihalcea and Nastase, 2012), the authors introduced the task of identifying changes in word usage over time, disambiguating the epoch at word-level.

## 3 Approach

### 3.1 Datasets used

In order to investigate the diachronic changes and variations in the Romanian lexicon over time, we used copora from five different stages in the evolution of the Romanian language, from the $16^{\text{th}}$ to the $20^{\text{th}}$ century. The $16^{\text{th}}$ century represents the beginning of the Romanian writing. In (Dimitrescu, 1994, p. 13) the author states that the modern Romanian vocabulary cannot be completely understood without a thorough study of the texts written in this period, which should be considered the source of the literary language used today. In the $17^{\text{th}}$ century, some of the most important cultural events which led to the development of the Romanian language are the improvement of the education system and the establishing of several printing houses (Dimitrescu, 1994, p. 75). According to (Lupu, 1999, p. 29), in the $18^{\text{th}}$ century a diversification of the philological interests in Romania takes place, through writing the first Romanian-Latin bilingual lexicons, the draft of the first monolingual dictionary, the first Romanian grammar and the earliest translations from French. The transition to the Latin alphabet, which was a significant cultural achievement, is completed in the $19^{\text{th}}$ century. The Cyrillic alphabet is maintained in Romanian writing until around 1850, afterwards being gradually replaced with the Latin alphabet (Dimitrescu, 1994, p. 270). The $19^{\text{th}}$ century is marked by the conflict (and eventually the compromise) between etymologism and phonetism in Romanian orthography. In (Maiorescu, 1866) the author argues for applying the phonetic principle and several reforms are enforced for this purpose. To represent this period, we chose the journalism texts of the leading Romanian poet Mihai Eminescu. He had a crucial influence on the Romanian language and his contribution to modern Romanian development is highly appreciated. In the $20^{\text{th}}$ century, some variations regarding the usage of diacritics in Romanian orthography are noticed.

| **Century** | **Corpus** | **Nwords** | |
|---|---|---|---|
| | | **type** | **token** |
| 16 | Codicele Todorescu | 3,799 | 15,421 |
| | Codicele Martian | 394 | 920 |
| | Coresi, Evanghelia cu învăţătură | 10,361 | 184,260 |
| | Coresi, Lucrul apostolesc | 7,311 | 79,032 |
| | Coresi, Psaltirea slavo-română | 4,897 | 36,172 |
| | Coresi, Târgul evangheliilor | 6,670 | 84,002 |
| | Coresi, Tetraevanghelul | 3,876 | 36,988 |
| | Manuscrisul de la Ieud | 1,414 | 4,362 |
| | Palia de la Orăştie | 6,596 | 62,162 |
| | Psaltirea Hurmuzaki | 4,851 | 32,046 |
| 17 | The Bible | 15,437 | 179,639 |
| | Miron Costin, Letopiseţul Ţării Moldovei | 6,912 | 70,080 |
| | Miron Costin, De neamul moldovenilor | 5,499 | 31,438 |
| | Grigore Ureche, Letopiseţul Ţării Moldovei | 5,958 | 55,128 |
| | Dosoftei, Viaţa si petreacerea sfinţilor | 23,111 | 331,363 |
| | Varlaam Motoc, Cazania | 10,179 | 154,093 |
| | Varlaam Motoc, Răspunsul împotriva Catehismului calvinesc | 2,486 | 14,122 |
| 18 | Antim Ivireanul, Opere | 11,519 | 123,221 |
| | Axinte Uricariul, Letopiseţul Ţării Românesti şi al Ţării Moldovei | 16,814 | 147,564 |
| | Ioan Canta, Letopiseţul Ţării Moldovei | | |
| | Dimitrie Cantemir, Istoria ieroglifică | 13,972 | 130,310 |
| | Dimitrie Eustatievici Braşoveanul, Gramatica românească | 5,859 | 45,621 |
| | Ion Neculce, O samă de cuvinte | 9,665 | 137,151 |
| 19 | Mihai Eminescu, Opere, v. IX | 27,641 | 227,964 |
| | Mihai Eminescu, Opere, v. X | 30,756 | 334,516 |
| | Mihai Eminescu, Opere, v. XI | 27,316 | 304,526 |
| | Mihai Eminescu, Opere, v. XII | 28,539 | 308,518 |
| | Mihai Eminescu, Opere, v. XIII | 26,242 | 258,234 |
| 20 | Eugen Barbu, Groapa | 14,461 | 124,729 |
| | Mircea Cartarescu, Orbitor | 35,486 | 306,541 |
| | Marin Preda, Cel mai iubit dintre pământeni | 28,503 | 388,278 |

Table 1: Romanian corpora: words

For preprocessing our corpora, we began by removing words that are irrelevant for our investigation, such as numbers. We handled word boundaries and lower-cased all words. We computed, for each text in our corpora, the number of words (type and token). The results are listed in Table 1. For identifying words from our corpora in dictionaries, we performed lemmatization. The information provided by the machine-readable dictionary *dexonline* [1] regarding inflected forms allowed us to identify lemmas (where no semantic or part-of-speech ambiguities occurred) and to further lookup the words in the dictionaries. In our investigations based on *dexonline* we decided to use the same approach as in (Mihalcea and Nastase, 2012) and to account only for unambiguous words. For example, the Romanian word *ai* is morphologically ambiguous, as we identified two corresponding lemmas: *avea* (verb, meaning *to have*) and *ai* (noun, meaning *garlic*). The word *amânare* is semantically ambiguous, having two different associated lemmas, both nouns: *amânar* (which means *flint*) and *amâna* (which means *to postpone*). We do not use the POS information di-

[1] http://dexonline.ro

rectly, but we use dictionary occurrence features only for unambiguous words.

The database of *dexonline* aggregates information from over 30 Romanian dictionaries from different periods, from 1929 to 2012, enabling us to investigate the diachronic evolution of the Romanian lexicon. We focused on four different subfeatures:

- words marked as obsolete in *dexonline* definitions (we searched for this tag in all dictionaries)
- words which occur in the dictionaries of archaisms (2 dictionaries)
- words which occur in the dictionaries published before 1975 (7 dictionaries)
- words which occur in the dictionaries published after 1975 (31 dictionaries)

As stated before, we used only unambiguous words with respect to the part of speech, in order to be able to uniquely identify lemmas and to extract the relevant information. The aggregated counts are presented in table 2.

| Sub-feature | | 16 | 17 | 18 | 19 | 20 |
|---|---|---|---|---|---|---|
| **archaism** | type | 1,590 | 2,539 | 2,114 | 1,907 | 2,140 |
| | token | 5,652 | 84,804 | 56,807 | 120,257 | 62,035 |
| **obsolete** | type | 5,652 | 8,087 | 7,876 | 9,201 | 8,465 |
| | token | 172,367 | 259,367 | 199,899 | 466,489 | 279,654 |
| **$<$ 1975** | type | 11,421 | 17,200 | 16,839 | 35,383 | 34,353 |
| | token | 311,981 | 464,187 | 337,026 | 885,605 | 512,156 |
| **$>$ 1975** | type | 12,028 | 18,948 | 18,945 | 42,855 | 41,643 |
| | token | 323,114 | 480,857 | 356,869 | 943,708 | 541,258 |

Table 2: Romanian corpora: *dexonline* subfeatures

### 3.2 Classifiers and features

The texts in the corpus were split into chunks of 500 sentences in order to increase the number of sample entries and have a more robust evaluation. We evaluated all possible combinations of the four feature sets available:

- **lengths**: average sentence length in words, average word length in letters
- **stopwords**: frequency of the most common 50 words in all of the training set:

  de și în a la cu au no o să că se pe din s ca i lui am este fi l e dar pre ar vă le al după fost într când el dacă ne n ei sau sunt

| Century | Precision | Recall | F1-score | texts |
|---|---|---|---|---|
| 16 | 1.00 | 1.00 | 1.00 | 16 |
| 17 | 1.00 | 0.88 | 0.94 | 17 |
| 18 | 0.88 | 1.00 | 0.93 | 14 |
| 19 | 1.00 | 1.00 | 1.00 | 23 |
| 20 | 1.00 | 1.00 | 1.00 | 21 |
| average/ total | 0.98 | 0.98 | 0.98 | 91 |

Table 4: Random Forest test scores using all features and aggregating over 50 trees

- **endings**: frequency of all word suffixes of length up to three, that occur at least 5 times in the training set
- **dictionary**: proportion of words matching the *dexonline* filters described above

The system was put together using the *scikit-learn* machine learning library for Python (Pedregosa et al., 2011), which provides an implementation of linear support vector machines based on *liblinear* (Fan et al., 2008), an implementation of random forests using an optimised version of the CART algorithm.

## 4 Results

The hyperparameters (number of trees, in the random forest case, and $C$, for the SVM) were optimized using 3 fold cross-validation for each of the feature sets. For the best feature sets, denoted with an asterisk in table 3, the test results and hyperparameter settings are presented in tables 4 and 5.

The results show that the nonlinear nature of the random forest classifier is important when using feature sets so different in nature. However, a linear SVM can perform comparably, using only the most important features. The misclassifications that do occur are not between very distant centuries.

## 5 Conclusions

We presented two classification systems, a linear SVM one and a nonlinear random forest one, for solving the temporal text classification problem on Romanian texts. By far the most helpful features turn out to be lexical, with dictionary-based historical information less helpful than expected. This is probably due to inaccuracy and incompleteness of

| lengths | stopwords | endings | dictionary | RF | SVM |
|---|---|---|---|---|---|
| False | False | False | False | 25.38 | 25.38 |
| False | False | False | True | 86.58 | 79.87 |
| False | False | True | False | 98.51 | 95.16 |
| False | False | True | True | 97.76 | 97.02 |
| False | True | False | False | 98.51 | 96.27 |
| False | True | False | True | 98.51 | 94.78 |
| False | True | True | False | 98.88 | *98.14 |
| False | True | True | True | 98.51 | 97.77 |
| True | False | False | False | 68.27 | 22.01 |
| True | False | False | True | 92.92 | 23.13 |
| True | False | True | False | 98.14 | 23.89 |
| True | False | True | True | 98.50 | 23.14 |
| True | True | False | False | 98.14 | 23.53 |
| True | True | False | True | 98.51 | 25.00 |
| True | True | True | False | 98.88 | 23.14 |
| True | True | True | True | *99.25 | 22.75 |

Table 3: Cross-validation accuracies for different feature sets. The score presented is the best one over all of the hyperparameter settings, averaged over the folds.

| Century | Precision | Recall | F1-score | texts |
|---|---|---|---|---|
| 16 | 1.00 | 1.00 | 1.00 | 16 |
| 17 | 1.00 | 1.00 | 1.00 | 17 |
| 18 | 1.00 | 0.93 | 0.96 | 14 |
| 19 | 1.00 | 1.00 | 1.00 | 23 |
| 20 | 0.95 | 1.00 | 0.98 | 21 |
| average/ total | 0.99 | 0.99 | 0.99 | 91 |

Table 5: Linear SVC test scores using only stopwords and word endings for $C = 10^4$.

dictionary digitization, along with ambiguities that might need to be dealt with better.

We plan to further investigate feature importances and feature selection for this task to ensure that the classifiers do not actually fit authorship or genre latent variables.

## Acknowledgements

The authors thank the anonymous reviewers for their helpful and constructive comments. The contribution of the authors to this paper is equal. Research supported by a grant of the Romanian National Authority for Scientific Research, CNCS – UEFISCDI, project number PN-II-ID-PCE-2011-3-0959.

## References

Angelo Dalli and Yorick Wilks. 2006. Automatic dating of documents and temporal text classification. In *Proceedings of the Workshop on Annotating and Reasoning about Time and Events, Sydney,*, pages 17—-22.

Franciska de Jong, Henning Rode, and Djoerd Hiemstra. 2005. Temporal language models for the disclosure of historical text. In *Humanities, computers and cultural heritage: Proceedings of the XVIth International Conference of the Association for History and Computing*.

Florica Dimitrescu. 1994. *Dinamica lexicului românesc - ieri şi azi*. Editura Logos. In Romanian.

Rong-En Fan, Kai-Wei Chang, Cho-Jui Hsieh, Xiang-Rui Wang, and Chih-Jen Lin. 2008. LIBLINEAR: A library for large linear classification. *Journal of Machine Learning Research*, 9:1871–1874, June.

Nattiya Kanhabua and Kjetil Nørvåg. 2009. Using temporal language models for document dating. In *ECML/PKDD (2)*, pages 738–741.

Abhimanu Kumar, Matthew Lease, and Jason Baldridge. 2011. Supervised language modeling for temporal resolution of texts. In *CIKM*, pages 2069–2072.

Abhimanu Kumar, Jason Baldridge, Matthew Lease, and Joydeep Ghosh. 2012. Dating texts without explicit temporal cues. *CoRR*, abs/1211.2290.

Coman Lupu. 1999. *Lexicografia românească în procesul de occidentalizare latino-romanică a limbii române moderne*. Editura Logos. In Romanian.

Judit Martinez Magaz. 2006. Tradi imt (xx-xxi): Recent proposals for the alignment of a diachronic parallel corpus. *International Computer Archive of Modern and Medieval English Journal*, (30).

Titu Maiorescu. 1866. Despre scrierea limbei rumăne. *Edițiunea și Imprimeria Societății Junimea*. In Romanian.

Roland Meyer. 2011. New wine in old wineskins? tagging old russian via annotation projection from modern translations. *Russian Linguistcs*.

Rada Mihalcea and Vivi Nastase. 2012. Word epoch disambiguation: Finding how words change over time. In *ACL (2)*, pages 259–263. The Association for Computer Linguistics.

Fernando Mourão, Leonardo Rocha, Renata Araújo, Thierson Couto, Marcos Gonçalves, and Wagner Meira Jr. 2008. Understanding temporal aspects in document classification. In *WSDM '08 Proceedings of the 2008 International Conference on Web Search and Data Mining*, pages 159–170.

F. Pedregosa, G. Varoquaux, A. Gramfort, V. Michel, B. Thirion, O. Grisel, M. Blondel, P. Prettenhofer, R. Weiss, V. Dubourg, J. Vanderplas, A. Passos, D. Cournapeau, M. Brucher, M. Perrot, and E. Duchesnay. 2011. Scikit-learn: Machine learning in Python. *Journal of Machine Learning Research*, 12:2825–2830, Oct.

Thiago Salles, Leonardo Rocha, Fernando Mourão, Gisele L. Pappa, Lucas Cunha, Marcos Gonçalves, and Wagner Meira Jr. 2010. Automatic document classification temporally robust. *Journal of Information and Data Management*, 1:199–211, June.

# Multilingual access to cultural heritage content on the Semantic Web

**Dana Dannélls** and **Aarne Ranta** and **Ramona Enache**
University of Gothenburg and Chalmers University of Technology
SE-412 96 Gothenburg, Sweden
{dana.dannells, aarne.ranta, ramona.enache}@chalmers.se

**Mariana Damova** and **Maria Mateva**
Ontotext
Sofia 1784, Bulgaria
{mariana.damova,maria.mateva}@ontotext.com

## Abstract

As the amount of cultural data available on the Semantic Web is expanding, the demand of accessing this data in multiple languages is increasing. Previous work on multilingual access to cultural heritage information has shown that at least two different problems must be dealt with when mapping from ontologies to natural language: (1) mapping multilingual metadata to interoperable knowledge sources; (2) assigning multilingual knowledge to cultural data. This paper presents our effort to deal with these problems. We describe our experiences with processing museum data extracted from two distinct sources, harmonizing this data and making its content accessible in natural language. We extend prior work in two ways. First, we present a grammar-based system that is designed to generate coherent texts from Semantic Web ontologies in 15 languages. Second, we describe how this multilingual system is exploited to form queries using the standard query language SPARQL. The generation and retrieval system builds on W3C standards and is available for further research.

## 1 Introduction

As the amount of cultural data available on the Semantic Web is expanding (Dekkers et al., 2009; Brugman et al., 2008), the demand of accessing this data in multiple languages is increasing (Stiller and Olensky, 2012).

There have been several applications that applied Natural Language Generation (NLG) technologies to allow multilingual access to Semantic Web ontologies (Androutsopoulos et al., 2001; O'Donnell et al., 2001; Androutsopoulos and Karkaletsis, 2005; Androutsopoulos and Karkaletsis, 2007; Davies, 2009; Bouayad-Agha et al., 2012). The above authors have shown it is necessary to have an extensive lexical and syntactic knowledge when generating multilingual natural language from Semantic Web ontologies. However, because previous applications are mainly concerned with two or three languages, it is still not clear how to minimize the efforts in assigning lexical and syntactic knowledge for the purpose of enhancing automatic generation of adequate descriptions in multiple languages.

This paper presents our work on making Cultural Heritage (CH) content available on the Semantic Web and accessible in 15 languages using the Grammatical Framework, GF (Ranta, 2011). The objective of our work is both to form queries and to retrieve semantic content in multiple languages. We describe our experiences with processing museum data extracted from two different sources, harmonizing this data and making its content accessible in natural language (NL). The generation and retrieval system builds on the World Wide Web Consortium (W3C) standards and is available for further research.[1]

The remainder of this paper is structured as followed. We present the related work in Section 2. We describe the underlying tech-

[1]The generation and retrieval system is available online: http://museum.ontotext.com/

nology in Section 3. We provide a detailed description of the data and present the approach taken to make this data accessible in the Linked Open Data (LOD) in Section 4. We outline the multilingual approach and discuss the challenges we faced in Section 5. We discuss the results in Section 6. We end with some conclusions and pointers to future work in Section 7.

## 2 Related work

Lately there has been a lot of interest in enabling multilingual access to cultural heritage content that is available on the Semantic Web. Androutsopoulos et al. (2001) and O'Donnell et al. (2001) have shown that accessing ontology content in multiple languages requires extensive linguistic data associated with the ontology classes and properties. However, they did not attempt to generate descriptions in real time from a large set of ontologies.

Similar to Bouayad-Agha et al. (2012), our system relies on a multi-layered ontology approach for generating multilingual descriptions. In contrast to Dekkers et al. (2009) and Brugman et al. (2008) whose systems make use of Google translation services, which are data driven, our system is grammar driven.

Moreover, we present a multilingual grammar-based approach to SPARQL (SPARQL Protocol and RDF Query Language) (Garlik and Andy, 2013). The method differs from the verbalization methods presented by Ngonga Ngomo et al. (2013) and Ell et al. (2012) in that it realizes the ontology content rather than the ontology axioms. Thus providing a more natural realization of the query language.

## 3 The technological infrastructure

Although the architecture of the Semantic Web and Linked Open Data provides access to distributed data sets,[2] many of the resources available in these sets are not accessible because of cross-language meta-data. To overcome this limitation, the knowledge representation infrastructure adopted in our approach is designed as a Reason-able View of the Web of Data. The Reason-able View is a compound dataset composed of several Resource Description Frameworks (RDFs). To query such a compound dataset, the user has to be intimately familiar with the schemata of each single composing dataset. That is why the Reason-able View approach is extended with the so called ontological reference layer, which introduces a unification ontology, mapped to the schemata of all single datasets from a given Reason-able View and thus provides a mechanism for efficient access and navigation of the data.

### 3.1 Museum Reason-able View (MRV)

The Museum Reason-able View is an assembly of cultural heritage dominated RDF datasets (Dannélls et al., 2011). It is loaded into OWLIM-SE (Bishop et al., 2011) with inference preformed on the data with respect to OWL Horst (ter Horst, 2005).

### 3.2 The ontological reference layer

The Museum Reason-able View gathers: (a) datasets from LOD, including DBpedia;[3] (b) the unification ontology PROTON,[4] an upper-level ontology, consisting of 542 classes and 183 properties; (c) two cultural heritage specific ontologies: (i) CIDOC-CRM (Crofts et al., 2008),[5] consisting of 90 classes and 148 properties; (ii) Museum Artifacts Ontology (MAO),[6] developed for mapping between museum data and the K-samsök schema.[7] It has 10 classes and 20 properties; (d) the Painting ontology,[8] an application ontology developed to cover detailed information about painting objects in the framework

[2] http://linkeddata.org

[3] DBPedia, structured information from Wikipedia: http://dbpedia.org.

[4] http://www.ontotext.com/proton-ontology

[5] http://www.cidoc-crm.org/

[6] It is just a coincidence that this ontology has the same name as the Finnish MAO (Hyvyonen et al., 2008), which also describes museum artifacts for the Finnish museums.

[7] K-samsök http://www.ksamsok.se/in-english/), the Swedish Open Cultural Heritage (SOCH), provides a Web service for applications to retrieve data from cultural heritage institutions or associations with cultural heritage information.

[8] http://spraakdata.gu.se/svedd/painting-ontology/painting.owl

of the Semantic Web. It contains 197 classes and 107 properties of which 24 classes are equivalent to classes from the CIDOC-CRM and 17 properties are sub-properties of the CIDOC-CRM properties.

### 3.3 Grammatical Framework (GF)

The Grammatical Framework (GF) (Ranta, 2004) is a grammar formalism targeted towards parsing and generation. The key feature of GF is the distinction between an abstract syntax, representing the domain, and concrete syntaxes, representing linearizations in various target languages, natural or formal.

GF comes with a resource grammar library (RGL) (Ranta, 2009) which aids the development of new grammars for specific domains by providing syntactic operations for basic grammatical constructions (Ranta, 2011). More than 30 languages are available in the RGL. Our application targets 15 of those, including: Bulgarian, Catalan, Danish, Dutch, English, Finnish, French, Hebrew, Italian, German, Norwegian, Romanian, Russian, Spanish, and Swedish.

## 4 Cultural heritage data

The data we have been experimenting with to enable multilingual descriptions of museum objects and answering to queries over them is a subset of the Gothenburg City Museum (GCM) database,[9] and a subset of the DBpedia dataset. Because these two datasets are very different in size and nature, the pre-processing of each set differs substantially. In the following we describe each of the sets and the pre-processing steps in more details.

### 4.1 Gothenburg City Museum (GCM)

The set from the GCM contains 48 painting records. Its content, both the metadata and data that were originally in Swedish, were translated to English. An example of a record from GCM is shown in Table 1.

### 4.2 DBpedia

The set from DBpedia contains 662 painting records, the data covers at least 5 languages, the metadata is in English. An example of a record from DBpedia is shown in Table 2.

| Record field | Value |
|---|---|
| Field nr. | 4063 |
| Prefix | GIM |
| Object nr. | 8364 |
| Search word | painting |
| Class nr | 353532 |
| Classification | Gothenburg portrait |
| Amount | 1 |
| Producer | E.Glud |
| Produced year | 1984 |
| Length cm | 106 |
| Width cm | 78 |
| Description | oil painting<br>represents a studio indoors |
| History | Up to 1986 belonged to Datema AB, Flöjelbergsg 8, Gbg |
| Material | oil paint |
| Current keeper | 2 |
| Location | Polstjärnegatan 4 |
| Package nr. | 299 |
| Registration | 19930831 |
| Signature | BI |
| Search field | Bilder:TAVLOR PICT:GIM |

Table 1: A painting object representation from the GCM database.

### 4.3 Transition of data to the MRV

Making the museum data available through the knowledge infrastructure required translations of the record fields and values, and mapping to a unified ontology. This process also required pre-processing of the free text fields such as *Description* and *History* (see Table 1) to enrich the data content.

To make the DBpedia data accessible through the knowledge infrastructure, it required some preprocessing, cleaning, and mapping to the Painting ontology for data consistency. This unification was needed to use a consistent SPARQL queries from where NL descriptions could be generated.

Firstly, we attempted to clean data noise and results that would make a single painting reappear in the query results. Then, we transformed year and size strings into only numbers. For each painter, museum and painting literal we had a single representation in the data. All names were normalized, for example, Salvador Dalí was converted

[9]`http://stadsmuseum.goteborg.se/wps/portal/stadsm/english`

```
<result>
<binding name='painting'>
<uri>http://dbpedia.org/resource/
Virgin_of_the_Rocks</uri> </binding>
<binding name='museum'>
<literal xml:lang='en'>Musée du Louvre
</literal> </binding>
<binding name='author'>
<literal xml:lang='en'>da Vinci, Leonardo
</literal> </binding>
<binding name='height'>
<literal datatype=
'http://www.w3.org/2001/XMLSchema#int'>
190</literal> </binding>
<binding name='width'>
<literal datatype=
'http://www.w3.org/2001/XMLSchema#int'>
120</literal>mateva </binding>
<binding name='title'>
<literal xml:lang='en'>London version
</literal> </binding>
<binding name='type'>
<literal xml:lang='fr'>Huile sur panneau
</literal> </binding>
<binding name='year'>
<literal datatype=
'http://www.w3.org/2001/XMLSchema#int'>
1495</literal> </binding> </result>
```


Table 2: A painting object representation from DBpedia

to *Salvador_Dal_*. For different Uniform Resource Identifiers (URIs) pointing to the same painting, we used the OWL (W3C, 2012) construct *owl:sameAs*. With this construct we were able to keep the data linked in the other graphs in the LOD cloud.

## 5 Multilingual linked data

Our application is targeted towards lay users who wish to formulate queries and retrieve information in any language. Such users do not have any knowledge about ontologies or semantic data processing. For us it was therefore necessary to enable interactions in a simple use.

The work towards making Semantic Web data accessible to different users required lexicalizations of ontology classes, properties and individuals (literal strings associated with a certain class).

Following the GF mechanism, lexicalizations is accomplished through linearizations of functions. Linearization of functions varies depending on the language.

### 5.1 Lexicalizations of classes and properties

Most of the ontology classes defined in our grammar are linearized with noun phrases in the concrete syntaxes. These were translated manually by a native speaker of the language. Examples from four languages are shown below. In the examples we find the following RGL constructions: *mkCN* (Common noun) and *mkN* (Noun).

```
Class: Painting
Swe. mkCN (mkN "målning");
Fre. mkCN (mkN "tableau");
Fin. mkCN (mkN "maalaus");
Ger. mkCN  mkN "Bild"
     "Bilder" neuter;

Class: Portrait
Swe. mkCN (regGenN "porträtt"
                   neutrum);
Fre. mkCN (mkN "portrait");
Fin. mkCN (mkN "muoto"
              (mkN "kuva"));
Ger. mkCN (mkN "Porträt"
        "Porträts" neuter);
```

Two of the ontology classes that are not linearized with a noun phrase are: *Year* and *Size*. These are linearized with prepositional phrases in which the preposition is language dependent. Below are some examples which show how the *Year* string, i.e. *YInt* function, is realized in six languages. In the examples we find the following RGL constructions: *mkAdv* (Verb Phrase modifying adverb), *Prep* (Preposition) and *symb* (Symbolic).

```
Bul. YInt i = mkAdv prez_Prep
     (symb (i.s ++ year_Str));
Fin. YInt i = mkAdv (prePrep
  nominative "vuonna") (symb i);
Fre. YInt i = mkAdv en_Prep (symb i);
Ger. YInt i = mkAdv in_Prep (symb i);
Swe. YInt i = mkAdv noPrep
     (symb ("år" ++ i.s));
Rus. YInt i = mkAdv in_Prep
     (symb (i.s ++ godu_Str));
```

The ontology properties are defined with operations in the concrete syntaxes. Because

Table 3: The amount of lexicalized literals in a subset of the MRV

| Class | literals |
|---|---|
| Title | 662 |
| Painter | 116 |
| Museum | 104 |
| Place | 22 |

an ontology property is linearized differently depending on how it is realized in the target language, these operations are of type: verbs (e.g. *paint_V2*), adverbs (e.g. *painted_A*) and prepositions (e.g. *Prep*). Examples from three languages are shown below.

```
Swe. paint_V2 : V2 = mkV2 "måla";
     painted_A : A = mkA "målad";
     at_Prep = mkPrep "på" ;
Fin. paint_V2 = mkV2 "maalata";
     painted_A = mkA "maalattu";
Ger. paint_V2 : V2 = mkV2
                (mkV "malen");
     painted_A : A = mkA "gemalt";
     at_Prep = in_Prep ;
```

The above functions correspond to three ontological properties, namely *painted_by*, *painted* and *created_in*. This approach to ontology lexicalization permits variations regarding the lexical units the ontology properties should be mapped to. It allows to make principled choices about the different realizations of an ontology property.

### 5.2 Lexicalizations of literals

The part of the MRV to which we provide translations for consists of 906 individuals, their distribution across four classes is provided in Table 3. The lexical units assigned to paining titles, painters and museum literals are by default the original strings as they appear in the data. The majority of strings are given in English. However, because without translations of the name entities the results can become artificial and for some languages ungrammatical, we run a script that translates museum literals from Wikipedia automatically.

Automatic translation was done by: (1) curling for Web pages for a museum string; (2) extracting the retrieved translated entry for each string; (3) reducing the retrieved list by removing duplicated and ambiguous entries. This process was repeated for each language.

Table 4: The number of automatically translated museum names from Wikipedia

| Language | Translated names |
|---|---|
| Bulgarian | 26 |
| Catalan | 63 |
| Danish | 33 |
| Dutch | 81 |
| Finnish | 40 |
| French | 94 |
| Hebrew | 46 |
| Italian | 94 |
| German | 99 |
| Norwegian | 50 |
| Romanian | 27 |
| Russian | 87 |
| Spanish | 89 |
| Swedish | 58 |

As a result of the translation process, a list of lexical pairs was created for each language. Museum literals were then linearized automatically by consulting the created list for each language. In the cases where no translation was found, the original string, as it appears in the dataset was used.

Unfortunately, the amount of the translated museum names was not equal for all languages. The distribution of the translated names is given in Table 4. Below follow some examples of how museum names are represented in the grammar:

```
Swe. MGothenburg_City_Museum =
 mkMuseum "Göteborgs stadsmuseum";
 MMus_e_du_Louvre =
                 mkMuseum "Louvren";
Ita. MGothenburg_City_Museum =
  mkMuseum
    "museo municipale di Goteburgo";
 MMus_e_du_Louvre =
        mkMuseum "Museo del Louvre";
Fre. MGothenburg_City_Museum =
  mkMuseum
      "musée municipal de Göteborg";
 MMus_e_du_Louvre =
        mkMuseum "Musée du Louvre";
Cat. MGothenburg_City_Museum =
 mkMuseum "Gothenburg_City_Museum";
 MMus_e_du_Louvre =
```

```
      mkMuseum "Museu del Louvre";
Ger. MGothenburg_City_Museum =
 mkMuseum "Gothenburg_City_Museum";
 MMus_e_du_Louvre =
             mkMuseum "Der Louvre ";
```

Where the construct *mkMuseum* has been defined to build a noun phrase from a given string. A special case of *mkMuseum* appears in four languages: Italian, Catalan, Spanish and French, where a masculine gender is assigned to the museum string to get the correct inflection form of the noun.

### 5.3 Realization of sentences

To generate sentences from a set of classes we had to make different judgements about how to order the different classes. Below we provide an example of a sentence linearization from four languages. The sentence comprises four semantic classes: *Painting, Material, Painter* and *Year*. In the examples we find following RGL constructors: *mkText* (Text), *mkS* (Sentence), *mkCl* (Clause), *mkNP* (Noun Phrase), and *mkVP* (Verb Phrase).

```
Ita. s1 : Text = mkText (mkS
 (mkCl painting (mkVP (mkVP (mkVP
 (mkVP dipinto_A) material.s)
 (SyntaxIta.mkAdv by8agent_Prep
 (title painter.long))) year.s))) ;
Fre. s1 : Text = mkText
 (mkS anteriorAnt
 (mkCl painting (mkVP (mkVP (mkVP
 (passiveVP paint_V2) material.s)
 (SyntaxFre.mkAdv by8agent_Prep
 (title painter.long))) year.s))) ;
Ger. s1 : Text = mkText
 (mkS pastTense
 (mkCl painting (mkVP (mkVP
 (mkVP (passiveVP paint_V2) year.s)
 (SyntaxGer.mkAdv von_Prep
 (title painter.long))) material.s)));
Rus. s1 : Text = mkText
 (mkS pastTense
 (mkCl painting (mkVP (mkVP (mkVP
 (passiveVP paint_V2)
 (SyntaxRus.mkAdv part_Prep
 (title painter.long
 masculine animate)))
 material.s) year.s))) ;
```

Some of the distinguishing differences between the languages are: in Finnish the use of an active voice, in Italian, present tense, in French, past participle, in Spanish, present simple. The order of the categories is also different. In German the material string appears at the end of the sentence as opposed to the other languages where year is often the last string.

### 5.4 Realizations of texts

The text grammar has been designed to generate a coherent natural language descriptions from a selected set of the returned triples. More specifically, our grammar covers eight concepts that are most commonly used to describe a painting, including: Title, Painter, Painting type, Material, Colour, Year, Museum and Size. In the grammar module called *TextPainting* they are defined as categories and are captured in one function *DPainting* which has the following representation in the abstract syntax.

```
DPainting :
 Painting -> Painter ->
 PaintingType -> OptColours ->
 OptSize -> OptMaterial ->
 OptYear -> OptMuseum -> Description;
```

In the function *DPainting* five arguments have been implemented as optional, i.e. *OptColour, OptSize, OptMaterial, OptYear* and *OptMuseum*. Each of these categories can be left out in a text.

In the current implementation we limited the length of a description to three sentences. A minimal description consists of only one sentences. Below follow some examples of texts generated in English to exemplify the different descriptions we are able to generate from one single function call with a varying number of instantiated parameters.

- Interior was painted on canvas by Edgar Degas in 1868. It measures 81 by 114 cm and it is painted in red and white. This painting is displayed at the Philadelphia Museum of Art.

- Interior was painted by Edgar Degas in 1868. It measures 81 by 114 cm. This painting is displayed at the Philadelphia Museum of Art.

- Interior was painted on canvas by Edgar Degas in 1868. It is painted in red and white. This painting is displayed at the Philadelphia Museum of Art.

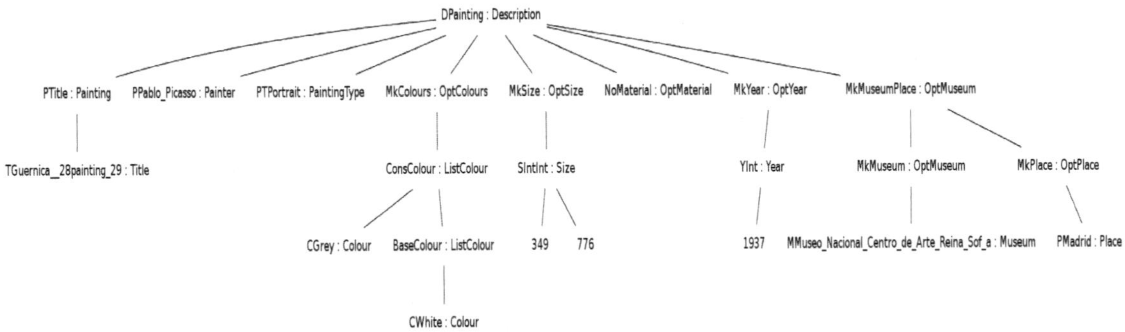


Figure 1: A semantic tree realization of nine ontology classes

- Interior was painted by Edgar Degas. It measures 81 by 114 cm and it is painted in red and white. This painting is displayed at the Philadelphia Museum of Art.
- Interior was painted on canvas by Edgar Degas. It measures 81 by 114 cm and it is painted in red and white.
- Interior was painted by Edgar Degas in 1868. This painting is displayed at the Philadelphia Museum of Art.
- Interior was painted by Edgar Degas.

### 5.5 Multilingual querying

Semantic Web technologies offer the technological backbone to meet the requirement of integrating heterogeneous data easily, but they are still more adapted to be consumed by computers than by humans. As a consequence, to retrieve semantic content from the knowledge base the user must: 1. master SPARQL, the query language for RDF; 2. have knowledge about each integrated dataset in the knowledge base.

Ngonga Ngomo et al. (2013) have shown that realizations of SPARQL queries in natural language enhance the user understanding of the formulated queries and the retrieved results.

We have implemented an extra SPARQL module that allow us to map from any of the 15 supported languages to SPARQL and from SPARQL to any of the 15 supported languages. The grammar reuses a more generic query module that allows to form both domain specific and domain independent queries. Some examples of the queries that can be formulated with the multilingual grammar and transformed to SPARQL are:

1. Some X
2. All About X
3. Show everything about X
4. All X painted by Y
5. Some X painted on Y
6. What is the material of X
7. Show everything about all X that are painted on Y

In GF, realization of SPARQL queries is done by introducing new parameters, for example:

```
QPainter p = {
 wh1 = "?author";
 prop = p ;
 wh2 ="painting:createdBy ?painter.
 ?painter rdfs:label ?author ."} ;
```

The function *QPainter* defined to formulate a query such as *who painted Mona Lisa?* has been added two additional parameters, i.e. *wh1* and *wh2*. With these parameters it is possible to formulate SPARQL queries such as the one below.

```
SELECT ?author
WHERE {
 ?painting rdf:type
          painting:Painting ;
 painting:createdBy ?painter ;
 rdfs:label ?title
 FILTER (str(?title)="Mona_Lisa").
 ?painter rdfs:label ?author.
}
```

```
TextPainting: DPainting (PTitle TInterior__28Degas_29) PEdgar_Degas PTPainting NoColours (MkSize (SIntInt 50 103)) NoMaterial (MkYear (YInt 1890)
TextPaintingBul: Interior е нарисувана от Edgar Degas през 1890 година. Тя е с размер 50 см на 103 см. Този експонат е изложен в Лувър.
TextPaintingCat: Interior fou pintat per Edgar Degas en 1890. Mesura 50 per 103 cm. Aquesta pintura està exposada al Museu del Louvre.
TextPaintingDan: Interior blev malet af Edgar Degas i 1890. Det er 50 ganger 103 cm. Dette maleri er udstillet på Louvre.
TextPaintingDut: Interior werd in 1890 door Edgar Degas geschilderd. Het werk is 50 bij 103 cm. Dit schilderij wordt in Musée du Louvre getoond.
TextPaintingEng: Interior was painted by Edgar Degas in 1890. It measures 50 by 103 cm. This painting is displayed at the Musée du Louvre.
TextPaintingFin: maalauksen Interior on maalannut Edgar Degas vuonna 1890. Se on kokoa 50 kertaa 103 cm. Tämä maalaus on esillä Louvressa.
TextPaintingFre: Interior a été peint par Edgar Degas en 1890. Il est de 50 sur 103 cm. Ce tableau est exposé au Musée du Louvre.
TextPaintingGer: Interior wurde in 1890 von Edgar Degas gemalt. Das Werk ist 50 mal 103 cm. Dieses Bild ist ausgestellt im Der Louvre .
TextPaintingHeb: פים האציור של דגס מצית 1890. ה אבוד ל 50 על 103 סטמת. יציר הזו מצגת במוזיאון הלובר.
TextPaintingIta: Interior è dipinto da Edgar Degas in 1890. Misura di 50 su 103 cm. Questo dipinto è esposto al Museo del Louvre.
TextPaintingNor: Interior ble malt av Edgar Degas i 1890. Det er 50 ganger 103 cm. Denne malerien er utstillt på Musée du Louvre.
TextPaintingRon: Interior este pictat de către Edgar Degas în 1890. Este din 50 pe 103 cm. Acest tablou este expus în Musée du Louvre.
TextPaintingRus: Interior нарисовалося Edgar Degas в 1890 году. Она с размером 50 см на 103 см. Эта картина видится в Лувр.
TextPaintingSpa: Interior fue pintado por Edgar Degas en 1890. Mide 50 por 103 cm. Esta pintura está expuesta en el Museo del Louvre.
TextPaintingSwe: Interior målades av Edgar Degas år 1890. Den är 50 gånger 103 cm. Den här målningen är utställd på Louvren.
```

Figure 2: Multilingual generation results

### 5.6 Multilingual text generation

Our approach allows different texts to be generated depending on the information that is available in the ontology. A minimal description consists of three classes: a title, a painter and a painting type. A complete description consists of nine classes, as illustrated in Figure 1. With only one function *DPainting* our system is able to generate 16 different text variants. Figure 2 illustrates a generation results in 15 languages.

## 6 Discussion

The majority of the challenges in the production of the CH data pool stemmed from the very nature of the Linked Open Data. The data in the LOD cloud are notoriously noisy and inconsistent.

The multilingual labels from the FactForge datasets and more precisely from DBpedia, are not always available in all the supported languages. Although DBpedia in its large pool of data provides access to multilingual content, it is inconsistent. Many of the entries it contains are missing translations. There is a mixture of numeric and string literals. There are many duplications, most of them occur because the same ID appears in different languages. The content of the data is verbose, for example place-names and museum-names are represented with one string, for example: "Rijksmuseum, Amsterdam", instead of two different strings linked by two separate concepts, i.e. *Museum* and *Place*. This kind of inconsistent data representation had an impact on the translation of museum names.

Another problem was that not all art objects are uniformly described with the same set of characteristics. For instance, some paintings were missing a title or a painter name. Because we constructed the grammar in such a way that disallows absence of this information, we had to replace titles with id numbers and empty painter names with the string *unknown*. Moreover, the data contained many duplications. This occurred because some of the property assertions were presented with different strings and triggered many RDF triples.

We also faced many linguistic challenges on different levels. Lexicalizations of ontology classes and properties regarding use of compounds, variations of verbs, adverbs and prepositions. On sentence level, order of classes, variations of tense and voice. On both sentence and discourse levels, aggregation variations and use of coreference elements.

## 7 Conclusions

We presented an ontology-based multilingual application developed in the Grammatical Framework and a cross-language retrieval system that uses this application for generating museum object descriptions in the Semantic Web.

The generation and retrieval system builds on W3C standards. It covers semantic data from the Gothenburg City Museum database and DBpedia. The grammar enables descriptions of paintings and answering to queries over them, covering 15 languages for baseline functionality.

## Acknowledgment

This research has been supported by MOLTO, the European Union's Seventh Framework Programme (FP7/2007-2013) under grant agreement FP7-ICT-247914.

## References

S. Kallonis Androutsopoulos and V. Karkaletsis. 2005. Exploiting OWL ontologies in the multilingual generation of object descriptions. In *The 10th European Workshop on NLG*, pages 150–155, Aberdeen, UK.

J. Oberlander Androutsopoulos and V. Karkaletsis. 2007. Source authoring for multilingual generation of personalised object descriptions. *Natural Language Engineering*, 13(3):191–233.

Ion Androutsopoulos, Vassiliki Kokkinaki, Aggeliki Dimitromanolaki, Jo Calder, Jon Oberl, and Elena Not. 2001. Generating multilingual personalized descriptions of museum exhibits: the M-PIRO project. In *Proceedings of the International Conference on Computer Applications and Quantitative Methods in Archaeology.*

B. Bishop, A. Kiryakov, D. Ognyanoff, I. Peikov, Z. Tashev, and R. Velkov. 2011. OWLIM: A family of scalable semantic repositories. *Semantic Web Journal, Special Issue: Real-World Applications of OWL.*

Nadjet Bouayad-Agha, Gerard Casamayor, Simon Mille, Marco Rospocher, Horacio Saggion, Luciano Serafini, and Leo Wanner. 2012. From Ontology to NL: Generation of multilingual user-oriented environmental reports. *Lecture Notes in Computer Science*, 7337.

Hennie Brugman, Véronique Malaisé, and Laura Hollink. 2008. A common multimedia annotation framework for cross linking cultural heritage digital collections. In *International Conference on Language Resources and Evaluation.*

Nick Crofts, Martin Doerr, Tony Gill, Stephen Stead, and Matthew Stiff, 2008. *Definition of the CIDOC Conceptual Reference Model.*

Dana Dannélls, Mariana Damova, Ramona Enache, and Milen Chechev. 2011. A Framework for Improved Access to Museum Databases in the Semantic Web. In *Recent Advances in Natural Language Processing (RANLP). Language Technologies for Digital Humanities and Cultural Heritage (LaTeCH).*

Rob Davies. 2009. EuropeanaLocal – its role in improving access to Europe's cultural heritage through the European digital library. In *Proceedings of IACH workshop at ECDL2009 (European Conference on Digital Libraries)*, Aarhus, September.

Makx Dekkers, Stefan Gradmann, and Carlo Meghini. 2009. Europeana outline functional specification for development of an operational european digital library. Technical report. Europeana Thematic Network Deliverables 2.5. Contributors and peer reviewers: Europeana.net WP2 Working Group members, Europeana office.

Basil Ell, Denny Vrandečić, and Elena Simperl. 2012. SPARTIQULATION – Verbalizing SPARQL queries. In *Proceedings of ILD Workshop, ESWC 2012.*

Steve Harris Garlik and Seaborne Andy, 2013. *SPARQL 1.1 Query Language*, March. `http://www.w3.org/TR/sparql11-query/`.

E Hyvyonen, E. Maekelae, M. Salminen, A. Valo, K. Viljanen, S. Saarela, M. Junnila, and S. Kettula. 2008. Museum finland. In *Finnihs Museum on the Semantic Web.*

Axel-Cyrille Ngonga Ngomo, Lorenz Bühmann, Christina Unger, Jens Lehmann, and Daniel Gerber. 2013. Sorry, i don't speak sparql: translating sparql queries into natural language. In *Proceedings of the 22nd international conference on World Wide Web*, WWW '13, pages 977–988, Republic and Canton of Geneva, Switzerland. International World Wide Web Conferences Steering Committee.

Michael J. O'Donnell, Chris Mellish, Jon Oberlander, and Alistair Knott. 2001. ILEX: An architecture for a dynamic hypertext generation system. *Natural Language Engineering*, 7(3):225–250.

Aarne Ranta. 2004. Grammatical Framework, a type-theoretical grammar formalism. *Journal of Functional Programming*, 14(2):145–189.

Aarne Ranta. 2009. The GF resource grammar library. *The on-line journal Linguistics in Language Technology (LiLT)*, 2(2). `http://elanguage.net/journals/index.php/lilt/article/viewFile/214/158`.

Aarne Ranta. 2011. *Grammatical Framework: Programming with Multilingual Grammars.* CSLI Publications, Stanford. ISBN-10: 1-57586-626-9 (Paper), 1-57586-627-7 (Cloth).

J. Stiller and M. Olensky. 2012. Europeana: A multilingual trailblazer. In *The W3C Workshop: The Multilingual Web - Linked Open Data and Multilingual Web-LT Requirements*, Dublin.

H. J. ter Horst. 2005. Combining RDF and Part of OWL with Rules: Semantics, Decidability, Complexity. In *Proceedings of The Semantic Web ISWC*, volume 3729 of *LNCS*, pages 668–684, Heidelberg. Springer Berlin.

W3C, 2012. *OWL Web Ontology Language Overview*, December. `http://www.w3.org/TR/owl2-overview/`.

# Author Index

**Association for Computational Linguistics**
209 N. Eighth Street
Stroudsburg, Pennsylvania 18360

CURRAN ASSOCIATES INC
proceedings.com

# First SIGHAN Workshop on Chinese Language Processing 2002

**Held at COLING 2002**

## Taipei, Taiwan
## 1 September 2002

ISBN: 978-1-62748-370-4